Anna Grabolle-Çeliker, a German-British anthropologist, received her PhD from Tübingen University. She has lived in Turkey since 1997, working first as a language teacher and translator, and then as a university lecturer.

KURDISH LIFE IN CONTEMPORARY TURKEY

MIGRATION, GENDER AND ETHNIC IDENTITY

ANNA GRABOLLE-ÇELIKER

I.B. TAURIS
LONDON · NEW YORK

New paperback edition published in 2015 by
I.B.Tauris & Co Ltd
London • New York
www.ibtauris.com

First published in hardback in 2013 by I.B.Tauris & Co Ltd

ISBN: 978 1 78453 215 4
eISBN: 978 0 85773 941 4

A full CIP record for this book is available from the British Library
A full CIP record is available from the Library of Congress

Library of Congress Catalog Card Number: available

Typeset by Newgen Publishers, Chennai

CONTENTS

ACKNOWLEDGEMENTS

This book would have been impossible to write without the support of many people. I would like to thank two professors at Tübingen University: Irmtraud Stellrecht, through her committed supervision of my PhD thesis, made this book possible. I would like to extend my sincerest gratitude to her. I am also grateful to Roland Hardenberg from the same university for critically engaging with my work and being part of the jury.

Miriam Geerse, Nazlı Öztürkler Somel, Catherine MacMillan, Anthony Pavlik, Chris Houston, Jelle Verheij, Ahmet Özer, Akile Gürsoy, Ayşe Betül Çelik, Fatih Bedirhanoğlu, Patricia Scalco, Ayten Arslan, and Siobhan Kızılkaya all contributed to this book with ideas or practical support and I extend my thanks to them. The Europäisches Zentrum für Kurdische Studien in Berlin was very helpful in helping me to locate sources. I am also grateful to the *muhtar* of Tepelik, as well as members of the Van Foundation, the Van Çataklılar Association, and the Van Province and Districts Association. I thank Mehmet Şenol for drawing the village plans for me. Two anonymous reviewers made constructive comments that allowed me to revise some of the manuscript. I am grateful to Amelie Soyka for her meticulous proofreading of the book. Any remaining faults are of course mine.

Vanlı interlocutors, friends, and family members in Gundême, Van, and Istanbul first sparked my interest through countless conversations and shared experiences. They have been extremely supportive. I hope they feel that I have created a realistic picture of the effects migration has had on their lives. *Xwedê ji we razi be.*

Writing this book would have been impossible without my parents, who offered practical and moral support throughout. I am deeply grateful. I also thank my brother Patrick for the editing of the manuscript and my sister Katherine for her help. Ayşe Abla's loving care of our daughters Aylin and Meryem made it possible for me to concentrate on this endeavour, and many conversations with her also clarified my ideas. Marriage to my husband Bayram made me a Vanlı *bûk* in the first place; he supported me in countless ways throughout this project. I dedicate this book to him, Aylin, and Meryem, with the hope that our daughters will cherish their multi-ethnic and multi-lingual background. *Û ji bo Apê Fadel û Xalê Haci Mustafa. Cihê wan cenet be.*

LIST OF FIGURES, TABLES, AND ILLUSTRATIONS

Figures

Tables

Illustrations

All photographs taken by the author. All figures and tables compiled by the author and Mehmet Şenol.

NOTES ON NAMES, SPELLINGS, AND PRONUNCIATION

All of the personal names (except for public persona) in this book are pseudonyms. When substituting personal names, I have tried to stay true to their associations. For instance, Kurdish names were replaced with Kurdish pseudonyms, and names with religious or worldlier associations were similarly substituted. The names of the village Gundême and the part of Istanbul I call Tepelik are also pseudonyms. The spelling of Gundême is Kurdish; it would normally be two words (Gundê me), but I have merged the two words for ease of reading. The district names of Van are all real. Throughout the book, I have used English spelling for Istanbul.

When using Turkish and Kurdish words, such as *dernek* (association) or *bûk* (bride), I have used English plurals for ease of reading, i.e. *derneks* and *bûks*. Several terms to describe sets of people have been used as one would use 'the French': thus Vanlı, Gundî, Acem, and Mirtip are the same in singular and plural, but would not be so in Turkish or Kurdish.

The Turkish and Kurdish words were spelt using the Turkish and Kurdish alphabet respectively; the latter is based on books by Bedir Xan and Lescot (2000) and Bedir Xan (n.d.). Below is a brief pronunciation guide that follows Yalçın's layout (1986). Some letters are pronounced the same in both languages, while in other cases there are divergences.

Letter	Turkish Pronunciation	Kurdish Pronunciation
a	like in 'far'	
e	like in 'bed'	
ê	—	long, like in 'page'
ı	short, like in 'mother'	—
i	long, like in 'sea'	short, like in 'fish'
î	—	long, like in 'sea'
o	like in 'toe'	
ö	like in the French 'peu'	—
u	short, like in the French 'tout'	
û	—	long, like in 'soon'
ü	like in the French 'tu'	—
c	like in 'jungle'	
ç	like in 'child'	
ğ	mostly silent, lengthens previous vowel	—
x	—	like in the Scottish 'loch'
j	like in the French 'jeux'	
q	—	unvoiced guttural stop
ş	like in 'shop'	
w	—	like in 'wish'

GLOSSARY OF TURKISH AND KURDISH TERMS

Much of the life of Kurdish Vanlı who have left their villages is lived in a bilingual context. The choice of terms below reflects the fact that their language use is contextualised.

Turkish Terms

abdest	Muslim ritual ablutions before prayer
abi	older brother
abla	older sister
acem	a Persian, but in Van used to refer to Azeri Turks from Iran
ağa	landowner
akraba	relative
akraba evliliği	marriage to a relative
alt kimlik	sub-identity
amca	paternal uncle
asimile	assimilated
aşiret	tribe
aşiret reisi	tribal leader
bakkal	grocery store, corner shop
baş örtü	head covering
bayram	(religious) holiday

belediye	city council
berdel	a marriage where young women from two families marry into the other family
bölücü	separatist
cahil	ignorant
cahillik	ignorance
cami	mosque
cem evi	place of worship for Alevi
cesaret	courage
çarşaf	the chador (literally 'sheet')
çokkültürlülük	multiculturalism
çok şükür	thank goodness
değirmen	mill
dernek	association
dershane	private cram school with university exam preparatory courses
düğün	wedding
ekmek kavgası	struggle to earn money
ev hanımı	housewife
ev kızı	an unmarried girl living with her parents and not working
ezan	call to prayer
ezik	inferior
gâvur	infidel
gecekondu	shanty housing (literally 'built by night')
gelin	bride, daughter-in-law
halay	dance where all dancers hold hands in long lines or form circles
hatım etmek	to read the Qur'an from start to finish
hemşehri	person with shared origin
hoca	Qur'an teacher or religious instructor
iftar	time for breaking the fast
il	province
ilçe	district
izin	leave from work
imam	Muslim religious leader

imam hatip okulu	school originally for training of imams, now school with religious focus
kaba	coarse, rude
kahve(hane)	men's café
kandil geceleri	nights with special religious significance
keçe	felt
kına gecesi	henna night (before a wedding)
kıro	colloquial and derogatory term for an uncouth migrant man
kız almak	taking a girl (in marriage)
kız vermek	giving a girl (in marriage)
korucu	village guard
kozmopolit	cosmopolitan
köy	village
köylü	villager, of the village
kuruş	unit of Turkish currency, 100 kuruş make one lira
Kürt	Kurd
lif	face cloth
lise	high school
mahalle	quarter (of a village or city)
market	shop
memleket	hometown, home region
mevlüd	recitation of a poem in honour of the prophet's birth
mezhep	Muslim religious tradition
millet	religious-based groups in the Ottoman Empire
mirtip	Roma, often used in a denigratory manner
muhtar	neighbourhood official
namaz	Muslim prayer
namus	honour
namuslu	honourable
okey	a game played with four people, using white playing stones that have coloured numbers
okul	school
öğlenci	pupil going to school in the afternoon

örtü	cover
öz Vanlı	original Vanlı, here: Turkish Vanlı
pardesü	an ankle-length loose-fitting coat
pimapen	plastic-framed double-glazed windows
pis	dirty
rahatlatıcı	comforting, relaxing
Ramazan	one of the Muslim lunar months, the month of fasting
sabah işleri	housework regularly performed in the morning
sabahçı	pupil going to school in the morning
sağlık ocağı	health centre
sandık	trunk used for keeping trousseau and other valuables
soba	stove
sohbet	a religious discussion
sofra	cloth or big tray put on the ground for eating on
sonradan gelme	late-comers
şuurlu	conscious
tapu	title deeds
tatil	holiday
temiz	clean, pure
terörist	terrorist
tesettür	the dress code for covered women
titiz	fastidious
torpil	connections
tövbe	repent (imperative)
tülbent	white cotton head covering
türban	head scarf
Türk	Turk
Türkiyeli	a citizen of Turkey
ümmet	the community of Muslims
vakıf	foundation
vali	governor
Van merkez	Van city

Vanlı	person/people from Van
varoş	(poor) suburb (derogatory)
yabancı	stranger
yazma	colourful cotton print head covering
yerli	literally 'local', here: the Turkish Vanlı
zina	adultery

Kurdish Terms

aş	mill
aşîret	tribe
bi dilê xwe zewicîn	to marry 'with one's heart'
bûk	bride, daughter-in-law
ceyran	electricity
file	Armenian (colloquial)
gundê me	our village
gundî	villager
kulav	felt
kur	son
laçik	a white cotton head covering
mal	household, lineage
mala Xwedê	literally 'house of Allah', i.e. mosque
malxê male	household head
mele	imam
meytep	school
mirtip/mitrip	gipsy
nan	bread
neh	nine
nehik	nine-day fast before the Feast of Slaughter
qabile	sub-tribe
qiz dayin	taking a girl (in marriage)
qiz xastin	giving a girl (in marriage)
sergîn	dried cow dung used as fuel
spas	thank you (newer word)
şeş	six
şeşik	six-day fast after Ramazan

tendûr	tandır oven
to	layer of cream on yoghurt
xanî	cooking outhouse
xun dîkele	the blood boils (i.e. people recognise each other)
Xwedê ji te razi be	may God approve of you (used for thanking)
welat	homeland

GLOSSARY OF ABBREVIATIONS
AND ACRONYMS

DPT	Devlet Planlama Teşkilatı	Ministry of Development
Göç-Der	Göç Edenler Sosyal Yardımlaşma ve Kültür Derneği	Migrants' Social Support and Culture Association
İBB	İstanbul Büyükşehir Belediyesi	Greater Istanbul Municipality
İHD	İnsan Hakları Derneği	Human Rights Association
PKK	Partiya Karkerên Kurdistan	Kurdistan Workers' Party
TESEV	Türkiye Ekonomik ve Sosyal Etüdleri Vakfı	Turkey Economic and Social Studies Foundation
TIHV	Türkiye İnsan Hakları Vakfı	Turkey Human Rights Foundation
TOBB	Türkiye Odalar ve Borsalar Birliği	Union of Chambers and Commodity Exchanges of Turkey
HTA		Hometown Association
HTO		Hometown Organisation

Political Parties

AKP	Adalet ve Kalkınma Partisi	Justice and Development Party
AP	Adalet Partisi	Justice Party
ANAP	Anavatan Partisi	Motherland Party
BDP	Barış ve Demokrasi Partisi	Peace and Democracy Party
CHP	Cumhuriyet Halk Partisi	Republican People's Party
DEHAP	Demokratik Halk Partisi	Democratic People's Party
DEP	Demokrasi Partisi	Democracy Party
DTP	Demokratik Toplum Partisi	Democratic Society Party
DYP	Doğru Yol Partisi	True Path Party
GP	Genç Parti	Young Party
HADEP	Halkın Demokrasi Partisi	People's Democracy Party
MHP	Milliyetçi Hareket Partisi	Nationalist Movement Party
YTP	Yeni Türkiye Partisi	New Turkey Party

1

INTRODUCTION

This book portrays the lives of Kurds originally from the eastern province of Van in Turkey, many of whom have migrated, either from villages to the province capital or from the province to larger cities further west. They have moved from all-Kurdish villages to the more ethnically mixed Van city or to areas in Turkey that are predominantly Turkish. Since in Turkey it is common to identify oneself according to province of origin and my Kurdish interlocutors often refer to themselves, in Turkish, as 'Vanlı', people from Van, I follow this usage throughout the book.

In a regional context, this work on Vanlı migration represents a much-needed addition to the ethnographic body of knowledge on Kurds, specifically those living in Turkey. Furthermore, it offers a case study of relatively recent internal migration within Turkey, discussing push and pull factors. Finally, borrowing concepts from the study of transnational migration, this book considers both migrants and those who have remained in the villages as part of one social field with 'interdependencies' (Cohen 2001: 955).

One contribution of the transnational perspective has been a move away from a unidirectional model of rural-urban migration to a consideration of migrants and non-migrants as positioned in the same social spaces. In addition, this approach makes allowances for fluidity and ambiguity within these social spaces. While certain macro-processes affect migrant and non-migrant lives alike, there is nevertheless variation in migration outcomes. Social scientist Smith captures this ambiguity in his foreword to a book on transnational migration; he warns of 'overly celebratory narratives of transnational cultural hybridity', while also pointing out that migrant communities are not homogeneous (2002: xii–xiii).

The aim of this book is to show changes that migration has brought to the lives of Vanlı villagers over the last three decades. My long-term involvement with migrant and non-migrant Kurdish Vanlı for more than 12 years has led me to realise that there are certain structural constraints that have affected their lives. As villagers they have had limited access to health care and education. As Kurds they have faced discrimination by the state and by Turkish society. As women and men they have been constrained by a dominant Kurdish age-gender hierarchy. As migrants to cities they have often been limited in their choice of residential area or jobs. Whether they have migrated or remained in the province, these Kurdish Vanlı form a social field where networks are formed, discourses are perpetuated, and religious and social practices are performed. This creates a certain commonality of experiences.

At the same time, however, there is great variety in how these experiences have translated into outcomes, largely due to the ever-accelerating rural-urban migration in the province, which has been a major cause of change in the lives of Kurdish Vanlı; it has led to socio-economic differentiation among them, as well as coexisting yet contradictory discourses on village life, Kurdishness, gender relations, and religion. This means that Kurdish Vanlı may now live quite different lives, hold different ideas, and take part in different practices. In comparing and contrasting constraining structures and variety of experiences, a spectrum of migratory lives has been presented in this book.

Kurds in Turkey

There are both Turks and Kurds living in Van, but my research is mostly based on the experiences and narratives of Kurdish Vanlı. Although I do not focus exclusively on the issue of Kurdish ethnic identity, it is an integral aspect of the everyday lives of Vanlı and thus deserves some preliminary discussion. A debate on and the silencing of Kurdishness have played an important role in Turkey's public discourses and impinge on the way in which Kurdishness has been experienced by my interlocutors.

Through my frequent visits to the eastern province of Van from 1997 onwards, I became increasingly aware of parallel universes existing in Turkey. I was living and socialising with Kurds in Istanbul, in the west of the country. Both there and in Van, I was listening to people singing, swearing, joking, and chatting in Turkish and Kurdish and expressing political opinions in private that could not be voiced in public. On the other hand, I was teaching young, mostly Turkish, students at universities in Istanbul as a language instructor. When at work, so went the unspoken caution, the words 'Kurdish' (*Kürt*) or 'Kurdish language' (*Kürtçe*) were unmentionable. Discussions of current affairs in lessons meticulously bypassed any mention of the war raging in the east of the country between the Turkish army and the militant Kurdistan Workers' Party (Kurdish: *Partiya Karkerên Kurdistan*, PKK) since the 1980s—but it became very real for some, such as my student whose brother was killed in action during his military service.

Everyone was aware of these issues and just as aware of the fact that they were not to be talked about. We foreign teachers were warned not to provoke reactions by questioning the official line that tarred even Kurds lobbying for political and linguistic rights non-violently as 'terrorists' (*terörist*) or 'separatists' (*bölücü*). Mostly these things were not even discussed with Turkish colleagues. The word '*Kürt*' was hardly ever used, but there were veiled references to 'the culture of the East' (*Doğu'nun kültürü*); this 'culture' was portrayed as one of violence, ignorance, and political extremism. I met young men who were scared of doing their military service in case they were sent to fight in the east of Turkey, and I heard and read about soldiers who came back broken souls after the traumas of war. Incidentally, a book interviewing soldiers who had done their military service in the East, describing their fears and experiences, was banned by the government.[1]

The first time I visited the East, I went by intercity bus with my future husband. I felt the fear of the young soldier who entered the bus at a checkpoint in Elazığ, eastwards of which the provinces then

still under emergency law began. I also felt the fear of the villagers
on the bus who studiously looked at the seat ahead of them while
the collected ID cards were being sifted through, felt the seething
anger when an old man was taken off the bus and not let on again,
and felt the frustration when these controls were repeated at numerous checkpoints the closer we got to Van. On this first visit I met my
future mother-in-law and many other middle-aged villager women
who could speak no Turkish, but were expressive, funny, scathing, and
poetic in Kurdish.

In Beyoğlu, a quarter in Istanbul, I saw the 'Saturday mothers',[2]
many of them Kurdish, holding up pictures of relatives who had disappeared after being detained by police or gendarmerie. Sometimes,
busloads of police in riot gear stood at the ready on their regular pro-
test spot to discourage even the beginnings of such peaceful dem-
onstrations. The protesters' struggle to find out the fate of the many
'disappeared' relatives from the 1990s was not covered by the mainstream media, and they seemed to be viewed with suspicion rather
than compassion or solidarity by passers-by.

I attended a wedding in Istanbul at which we were told to switch
off the Kurdish folk song people were dancing to or leave the rented
hall. Many Kurds told me about how they used to listen to Kurdish
music secretly, hiding cassettes if there were army searches in their village homes or switching off the tape in the car before approaching one
of the many army road blocks in the East. People in Istanbul I had just
met would feel free to tell me not to learn Turkish from my 'eastern'
husband since his accent was 'broken' (bozuk) or to ask me whether he
beat me.

This is not to suggest that there was constant hostility between
Turks and Kurds. Indeed, I often heard western Turks say, 'Turk or
Kurd, it did not use to matter. We all used to live together peace-
fully' (implied: before the armed conflict between the army and the
PKK began). Indeed, there have been countless interethnic friendships, marriages, and business partnerships. There have also been
successful Kurdish businesspeople, actors, singers, and parliamentarians. However, a basic condition for their success seemed to be not
mentioning 'the K word'. In 1979, cabinet minister Şerafettin Elçi

had claimed in public, 'There are Kurds in Turkey. I too am a Kurd.' He was later sentenced to two years and four months of hard labour (McDowall 1997: 413). Kurdish singer-songwriters sang in Turkish, Kurdish writers wrote in Turkish, and Kurdish parliamentarians joined mainstream parties and also government cabinets.[3] Haig describes this as the 'invisibilisation' of Kurdish ethnicity: '[Turkish state policy] has been characterised precisely by a *lack* of overt policy formulation, by indirect or masked reference, or systematic lack of reference to Kurdish, rather than officially formulated agendas, or public debate' (2004: 122). Yeğen also writes about the 'masked references' the Turkish state has used:

> Whenever the Kurdish question was mentioned in Turkish state discourse, it was in terms of reactionary politics, tribal resistance or regional backwardness, but never as an ethno-political question. In Turkish state discourse, the Kurdish resisters were not Kurds with an ethno-political cause, but simply Kurdish tribes, Kurdish bandits, Kurdish sheikhs—all the evils of Turkey's premodern past.
>
> (1999: 555)

This invisibilisation and masking of anything pertaining to Kurds was present in both private and public discourses; people in the west of Turkey made sure of friendships before 'outing' themselves as Kurds or proffering criticism of the lack of cultural rights for Kurds, let alone any more radical opinions. Anthropologist Neyzi notes that individuals from different linguistic, religious, or ethnic backgrounds in Turkey experience a conflict between the official national identity or historiography and that of their own family. This leads to a silencing in public, which sometimes also extends to the private realm (2004: 9). A manifestation of such parallel worlds is the common Kurdish childhood memory of living in a virtually monolingual Kurdish village, growing up speaking Kurdish, and then being beaten by the lone Turkish teacher if one is unable to speak Turkish. Neyzi rightly points to the penetration of such public denigration into the private realm; anecdotal evidence from my interlocutors showed that Kurdish children often became embarrassed by their families' linguistic background and perceived ignorance.

In this context it does not come as a surprise that much of the literature on Kurds has been produced outside of the country. Centres of Kurdology are found in Europe and the USA rather than in Turkey. According to a recent review of Kurdology, there have been different 'generations' of academics in Kurdology,[4] and each generation has had a different focus. The first generation, exemplified by Russian scholars such as Nikitine and Minorsky, as well as some Kurds in exile themselves, offer a somewhat essentialised portrait of 'the Kurd' and 'his character'. The second generation, from the 1960s onwards, has framed the study of Kurds in terms of a 'national struggle' or 'minority rights'. This perspective has been shaped by political events in Turkey, Iran, Iraq, and Syria, the four countries with large Kurdish populations, as well as by a growing diaspora of Kurds in Europe; many of the contributors to the literature were either Kurdish themselves or sympathetic to their struggle. The authors of the review argue that the aim of such studies was 'not to understand the Kurds themselves but rather to understand the relationships between the Kurds (either considered as minorities or as national movements) and the states' (Scalbert-Yücel and Le Ray 2006: §8–17). Thus, internationally,[5] Kurds have often been constructed as an oppressed people without a nation.[6] There have been attempts at formulating solutions[7] to the so-called 'Kurdish Question', sometimes with reference to ethnic conflicts in other countries, such as the Basques in Spain, the Northern Irish,[8] or the Chechens.[9] Research on Kurds has thus often focused on social and political macro-analyses. Reasons for this may be that the oppression of Kurds in Turkey and its neighbouring countries took precedence over small-scale studies and, indeed, that it was difficult to gain access to communities and individuals in the east of Turkey for research.

It is important to note here that not only the Turkish state made it difficult to study Kurds, but that 'Kurdish nationalist movements themselves impose an ideological mortgage on the Kurdish studies,' frowning upon the discussion of religious, linguistic, and other diversity (Bozarslan n.d.). Such diversity was thought to damage the cause of ethnic identity politics.

According to Houston, 'many of the more recent books on the Kurdish question are uninterested in ethnographic research and are obsessed with questions of geo-politics and international relations' (2001b: 1). MacDonald, however, claims that there has been 'a transition in Kurdish studies from primarily historical and political presentations to a modern focus on the "construction" of the Kurdish identity and an attempt to scientifically examine Kurds in their broadest social context' (1998). In other words, Kurds are beginning to be seen not only as acted upon, but also as actors, and they do not act as a homogenous group, but display diversity.

Early anthropological works on the Kurds by Leach (1940) and Barth (1953) were not followed by other works from the same authors; there was a general decline in interest in the Kurds until the 1960s and 1970s, argued by Bozarslan to be due to the 'pacification' of the Kurdish populations by the Turkish, Iranian, and Iraqi states at the time (Bozarslan n.d.).

Finally, a third generation of Kurdologists has offered work that considers 'nations', 'ethnicity', and 'identity' as constructions. This perspective has allowed for historically contextualised and more differentiated pictures of 'Kurdishness' to emerge. Since the late 1970s, Dutch academic Bruinessen is perhaps the best-known Kurdologist internationally; he has published extensively on Kurdish social organisation and identity based on fieldwork in Turkey, Iran, Iraq, and Syria; he is a first point of reference for scholars in the field. His work has also been helpful because he points to the fragmentation of the Kurdish 'community' in Turkey (e.g. 1997a). Today, scholars pursue a wide variety of research interests related to Kurds: the languages and oral and written literature (e.g. Allison 1996, Blau 1996, Chyet 2002, Kreyenbroek 1992), material culture (e.g. Aristova 2002, Kren 1996, O'Shea 1996), religions (Kreyenbroek 1996, Mir-Hosseini 1996), women and gender (e.g. Hajo et al. 2004, Mojab 2001, Savelsberg et al. 2000, Wedel 1997), social organisation (e.g. Bruinessen 1978, 1989a, Yalçın 1986), the use of Kurdish media (e.g. Hassanpour 1996, 1997), the history of Kurdish nationalism (Olson 1989, Strohmeier 2004), the linguistic policy of the Turkish state (Haig 2004, Skutnabb-Kangas and Bucak 1994), the Kurdish diaspora (Ammann 1997, 2000, 2004, Wahlbeck 1999), the pro-Kurdish political movement (e.g. Casier et al. 2011), and Kurds in urban centres (Houston 2001a, 2001b, Seufert 1997, Wedel 1997).

Today, most academics show no ambition to study Kurds in all four states (Turkey, Iran, Iraq, and Syria) at once or to try to compare them all; rather, there is more focus on Kurds in each individual state. Arguably, this change in perspective reflects ideological changes. The attempt to write about Kurds in all four states together implies a sense of unity and common purpose, perhaps even national ambitions. Studying Kurds in a certain state, on the other hand, means that more attention is paid to interactions with other ethnic groups within the state. It offers the potential to de-reify the concept of ethnicity and analyse how Kurdishness is shaped through these interactions. In fact, the subjects of Kurdology, 'Kurds', have been deconstructed to a certain extent (Scalbert-Yücel and Le Ray 2006: §22–3).

In Turkey, academic research on Kurds has often been hampered by state control. The following examples show how much was at stake for researchers of Kurdish issues. A Turkish academic now inextricably associated with the study of Kurds, İsmail Beşikçi, lost his position at Erzurum University for writing about Kurds and was imprisoned after the military coup of 1971. He wrote a series of books criticising the dominant Kemalist discourse on Turkish history and tried to bring to attention issues relating to Kurds.[10] However, his books were banned, and he faced trials for each one of them (Bruinessen 1997b: 18, cf. Scalbert-Yücel and Le Ray 2006: §52). According to Bruinessen, 'Most Turkish academics discovered only after 1991, when ethnicity could be openly discussed, that it was a relevant factor after all' (1997b: 24). Whether it could be openly discussed even then is debatable; one academic report deserves mention for causing uproar at its publication in 1995. The Union of Chambers and Commodity Exchanges of Turkey (TOBB) had commissioned a study on Kurds in Turkey. The report, written by a research team under political scientist Doğu Ergil, was a surprisingly candid document, asking over 1,000 Kurds living in the east or the west of Turkey about their attitude towards government policies, language, and the PKK. It seems that some interviewees were too scared to answer certain questions.[11] The State Security Court reacted to the report by investigating whether a charge of separatist propaganda could be brought against the authors (İncesu and Meresh 1995, cf. Scalbert-Yücel and Le Ray 2006: §60). It is clear that in such a climate, academic research has been stifled, and only research matching the official discourse passed muster.[12] Houston says:

> For intellectuals, especially those employed at the state universities, the Kurdish problem represents an uncomfortable taboo that haunts the post 1980 coup reorganisation of the tertiary education sector with its self-aggrandising discourse of the independence of science and research.
>
> (2001b: 2)

At one point, a popular endeavour for some Turkish academics was to prove that Kurds were really Turks; such 'research' was rewarded by stable academic positions at a time when academics with more critical attitudes lost their jobs (Scalbert-Yücel and Le Ray 2006: §45).

Although there now exist studies focusing on the forced migration of Kurds to regional centres and to the west of Turkey, there is still not complete academic freedom. First of all, there is still a tendency to consider the *effects* of this displacement of people rather than the *causes* as the latter would involve a discussion of who initiated the migration, how well or badly it was organised, and whether it was legal. In short, there would be blame apportioned, not only to the PKK, but also to the army and the state. Kurban, a co-author of a report on forced migration by the research foundation TESEV, criticises exactly this silence (Kurban 2007) in a recent Hacettepe University report on internal migration (Hacettepe Üniversitesi Nüfus Etüdleri Enstitüsü 2006). Second, publishing in Turkish can still lead to repercussions beyond academic or public debate. For instance, the TESEV report writers experienced the dangers of too much candour at first hand, when their book launch in July 2006 was hijacked by a group of nationalists who threatened violence. Third, this kind of research is mostly carried out at non-state universities as state-employed academics must still fear dismissal more readily (Gambetti 2006: §65).[13] As a result, academic writing on the Kurdish issue still involves auto-censorship (Gambetti 2006: §64, Scalbert-Yücel and Le Ray 2006: §74).

Considering the political sensitivity of the Kurdish issue, it is not surprising that there has not been much extensive fieldwork in rural Kurdish areas in Turkey. Yalçın-Heckmann's fieldwork in a village in Hakkâri resulted in a book on kinship and tribal organisation of that village (Yalçın 1986), which has provided me with data to compare. The village that she studied does not exist any longer; the villagers were recruited as *korucus* (village guards) by the army in the conflict between the PKK and the army. Some villagers claim that the army started mistrusting them after a clash with the PKK in which a *korucu* and soldiers died. Apparently, the army ordered the villagers to leave after the clash (Strohmeier and Yalçın-Heckmann 2000: 221–7).

A more recent study by Wießner (1997) combines fieldwork in Van and research into Turkish, Armenian, and Russian archives in order to describe the transformation of formerly Armenian villages in Van province into (mostly) Kurdish settlements after the First World War. He describes the care with which he had to proceed in order to ask questions concerning Armenians to Kurdish villagers. While he was offered the cooperation of the land registry in Van, I would hazard the guess that this was done unofficially. It has to be remembered that the State Security Council (*Milli Güvenlik Kurulu*) is still preventing Ottoman land registers from being published, arguably fearing that the hegemonic discourse on the 'Armenian issue' (and the treatment of other non-Muslim minorities) could then not be maintained (Düzel 2006).

A third study, though minor, is interesting since it was written by a Kurdish undergraduate student from Van in 1970. He wanted to research the Ertoşi tribe from Hakkâri, many members of which today live in Van. He touches on the difficulties he had, despite being a Kurd himself, of gaining the trust of the locals, putting this down to the presence of gendarmerie agents in the area (Müküs 1970).

A fourth study by Turkish sociologist Özgen in villages in the province of Van, looks at ways of collective remembering and forgetting. She has published a book on an event that is remembered in Turkey as the '33 bullets event' (*33 kurşun olayı* in Turkish, *Geliyê Sefo* in Kurdish). In 1943, 33 villagers, who had been arrested on charges of smuggling, were shot dead without trial. She shows how the event has been forgotten and remembered at different times in different local and national discourses (Özgen 2003, cf. Başlangıç 2003, Scalbert-Yücel and Le Ray 2006: §50). It was not easy for her to gain the trust of the villagers, some of whom 'shopped' her to the army as an alleged PKK member (Başlangıç 2003).

It is in this context of a relative dearth of long-term ethnographic studies on Kurds in Turkey that my study needs to be situated. Although my research has not focused on Kurdish ethnicity exclusively, a generally repressive atmosphere permeated all initial exchanges with Vanlı and Turks, be they villagers, migrants to the city, academics, or officials. Research into the lives of Vanlı was met with an initial 'Why?' of distrust, a questioning of motives, and suspicion of political alliances. A researcher from Germany looking at Kurds was the stereotypical 'separatist' for some Turks, while some Kurdish interlocutors had unspecific yet real fears about the possible consequences of speaking to me.

The capture of PKK leader Abdullah Öcalan in 1999 and the subsequent ceasefire led to a relative relaxation in attitudes towards Kurdishness and even to a public debate on ethnic 'sub-identities' (alt kimlik) that could possibly coexist with a supra-identity of Turkish citizenship (Türkiyelilik). However, when armed fighting resumed in around 2005, there was a public backlash against the expression of Kurdish identity.

Since 2009, the public climate has changed again, with the government announcing a 'democratic ouverture' that is to lead to more cultural recognition of Kurds and other groups such as Alevis and Roma, as well as political acknowledgement of previous discrimination against them. The government promised to change the current constitution, a product of the military coup of 1980, and make it more democratic. It became more commonplace to discuss the Kurdish question openly in newspapers and the media. However, Turkish nationalists reacted strongly against a perceived threat to the unity and homogeneity of the Turkish state. Left-leaning activists, meanwhile, were cynical about what they perceived as token gestures, accusing the ruling party, the Justice and Development Party (AKP), of wanting to maximise election support from different groups in society.

In the days leading up to the general election of June 2011, the promise of a more democratic and open society became largely forgotten as parties of the political centre vied for the Turkish nationalist vote with increasingly chauvinist rhetoric. After the landslide victory of the AKP, there has been a clampdown on political activists, many of them alleged to be members of the KCK (*Koma Civakên Kurdistan* in Kurdish, Union of Communities in Kurdistan), described as the 'urban division of the PKK' in the media. There is much less optimism about democratic change, and the continuing promise of constitutional change does not seem to be taken seriously by the general public. As so often in Turkey, it remains to be seen in what direction the political and cultural landscapes change.

Migration within Turkey

The focus of this book is on the effects that rural-urban labour migration of Kurds from eastern Turkey has had on their everyday lives. Within Turkey, rural-urban migration has been taking place for centuries, as the following extract shows:

> Labor migration is an old phenomenon in the Ottoman world that, according to some, can be traced back to Byzantine times. Connecting underdeveloped areas with population surpluses to more developed areas suffering from a scarcity of labor is the economic rationale behind labor migration. [...] According to population counts around 1850 more than 75,000 temporary labor migrants worked in Istanbul amounting to more than 35 per cent of the city's male population at the time.
>
> **(Riedler 2008: 235)**

This rural-urban migration was accelerated in the 20th century. While the urban population of Turkey was 20 per cent in 1955, it had risen to 65 per cent by 1997 (Strohmeier and Yalçın-Heckmann 2000: 181) and to 70 per cent by 2007 (TÜİK 2007). In the early 1970s, anthropologist Magnarella already observed a 'culture of discontent' in the town of Susurluk, northwestern Anatolia, 'a manifest dissatisfaction with locally available income and consumption opportunities and a pressing desire to abandon Susurluk and even Turkey in pursuit of a "better life"' (1974: 180). His findings are exemplary for rural Turkey. Indeed, Paul Stirling, when doing research near Kayseri in central Anatolia around 60 years ago, already found sons going to towns and cities to work (Stirling 1994, see also Stirling and İncirlioğlu 1996: 61–82). Writing about villagers in Subay, in the northern province of Kastamonu, Schiffauer said that seasonal migration among men was common until the 1950s to supplement the income of farms, but that wage labour later became an end in itself and led to more people leaving the village completely (1987: 151–8).

Thus, when a young Kurdish man, Mücahit Çetin, left Gundême, the village of my study, to work in the construction industry around 25 years ago, he was joining a stream of migrants from all over rural Anatolia looking for work in the cities. These migrants fit the typical profile of rural-urban migrants all over the world: they were in their late teens or early twenties, they were male and often single, and they often left for economic reasons. They entered the unskilled job markets of the cities, where they nevertheless earned more than they would have if they had remained in the village. Finally, they initiated and benefited from chain migration (Gmelch 1980: 137). Mücahit Çetin also initiated a stream of men from Gundême who then joined the unskilled (and later also skilled) labour market in the construction industry.

Labour migrants, temporary or permanent, have always been viewed with an attitude of distaste or mistrust by established urban populations (cf. Çelik 2005: 142, Erman 2004: §6, Karpat 2004: §24, Riedler 2008: 236–7). They are stereotyped as an invasion of uncouth peasantry that is neither able nor willing to adapt to urban life. Writing about Greece, Just describes Athens as having become a 'city of erstwhile country folk' by the 1970s; he says that 'true Athenians, old Athenians, those who can claim their roots in the city for several generations, are a rare breed' (2000: 27). In the same way, the concept of *eski İstanbullu*, an established Istanbulite, refers to a genealogy that is considered superior in its rooted urbanity, but does not reflect the life experience of most of the people living in Istanbul (and other large cities) any more. Indeed, according to a study by research institute KONDA, only 28.45 per cent of the inhabitants of Istanbul are such *eski İstanbullu*, all the others having migrated within one or two generations. This statistic is more dramatic for Istanbul than for other cities, but in the whole of Turkey, only 62 per cent of people live where they were born ('Biz Kimiz?').

In the case of migrant labourers from Van and other provinces in the east and southeast of Turkey, the fact that they are Kurdish may add to the tensions arising between migrants and more established urbanites. In Turkish, the word *kıro*, adapted from the Kurdish *kur* for 'son', has become a common label to refer to migrant men allegedly displaying conspicuously inappropriate behaviour in public urban spaces. Like other denigratory terms, *kıro* has become shorthand for a public discourse on 'the invasion of Istanbul's cultural spaces by outsiders who threaten its authenticity and purity' (Öncü 2002: 184).

This same discourse does not ask why people feel the need to migrate. Attention is thus drawn away from the disparate distribution of national resources and drawn towards the perceived threat to an elitist urban lifestyle. A publication by the Greater Istanbul Municipality (İBB) in 2007 exemplifies this attitude. Entitled 'Living in Istanbul in a Well-Mannered Way', it was envisaged as a 'travelling book' that people should pick up, read, and then leave in public spaces for others to read. The target audience was rural-urban migrants, who were supposed to learn manners from the book in order to fit in with city life. The book's preface reads:

> Of all our cities, Istanbul has received most migration. This migration has created a cosmopolitan living culture in Istanbul, but it has also weakened the sensitivity of people in shared living spaces. Istanbul has discarded its own living culture, based on a homogeneous culture, and is on the threshold of heterogeneous cultural chaos. This multiculturalism, which is not based on any shared living culture, has begun to damage our Istanbul of today.
>
> (İstanbul Büyükşehir Belediyesi 2007: 8,
> author's translation)

Ironically, terms such as 'cosmopolitan' and 'multiculturalism', words that conventionally imply approval of a variety of lifestyles, are used here to denote 'chaos', that is, something undesirable and unmanageable. Equally ironically, these terms are used to describe a cultural variety ignored in official discourses as differences are more often denied than expressed. It seems that the words '*kozmopolit*' and '*çokkültürlülük*' are here used rather self-consciously in an effort to set off the authors as more urban/urbane and sophisticated than the targeted audience.

It is true that cities with high immigration rates have faced difficulties. Because of the rapid urbanisation of only a few cities in Turkey, infrastructure has been challenged and unplanned buildings have mushroomed out of the ground. However, blaming migrants for the ensuing problems that growing cities face ignores the reasons why they come. A lack of investment in most of Anatolia means that unemployment is high outside of a few cities. Industry is concentrated in and around a few large cities. Belated attempts are being made at decentralising the country, for instance by setting up a university in each province. In addition, the Ministry of Development (*Devlet Planlama Teşkilatı*, DPT) announced in 2006 that it would create 'centres of attraction' (*cazibe merkezleri*) in Anatolia in order to channel migration there, away from the overcrowded large cities.

An added dimension of the internal migration in Turkey is the forced displacement of many people in the east and southeast of Turkey, mostly Kurds, but also Suryani Christians and Yezidis.[14] According to official numbers, 905 villages and 2,523 hamlets were evacuated by either the army or the PKK in their armed struggle in the late 1980s and 1990s (Ayata and Yükseker 2005: 14–5).[15] Thousands of people fled to Iraq and many others found refuge in the EU (Kurban et al. 2006: 17), but the vast majority was condemned to displacement within the country. There are estimates that half to two-thirds of the Kurdish population of Turkey today live in the west of the country, three million of them in Greater Istanbul (Wedel 1997: 155), the result of both labour and forced migration.

When the 'Kurdish issue' was discussed in Turkey in the past, human rights (violations) were never emphasised; rather, the problems of the area have been discussed in terms of terrorism and underdevelopment

(Yeğen 1996). Thus, internally displaced Kurds have often found themselves 'at the bottom of the barrel among the new urbanites' (Ayata
and Yükseker 2005: 21), without people in the cities recognising their
plight as anything but self-inflicted.[16]

It is in this national discursive context of urban contempt for rural
migrants in general and a silence on human rights pertaining to the
Kurdish question that my study of Kurdish rural-urban migrants in
and from the province of Van has to be placed. For the last 12 years, I
have observed life in Gundême, a Kurdish village from this province
in the east of Turkey, watching as it gradually emptied more and more
as people moved first seasonally for work and then often completely.
I have also been involved in the lives of people from Gundême who
have migrated to Van city and also some who came to Istanbul. In
Istanbul, I have done additional research among a cluster of Vanlı families, not from Gundême, in a neighbourhood I call Tepelik. Although
these particular migrants are not victims of forced displacement by
army or PKK, they have arguably been displaced by other factors
not always recognised by unwelcoming urbanites. In addition, they
may also experience discrimination as Kurds in western cities or high
unemployment in eastern ones.

This study thus represents an analysis of a relatively recent stream
of rural-urban migration of Kurdish Vanlı villagers. It focuses on the
effects that this migration has had both on migrants and in the sending province of Van.

Anthropological Perspectives on Migration

In recent reviews of the anthropology of migration, Vertovec and Brettell
point to shifts in the focus of the studies carried out. Initially, the
Manchester School was very influential in turning attention from the
study of social and cultural *orders* to processes of *change*, which allowed
for the emergence of studies on rural-urban migration in the first place.
Then a focus on identity formation and ethnicity was added to studies.
These were succeeded by a shift of attention towards migration and gender. The 1990s have also witnessed a 'transnationalist turn' in the study
of migration, a turn which has meant that anthropologists do not only

study the 'here' where migrants have moved, but the 'here-and-there', in order to arrive at more complete pictures of transnational networks (Brettell 2003: ix–x, Vertovec 2007a: 961–8, Vertovec 2009: 13).

Over time, there has been a shift in terminology. Where researchers once spoke of 'assimilation' or 'acculturation', the preferred term is now 'incorporation' (Brettell 2003: 103). A similar discursive shift can sometimes be observed in popular Turkish discourses on migration; as described above, there has long been a negative attitude towards migrants who have been perceived as resisting assimilation (i.e. urbanisation). In recent years, however, both media and academia have sometimes adopted a broader perspective that considers the reasons for and circumstances of migration and that goes beyond the 'village in the city' model when describing migrants. Migrants are thus portrayed as victims of greater circumstances (rural unemployment, lack of financial viability in farming, regional underdevelopment, forced displacement, gender inequalities), but at the same time as rational agents who react to their situation by making do in the best way they can (e.g. 'Biz Kimiz?'). Ethnographic research with small groups of people allows readers to partake in individual life experiences and leads to less sweeping statements about migrants (e.g. Çelik 2005 on Kurdish migrants in Istanbul, Şen 2005 on female migrants in Diyarbakır, Erman 1998a on rural migrants to Ankara, Wedel 1996 and 1997 on Kurdish migrants to Turkish cities, Neyzi 2004 on a female migrant from Tunceli). Erman also argues that there has been more attention paid to an indepth study of migrants, and particularly women, since the 1990s (2004: §30).

A move away from 'community studies' to an analysis of social networks has arguably facilitated the depiction of migrant life as varied, and has raised awareness of migrant interactions and transactions with other people from 'here' as well as 'there' (cf. Brettell 2003: 109, Levitt 1998: 927–8, Vertovec 2007a: 968); migrants inhabit 'multi-layered, multi-sited transnational social fields, encompassing those who leave and those who stay behind' (Levitt and Glick Schiller 2004: 1003). My research has thus made use of social network theory (Boissevain 1974, 1979, Bott 1971, Lin 1999, Mitchell 1969, Sanjek 1996) and the related concept of different types of capital (Bourdieu 1985, Lin 1999, 2000,

2001, Putnam 2000) in order to portray a less static picture of Vanlı migrants and non-migrants within such a migratory social field, which, in this case, is mostly not transnational, but rather 'translocational'.

Urban theorist Smith argues that transnational migration can be analysed according to different social spaces; he lists domestic, public, discursive, transactional, institutional, and global media spaces (2002: xii); in effect, he is dissecting the 'layers' of the migratory social field. I have borrowed and adapted the idea of such different social spaces in order to frame the data from my research. Thus, I discuss whether migration has had any effects on gender relations of migrating and remaining families. I have further used Smith's concept of a 'transactional space', merging it with the 'pathways, routes along which people, goods, and ideas travel' of Pnina Werbner (1999: 33). This has been helpful to discuss exchanges of goods and services, as well as marriage patterns, among migrant and non-migrant Vanlı. The concept of 'social remittances' (Levitt 1998) is used to discuss the transactions of ideas within the translocational migratory social field.

The analysis of discursive space also plays an important role in this book; my understanding of discursive space encompasses media and institutional spaces, and I discuss different levels of discourses on migration and, related to this, discourses on Kurdishness and Islam, ranging from those at state level to those created and perpetuated by individuals and groups themselves. Levitt and Glick Schiller differentiate between 'ways of being' and 'ways of belonging' in transnational migration; the former is 'actual social relations and practices', while the latter is a more conscious effort to 'signal or enact an identity' (2004: 1010). This distinction is particularly useful when discussing the explicit self-identifications of Vanlı as members of a tribe or as part of a province community, as 'conscious' Muslims, or as members of a Kurdish ethnic group.

'Ways of belonging' might be an explicit, discursive way of creating a 'home', a much-discussed concept in migration. A recent edition of articles on transnational migration refers to 'home' thus:

> The various chapters in this book expose conglomerate notions of 'home' including not only territorial attachment, but also

adherence to transportable cultural ideas and values. Often a great sense of belonging to a specific place is accompanied by the wish to reproduce and/or reinvent 'traditions' and 'cultures' associated with 'home'. It is not only national, cultural and social belongings, but also a sense of self, of one's 'identity', which corresponds to various conceptualizations of home.

(Al-Ali and Koser 2002: 7)

To my mind, there is a relationship between discourses at different levels (public, community, media, school, family...) and individual narratives that frame a person's life and that do the work of identification. Thus, a person who fronts certain identifications also acts upon them and creates a 'home' in a particular area of the migratory social field. Rapport and Overing point to the relation between practice and discourse (or 'stories') in relation to 'home':

[H]ome comes to be located in a routine set of practices, in a repetition of habitual social interactions, in styles of dress and address, in memories and myths, in stories carried around in one's head, in the ritual of a regularly used personal name.

(2000: 158)

While 'home' can evoke a sense of rootedness and singularity, it is actually possible to feel 'at home' in different places, spaces, or social fields, something that has become commonplace for translocational migrants. Elwert speaks of a 'switching process', or the 'polytactic potential' of humans, who are able to use different affiliations situationally (1995: §31). Similarly, Sökefeld discusses individuals 'embracing different identities', some of which may be in conflict with each other; he argues that a self is able to manage different identities and to create a relatively integrated whole in self-narratives (1999: 420–6). One can equate this successful management of different identifications 'amongst a global inventory of ideas and modes of expression' (Rapport and Dawson 1998: 25) with a constant repositioning of 'home'. People are thus 'at home' not in a fixed location but when they are able to create narratives of themselves that do not contain great ruptures.

For migrants, this involves positioning themselves in relation to the sending and receiving community, in relation to 'traditions' and 'innovations', and within networks of people.

Narratives and practices that connect the 'here' and the 'there' of migrant lives may 'ebb' and 'flow' during the lifetime of migrants, something that many short-term studies miss (Levitt and Glick Schiller 2004: 1012–3, cf. Gardner 1995: 5). Thus, migrants who seem to have cut ties with their sending community may, later in life, reconnect in the search for marriage partners, due to economic problems, for elections, or for other reasons. Children of migrants, who in my research context have mostly grown up without the active use of Kurdish, may later in life express a desire to learn to speak more Kurdish or spend more time in 'the village'. Transactions among migrants and between migrants and villages may vary in intensity over time. Indeed, according to a study in the USA, 'transnational practices were found to increase with time since immigration', an unexpected yet interesting finding. The argument is that an increase in economic (and other types of) capital over time allows a migrant to increase their interactions with and investments in the sending community (Portes and DeWind 2007: 10–2).

In my consideration of Vanlı migration I have thus found the recent anthropological literature on *transnational* migration relevant, despite the 'domestic' nature of the migration I have looked at. For one, since the sending area I am considering is virtually all Kurdish and the receiving areas are ethnically mixed, there is a real sense that the Kurdish migrants are crossing borders. Although these borders are denied by an official discourse of a homogeneous Turkey, they are imprinted in virtually everybody's mind and are reinforced by both Turkish and Kurdish nationalist discourses. Second, many of the concepts used and developed in recent transnational studies can be applied to migration in general and offer a more differentiated picture.

Research Locations and Methods

This book has emerged from long-term involvement with Kurdish Vanlı in three locations since 1997: a mountain village in the eastern province of Van, the city of Van, and Istanbul. In addition, I conducted research during a five-month period of fieldwork among a different set of Vanlı in Istanbul in 2006. This study is thus based on multi-sited fieldwork, something that has been called for (e.g. Marcus 1995) in order to avoid static pictures of bounded communities and to reflect the translocational networks that migrants and non-migrants maintain. Barth reminds us that large-scale processes are to be found in small-scale interactions (Just 2000: 25); thus, the macro-processes of rural-urban migration, the invasion of globalised capitalism, cultural assimilation, and changes in gender ideologies are here all considered from the point of view of Kurdish villagers or relatively recent villager migrants to cities in Turkey.

In the village of Gundême, I had close contact with five extended families of the Çetin lineage, numbering six elderly people (two widows and two couples), 17 couples ranging in age from 30 to 60, nine of their married children and countless younger children. I also met many women from other families when they visited or when we attended a celebration together. Although it was not acceptable for me to enter all the other households of the village on my own (cf. Abu-Lughod 1986), I gathered basic data on the household composition of Gundême and marriage alliances (both intra- and inter-village) over the last three generations. In 2005, there were 106 households[17] in the village.

In Van city, the main contacts I have are also members of the Çetin lineage from Gundême who had moved to the city. Some of them moved to Van as early as 25 years ago, while others only moved in 2007. The main reasons for moving are lack of work and income in the village, the lack of schooling opportunities in the village, and disagreements between family members. I had, and have, regular and close contact with three extended families, as well as six other households of their relatives. There were other families I visited more sporadically or other Vanlı I met when they visited the houses I stayed at.

In the village and in Van, I have had extensive opportunities for participant observation as well as some semi-structured interviews. I also noted information on households and marriages in Gundême, as well as the genealogies of Vanlı in Van and in the village.

In Istanbul, our home has witnessed a steady stream of visitors from Van, relatives, friends, or co-villagers. The number of visitors has grown with a relative increase in wealth among Vanlı as well as the decrease in prices for flights between the cities. While people used to come mostly for work and work-related tasks, university studies, or hospital visits, now Vanlı also come on holiday trips. Such visits have afforded me the opportunity to witness encounters between migrants and non-migrants and listen to discourses regarding migration, village life, Kurdish ethnicity, and religion.

In addition, in early 2006, I made contacts with Vanlı hometown organisations in Istanbul. Hometown organisations, or HTOs, are a common way for rural-urban migrants from any part of Turkey to organise themselves in the city (Çelik 2005, Narı 1999). Many Turks and Kurds have in common a strong attachment to their place of origin, called *memleket* in Turkish or *welat* in Kurdish. There are a great many hometown associations (Turkish: *hemşehri derneği*) in the big cities, serving as informal meeting points and, to differing degrees, offering a network of support. Both Turks and Kurds may self-identify as 'Vanlı', with the latter originally making up more of the rural population in the province. In Istanbul, there are different organisations that appeal to the two main different ethnic groups, reflecting their wary coexistence in Van. Although some of the Turkish Vanlı I met were very forthcoming with information and reminiscences, I felt that ultimately I had better background knowledge on the lives of Kurdish (villager) Vanlı and chose to pursue my research with them; however, information about Turkish Vanlı has sometimes been used to illuminate my data on Kurdish Vanlı.

At the initial stage of my research in Istanbul I used questionnaires to collect information, also asking some people at the centre of denser networks of (Turkish or Kurdish) Vanlı to ask their acquaintances to fill them in. In retrospect, the questionnaire[18] was an attempt on my behalf to be proactive when I only had contact with very few Vanlı in the city who were scattered and not necessarily known to each other. I had not yet found a suitable 'community' or place for more fruitful fieldwork. It turned out that the questionnaire made some Turkish Vanlı uncomfortable and reluctant to participate because of references to tribal membership, which is associated with Kurds and Kurdishness. For them, 'being Vanlı' did not include such concepts. Indeed, a common self- and other-description of Turkish Vanlı is *'yerli'*, that is, 'local'. Implied is an urbanity in contrast to the mostly Kurdish villager migrants who later moved to the province capital. As I became more focused on the phenomenon of rural-urban labour migration, I decided to limit my study to Kurdish Vanlı, whose lives in the village and in the cities I had easier access to.

I obtained 85 completed questionnaires from Vanlı outside of my Tepelik research location. Some of them were students whose studies are sponsored by the (Turkish) Van Foundation and a few Van Foundation members; the majority of respondents were accessed through another (Kurdish) Vanlı Association, which is located in Bağcılar, a district of Istanbul where there is quite a concentration of Kurdish Vanlı. Although I have calculated percentages for some of the responses, I would like to emphasise that I have only used the questionnaire responses when they confirm my general observations among Vanlı in Tepelik, in Van, and in Gundême, rather than to make any new claims. When I had found a suitable research location in Istanbul, I decided not to use the questionnaires with the people living there. My longer-term and more intensive involvement meant that a formal questionnaire would have been alienating. Finally, most of the questionnaire respondents were male, but most of my interlocutors in Tepelik were female.

Through the head of one of the Kurdish Vanlı hometown associations in Istanbul I was introduced to an estate of eight apartment blocks, with a total of 81 flats, the majority inhabited by people from Van. I chose this estate in an area I call 'Tepelik' as a research location and from March to July 2006 spent at least three days a week there. In the autumn of 2006 I revisited the estate several times to pursue some issues further.

In order to meet more Vanlı quickly and in order to make me a familiar figure on the estate, I decided to teach English to the inhabitants. As English lessons are a highly-valued commodity in Turkey, people were generally open to the idea. Many of them wanted to send their children, so I started teaching four different lessons on three days a week, spending the remainder of those days visiting households and talking to women.

As well as my teacher role, my identity as the wife of a Vanlı was invaluable. Indeed, it soon turned out that some of the inhabitants of the estate knew my husband or his family. First, Hediye, the wife of the Tepelik HTO leader, was the relative of the wife of my husband's relative, from a village near Muradiye district town. Second, a woman in her block, Gülşen Derman, turned out to be from the village of Gundême. She had not been back to Van for 20 years, and I had to jog her memory a bit to find shared acquaintances. On another day, when I was just leaving a block, a woman waved to me to come to her. When I did, the woman scolded me for not having come to them earlier; she turned out to be the niece of my husband's maternal grandmother. More generally, this grandmother's brother was well-known by all the families who came from the same district as my husband. He had been a self-made tribal leader whose influence had stretched widely throughout the villages. However, even women with no direct link of family or district welcomed me warmly in their midst as 'bizim gelin' or 'bûka me' ('our bride' in Turkish or Kurdish). My obvious interest in rural life in Van as well as the details of their life in the city sometimes amused them, but they also commended me for trying to learn about the ways of my husband's people. In order to obtain information, I mostly resorted to semi-structured interviews. I visited the women in their homes, and, after obtaining their permission, took notes during our conversation.

When evaluating conversations I had with people in all three research locations, I had to confront the question whether what I was told was 'really true'. Finally, I came to the same conclusion as Bora, who studied domestic helpers and their female employers in Turkey:

> Of course it cannot be claimed that what I was told reflected 'real life'. During each meeting, the women scrutinised their experiences and reassembled and reframed them as they saw fit. But since I considered exactly this scrutiny and reassembly as the 'source of information' of the research, I did not think I was facing a methodological problem.
>
> (2005: 31, author's translation)

Since identification is a process (Brubaker and Cooper 2000), it is never completed. Thus, to seek the absolute reality of people's lives is impossible, seeing as they continuously recreate their 'reality' themselves.[19] The descriptions of people's lives in this book should thus be read as a mêlée of self-descriptions, other-descriptions, and observations and interpretations on my part. I do, however, acknowledge the existence of certain dominant discourses, which in turn lead to certain behaviour being more likely and more acceptable.

In addition to the semi-structured interviews and recording of genealogies, I have used information and impressions gleaned from many less formal chats. Spending time with women in their homes and children at class in Tepelik, and with families in their homes in Van, Gundême, and Istanbul gave me scope for observation, too. Finally, having lived in Turkey since 1997, I have watched, read, and listened to Turkish (and sometimes Kurdish) media (TV, radio, newspapers, and magazines) and literature. During one year of my research I also worked as a translator and website editor for an independent Turkish news website, thus following national discourses on many issues closely. All of this represents invaluable background knowledge with which to contextualise my observations, conversations, and research.

2

GUNDÊME: A KURDISH VILLAGE IN EASTERN ANATOLIA

Why Start Here?

The pseudonym I have given to the village of my study, *Gundême*, is Kurdish for 'our village'. This is a deliberately generic term as my purpose is to convey a sense of an archetypical village. Since virtually all the migrant Kurdish Vanlı I have talked to speak frequently about 'our village', I am positing *the* village as a central cultural theme, a summarising key symbol (Ortner 1973). Similar observations have been made in other studies of Kurdish culture and migration (e.g. Ammann 2000, Kreyenbroek and Allison 1996, O'Shea 1998), and descriptions of village life are remarkably similar in these and other accounts (see also Yalçın 1986).

Although excessive generalisation about a whole society based on findings in a small community has long been frowned upon by anthropology, the presentation of *a* village as simultaneously *the* village is here meant to mirror the commonalities I have found in the references to rural life in conversations with Kurdish Vanlı over the last 12 years. Herzfeld points out:

In rightly rejecting the timeless perfections of structuralism, some anthropologists [...] have been too inclined to overlook how very similar are the models entertained by social actors in many societies, their own included.

(1990: 305)

I have always been struck by the similarity in the themes emerging when different Vanlı have talked about village life, which the majority of my interlocutors experienced first-hand. Indeed, in Turkey the concept of 'our village' is not limited to Kurds from Van, or even Kurds. Until quite recently, for instance, the concept of a 'holiday' (in Turkish: *tatil*) in a resort town was alien to all but the most affluent in Turkey. When people took 'leave' (*izin*) from work, it was to return to 'our village'. According to Andrews, more than 70 per cent of the population of the Kurdish-majority provinces in southeast Turkey were still villagers in 1965 (1989: 112). Thus, while the following is a description of *a* village as I have observed it, many of its features and activities also make it *the* village that Kurdish Vanlı use as a key symbol. Just as 'the American Way of Life' is cited by Ortner as a 'conglomerate of ideas and feelings' (1973: 1340), 'the village' for my Vanlı interlocutors is also a symbol that contains a multitude of ideas.

So, for instance, remembering the village can entail denigration or nostalgia. This apparent contradictory interpretation of a symbol can be understood better if one considers the dynamic function that discourses on village life have in the lives of migrant Vanlı. Rural-urban migrants use memories of rural life in their narratives in order to locate themselves spatially, temporally, and culturally in their migratory social field. They contemplate their current situation in terms of distance travelled from their village, time passed since migration, and changes made (or not made) in their lives. 'The village' is thus a constant point of reference, and representations of rural life are a means of self-presentation for migrants to the city (Rosenthal 2000: 24). Different interpretations of the key symbol 'the village' are discussed at the end of this chapter, following a description of Gundême location, material culture, activities, and population.

Location and Layout

Gundême is a village in the east of Turkey, in the province of Van. I have visited this village yearly over the past 12 years. These visits have afforded me a close relationship with several families there and have allowed me to observe the gradual migration of families from village to city. Together with my stays in Van city, these visits have also formed a meaningful background to my research among Vanlı migrants in Istanbul city.

The village is situated at least 2,000 metres above sea level, compared to the 1,727 metres of Van city. The road that winds up to Gundême from Van through the mountains was finally tarred in 2006; the previous dirt road had been difficult to navigate in rain and snow. In the past, the village was much more cut-off from other villages or district towns, let alone Van city, in the winter. Today, it takes about an hour to reach Gundême from Van. Haci[1] Fahrettin Çetin, a 70-year-old *Gundî* [2] who will be discussed in more detail later, remembers a winter in his childhood when over 25 babies and infants died from an infectious illness. Without telephones, clear roads to hospitals, or medical care in the village itself, there was nothing anyone could do.

The landscape on the way to the village is barren, made up of bare rounded mountainsides that are only green for a few months of the year. Snow caps the higher mountain tops until well into May, and new snowfall can be expected from November onwards. In winter, snow may be over a metre deep; however, all villagers, blaming global climate change, have noted that winters have become less severe in recent years. Trees can be seen surrounding houses and gardens in the villages that one passes, but the mountains themselves have long been stripped of them. Forests are very rare in Van province, today covering only 1 per cent of the province (Tarım ve Köyişleri Bakanlığı 2005: 25). This of course makes erosion a problem, creating a vicious circle of lack of trees to hold the earth and a resulting lack of top soil on the mountains to nurture trees and other plants. When it has rained a lot, there is thus a danger of mud brick houses sliding down the hill, and the winters bring the threat of avalanches.

Illustration 1: Gundême, Overlooking the Plain

Viewed as one approaches it from a plain in the northwest, Gundême is dwarfed by the mountains surrounding it in the southeast and west. It is situated on the edge of the plain, on the lower skirts of two mountains that rise in those two directions. On the plain, the villagers have fields of wheat and grass, but the mountain sides are quite bare, only offering grazing grounds for the cattle, sheep, and goats of Gundême. Due to inter-village marriages, many Gundî have relatives in other villages bordering the plain, and they are easily accessible on foot or by vehicle in the summer; some villagers also scale the mountains to walk to villages in the south.

When compared with other villages in the area, Gundême is typical in its architecture and household layout. Apart from the houses, outdoor kitchens, stables, and barns of each household, Gundême also has a few buildings for community use. First, there is a school (called *meytep* in the village), which has a teacher's house attached to it and is marked by a Turkish flag on its roof. The school is a small building of three rooms, in which five different classes are taught. Obligatory primary education was raised from five to eight years a few years ago.

However, the village school can still only offer five years of education, thus forcing Gundî children to give up their education, to attend regional boarding schools in other villages or towns, to stay with other relatives in bigger towns, or to migrate with their families. A bigger, three-storey boarding school has been built in Beyazlı, a nearby village on the plain, and was opened in 2007. It offers eight years of education.

Second, there is a mosque in the centre of the village, where most of the men congregate, at least on Fridays. It is called *cami* (Turkish for mosque) by most people, although some of the elder people may also refer to it as *mala Xwedê*, Kurdish for 'the house of Allah'. The *ezan* (prayer call) is in Arabic, like in the rest of Turkey, but announcements of other kinds are made in Kurdish. The current *mele* (Kurdish for *imam*, religious leader), who is from a different village, but Kurdish too, announces deaths of villagers or village meetings to be held in the mosque.

Third, the village has a health centre (*sağlık ocağı* in Turkish). In Turkey, nurses and doctors (as well as teachers) are sent to rural areas as part of their initial duty placements, but some manage to get out of this unpopular assignment, thus leaving many places in the East and Southeast without adequate medical attention. Some children in Gundême took me for a nurse initially as I spoke Turkish and did not cover my hair; they hid in case I would give them an injection. Indeed, most village children are now regularly inoculated. A midwife from the *sağlık ocağı* was called to a birth when I was in the village in August 2004, but for many births the mothers still rely on experienced fellow village women instead. It was rare for village women to be taken to give birth in hospital unless there was an emergency. One middle-aged woman told me how they 'butchered' her daughter in hospital, regretting that she was sent there. Unlike the trend in urban Turkey, where many women pressure their doctors for caesarean births (and pressure is also exerted by doctors), women in the village would feel sorry if such an operation were necessary.

Fourth, Gundême has three little shops (*market*) serving the community. One of them also has a men's *kahve* attached to it, but it is only open in the evenings and at the weekends. Fifth, there is a grain mill (*aş* in Kurdish). In fact, the mill is owned by two villagers in partnership and the others pay for its use.

Housing and Daily Routines

While the following descriptions refer to my observations in Gundême over many years, the reader should keep in mind that descriptions of buildings, fields, and mountains of the village, as well as its activities and sensory experiences, form a vital part of discourses on village life by migrants in the city, both by my interlocutors and others (cf. Ammann 2000: 100).

When I visited Gundême, most of the social gatherings took place in homes or, in the summer, in the garden. The Kurdish word for the house, *mal*, also denotes the members of the household and in some contexts the whole lineage (Yalçın 1986: 82). The significance of *mal* thus transcended the physical to include a sense of belonging. One's own home (*mala xwe*) represented the place where one found peace and could withdraw from the eyes of others. The home was the focal point of the household, with women going to and fro between house, outdoor kitchen, fountain, and stables, children coming in from school, play, or shepherding duties to grab a bite to eat, and men coming home from fieldwork or from trips to the city in the evenings. It was also the place where one played host to others, looking after their needs and encouraging them to relax. In summer, the *mal* provided a shady quiet retreat from the work in the sun, while in winter, with families gathered around the stove, it was a warm shelter from the snow and wind.

Traditionally, houses in the province of Van were made of sun dried mud bricks. The ceilings were supported by the stripped trunks of the slim, tall poplar tree. In the past, houses in the village were sometimes two storeys high, and the ground floor was used as a stable for the animals. This arrangement allowed the heat from the animals to rise and warm the living space of the family. However, with the arrival of modern building materials, two storeys became too expensive and people built only one storey. There were still numerous mud brick houses, but many were also made of breeze blocks and cement. They still featured the poplar beams across the ceiling (cf. Ammann 2000: 102),[3] exceptions being the school and the *sağlık ocağı* as they were built by the government. The *sağlık ocağı* was three storeys high. Where people could afford it, the traditional flat roof had given way to raised roofs (gabled or hipped) made of corrugated iron. It meant that rain water did not seep through the roof and that the snow, which had to be shovelled off laboriously from the flat roofs to prevent their collapse, slid off or was easily removed in winter. Windows were usually single-glazed and wood-framed, but I also saw a few examples of plastic-framed double-glazing, called '*pimapen*' and considered a sign of luxury.

The bare cement floors were covered with a thin, low-quality wall-to-wall carpet; they had replaced the traditional earthen floor covered by felt (Turkish: *keçe*, Kurdish: *kulav*). On top, there were factory-made carpets. Carpet production had completely died out in Gundême village, and I only saw older handmade carpets in two households in Van, but none in the village.[4] The handmade carpets that once adorned the houses were sold to shrewd traders who introduced machine-made woollen or nylon carpets. The inner walls of the houses were white-washed or painted; wallpaper was never used.

Room layout was very similar in all of the village houses. There were usually few, but large rooms. Married couples usually had a bed on a bedstead, but most household members, as well as guests, slept on homemade woollen mattresses with woollen bedding; both were laid out at night and folded up in big layers against a wall during the day (cf. Aristova 2002: 178, Ammann 2000: 104). Consequently, even rooms used for sleeping could be used as sitting rooms during the day. This was particularly important when large gatherings of men and women socialised separately. A typical house had a large rectangular sitting room with blankets and cushions arranged along the walls for sitting. A lot of homes had one or two sofas, too, but in female gatherings I noticed that the older women were often more comfortable sitting on a cushion on the ground. If the household contained an extended family, each married couple ideally had a room of their own, where they slept with their children. Older children would sleep in the sitting room, or they were separated according to gender.

Another common feature was a kitchen or kitchen area. Some houses had organised running water in the kitchen and had a sink they could use for washing dishes. Other houses' kitchen areas had a low cement basin with a drain, not unlike a shower basin, and the women brought in jugs of water to be used there. Most women used the kitchen for some cooking (if they had a gas or electric cooker), for the fridge, and to store crockery, cutlery, and provisions (e.g. tea, sugar, vegetables, pulses, pasta, and oil).

However, no household was complete without an outdoor kitchen (Kurdish: *xanî*). It was made of stone and had a *tendûr* oven, a hole in the ground lined with a hollow ceramic cylinder (cf. Ammann 2000: 100, Aristova 2002: 254). To make bread (Kurdish: *nan*), a fire was lit in the cylinder, heating the ceramic walls, and the risen yeast dough was shaped and slapped onto the walls with a kind of hard pillow. The *tendûr* was also used for heating water and slow-cooking foods. Vanlı in the city tended to miss the taste of the *tendûr* bread and the meat and vegetable stews cooked slowly over the fire. However, it is doubtful whether women miss the actual activity of baking the bread, which involved sitting in the smoky little room, kneading the dough, bending low to slap it onto the sides of the oven, and being careful not to burn their hands. Baking bread could be a day-long activity if the family was large or if one baked provisions for several days. The baking of the bread was often done by the mothers-in-law and the older *bûks* (Kurdish: brides) rather than the daughters of the house. This meant that young women, on getting married, had to learn this skill from their mothers-in-law.

The main house also had a little wash chamber with a drain leading outside into the ground. Water was either boiled on the *tendûr* in big aluminium jugs and carried to the chamber or heated in big plastic tanks with immersion heaters. The toilet was outside, further away from the house. It was a hole over a deep pit, surrounded by stone walls, and had a thatched roof. When villagers talked about physical hardship in the village, they tended to agree that an indoor toilet, canalisation, and running water would be great improvements, particularly in the long and harsh winter. In addition, some villagers considered buying solar water heating panels and tanks, which were very popular in Van city. Even in winter there is enough sun to heat water, although the cold may damage the fluid used in the equipment.

Visiting different families in the village, I had occasion to compare wall decorations. Generally there was not much furniture, so that most of the walls were exposed. Wall decorations were typically sparse and hung very high on the walls, and typically at least some of them had a religious theme. There were often representations of the holy cities of Mecca or Medina as posters, prayer rugs, or stained glass. Pictures of Hazreti Ali, the son-in-law and nephew of the Prophet Muhammed, were also very popular. This was curious as these pictures are typically found in Alevi households. Apparently a conservative teacher was once on duty in the village and saw all the pictures of Hazreti Ali. He later confessed his fear that he had been sent to an Alevi village.[5] Depicting the Prophet Muhammed is forbidden, and perhaps the pictures of Ali provided people with a focus for emotional attachment. In one household I also came across a pictorial dynasty of religious leaders.

In virtually every household there was a promotional calendar, a block of pages with one to be torn off every day, mounted on a cardboard advertisement for veterinary clinics, medicine, or petrol stations. The daily page was often the only reading material in the house apart from the Qur'an. A typical page contained a prayer, a suggested menu for the day, popular girls' and boys' names, the prayer times in different cities around Turkey, a religious story, or interesting facts about science. Apparently, these calendars were once very sought after when people did not often leave the village. Tacit Amca and Haci Şako from the Çetin lineage used to be the only Gundî regularly driving between Van and the village, and they were asked to bring the calendars to the village as special favours. Today, there are many minibuses driving to and from Van, and the calendars have become common.

Many homes also contained a clock. Clocks were important for school, minibus schedules, and the return of the sheep; on the other hand, people also measured the passing of the day according to the position of the sun (and the resulting shadows) and the *ezan*.[6]

Some households had one or two photos framed on the wall, but I never saw a picture of the resident family as a whole displayed. Rather, if there were any pictures at all, they seemed to be of a respected elder (perhaps deceased), and sometimes a picture of a young man in his military uniform, a typical occasion in a man's life when a rare photo used to be taken. With an increase in school attendance by the young generation, there were sometimes pictures of children in their school uniform. I once took photos of middle-aged married couples in Gundême, and there was much bashfulness and laughter during the proceedings. They were very pleased with the photos, but did not hang them on the wall. Many villagers in their thirties and forties lamented the fact that they did not own any childhood photographs, and there were many older people who had died with no photos remaining of them.

In only three households did I see wall decorations with a more (political) Kurdish flavour; in one home, there was a plait of red, green, and yellow cloth, that is, the colours of the Kurdish flag, unaccepted by the Turkish state. In three households I saw pictures of Yılmaz Güney, the Kurdish actor and film director whose works were long banned in Turkey. His films, such as 'Yol', depicted the lives of Kurds and other downtrodden people. Popular posters depict him in a macho pose with a gun and a stern look on his dark face, a well-known still taken from one of his films. In two households there were also pictures of Ahmet Kaya, a Kurdish singer who died in exile in 2000.

As mentioned above, the houses were sparsely furnished. The sitting rooms were virtually empty apart from the sitting cushions and possibly one or two sofas. In the bedrooms, the double bed for the married couple was sometimes matched by a wardrobe, but often their belongings were also stored under the raised bed. A copy of the Qur'an was often kept in a cloth bag hung from a nail high on the wall, and medicine and tablets were often stored in plastic bags hung up in the same way. In no house in the village did I see a desk for children to study at or a dining table with chairs. Children did their homework sitting or lying on the floor, and everyone ate from a big round metal tray or a vinyl tablecloth, called *sofra*, spread on the floor.

One piece of furniture seemed to be present in every village household and held great symbolic value: a wooden chest, *sandık* in Turkish and Kurdish. It was brought into the marriage by the bride, holding the trousseau she prepared. Since it was lockable, it was often used to safeguard gold jewellery and goods such as tea, sugar, biscuits, and sweets, the former from thieves, the latter from children. The key to the *sandık*, as well as the key to the *xanî*, was with the highest-ranking woman of the household. I often saw daughters or brides ask for the key from their mother or mother-in-law, who would fumble for the key under layers of skirts or under her blouse and hand it over, sometimes reluctantly. Adults have recounted childhood memories of trying to steal the keys to either *sandık* or *xanî* in order to feast on the sweets or on the *to*, the much-loved creamy layer that forms on freshly-made yoghurt.

Matching the move from handmade carpets to synthetic ones, there was a great popularity of plastic flowers in very lurid colours. They often adorned the shelves on which the TV stood and the little side and coffee tables that were stacked against the wall when not in use. The little furniture that there was (a shelf for TV and music set, side and coffee tables, perhaps another shelf or table for extra cups and glasses, and the *sandık*) were often covered with small square lace mats made by the women of the home as part of their trousseau.

Electricity came to Gundême as late as 1986, but every household I have visited since the 1990s had a television. Some villagers lamented the advent of TV and the demise of socialising it had caused. They still remembered the first television arriving in the village, in Tacit Çetin's household in 1988. People would crowd into the house to watch TV together. Interlocutors also recalled fondly how they used to pass the evenings without electricity. They had gasoline lamps that were not very bright, reserving a more powerful type of gasoline lamp for visitors. When that bright lamp lit up the windows, neighbours also came round to enjoy an evening together. Another pastime was to go to the *xanî* and sit around the still-warm *tendûr* in the dark or by candle light, dangling one's legs in the *tendûr*, covering the legs with a duvet, and telling stories or chatting. These memories were of course tinted with nostalgia; life without electrical light, water heaters, stoves, and heaters for physical comfort and without any radio and television to stay in touch with the outside world must have been difficult.

Television is now ubiquitous. At one point in the late 1990s I remember looking on in fascination as the married women, a lot of whom spoke little or no Turkish, watched Brazilian soap operas dubbed into Turkish. Not only was the Turkish language alien, but the domestic servants, the children out of wedlock, and the intrigues of the world of business seemed alien to village life, too. However, as I have realised over the years, scheming relatives, scandals, and family feuds are commonplace in the village, too, if not immediately apparent to the outsider. Indeed, people sometimes compared the soap opera characters to acquaintances. When television first arrived, it was such a novelty that people sometimes forgot to lock the animals up in time. In a neighbouring village, a man was said to have lost his flock to the wolves for that reason. 'Fernando' and 'Isabella' gradually made way for Kurdish broadcasting received by satellite (cf. Hassanpour 1997) from outside of Turkey and countless Turkish soap operas on dozens of private Turkish channels. Since 2009, Vanlı can also watch the state channel TRT 6, which broadcasts in Kurdish.

The arrival of the first telephone in the house of Haci Memo Çetin, an important elder of the village, was also still remembered by young adults. Today, all households have telephones. As for mobile phones, there only used to be a strong enough signal on the top of the mountain behind the village. Now one provider has made reception possible in the village, and Gundî have been quick to embrace the new technology. In Tepelik, and in Istanbul in general, I met several women who sent their mothers or relatives in the village or in Van call units by mobile phone so that they could keep in touch.

Population of Gundême

Gundême and many surrounding villages in Van province are (today) ethnically homogeneous, that is, they are exclusively Kurdish, with the exception of the Turkish civil servants who are sent to the villages as nurses, doctors, *imams*, or teachers.[7] However, government policy has sometimes been to settle non-Kurds in the rural areas of the province, resulting in a few non-Kurdish villages. Some are populated with Black Sea Turks (e.g. Emek and Dönerdere in the Özalp district of Van), some with so-called 'Acem' (in this context Azeri Turks from Iran), or Kyrgyz from Afghanistan.[8] These groups have formed their own villages. In the case of Gundême, I know that five women have married into a neighbouring *Acem* village, but no women from that village have come to Gundême in marriage. Generally, the term 'Acem' as used by the Kurds seems to have derogatory connotations.

Many of the Kurds from Van are members of tribes, but not necessarily so (cf. Bruinessen 1994: 7, McDowall 1997: 17). Bruinessen states very clearly that although social scientists have become wary of using the term 'tribe', it is a definite emic concept that many Kurds can relate to (Bruinessen 1999a and 2003). Yalçın's research in the Turkish province of Hakkâri confirms this; she points to the existence of different levels of Kurdish social organisation; they are, in ascending order, the *mal* as household, the *mal* as lineage or clan[9], the *qabile* as sub-tribe, and the *eşîret* as tribe. She also says, however, that tribal units have become smaller, with tribal confederacies dissolved and only tribes relevant today; up to 15 tribes are said to exist in Hakkâri (1986: 186–9). According to Özer, there are at least 43 tribes in the Van area (2003: 36). Of 55 Vanlı respondents to my questionnaire, all living in Istanbul, 21 said they did not belong to a tribe, whereas 32 said they did.

In Gundême, which has been settled by lineages from various tribes at different times, the level of the *qabile* seems irrelevant. Bruinessen has argued that for Kurds a distinction between what he denotes as lineage (*mal*) and clan (*qabile*) is rare as the actual political association with a kin group of patrilineal descent has mostly been more important than clan membership (1978: 60). As for tribal membership in Gundême, there have been conflicting statements about what tribe people belong to. This is arguably due to the fact that there are no prominent tribal leaders living in the area of Gundême today. It is thus more useful to introduce the lineages existing in Gundême and their relative sizes first, and then to discuss probable tribal membership.

When counting households, I have made use of the local concept of *mal* referred to earlier. The extended patrilocal patrilineal households may split when a son has established himself as sufficiently independent of his father or if the sons of a deceased father decide to separate. While *mal* sometimes also refers to the wider patrilineage, which is led by one male elder, the separation of housing is a highly symbolic act signalling, to a certain extent, the break-up of the extended family. *Mal* in the sense of 'house' thus implies separate household heads, who may act independently in many matters, and it is appropriate to count the separate residential units as separate households.

In the summer of 2006, there were 106 households in Gundême village, not counting the lodgings of the teachers and nurses or the household of the *mele*, who was Kurdish but from outside the village. There were lodgings for one teacher next to the school building; the other teachers and nurses lived in the health centre lodgings. The *mele* lived in a house near the mosque. All remaining households were linked to at least a few others through patrilineal or affinal ties. There were 11 self-identified patrilineages in the village (Table 1). Mostly they were easily identifiable because of the shared surname. In the case of lineages 7 and 11, there were some different surnames, but as people considered themselves part of the same lineage, I noted them down as one.

I was only able to collect exact information on the adult population of the village, shown in Table 1. My movements were somewhat restricted, and my interlocutors themselves sometimes lost count of the number of children in other households. In order to give an impression, however, I counted the number of children that was given as definite and used the lower number when I was given estimates, resulting in a conservative estimate of 410 children. Added to the adult population, this would mean a village population of 799. Again, just in order to give an impression, the average household size would be 7.6 people.

Table 1: Lineages in Gundême

Lineage	No. of Households (HH)	No. of Married and Widowed Adults[10]	Average No. of Adults per HH
1	2	4	2
2	3	11	3.7
3	3	9	3
4	3	10	3.3
5	4	13	3.3
6	6	26	4.3
7 (Çetin)	7	27[11]	3.9
8	9	21	2.3
9	12	34	2.8
10	13	44	3.4
11	44	190[12]	4.3
Total	106	389	average: 3.7

Of the 106 households, lineage 11 had both most households and most adults per household in 2006, adding up to 190 adults (around 49 per cent of the adults of the village). In comparison, lineage 7, the Çetin lineage with which I am most concerned, numbered 27 adults in the village at the time.

The members of lineage 11 are said to be Xanî, a tribe originally from the province of Hakkâri, south of Van. Lineages 2, 6, and 9 are said to be Şemsikî, but lineage 2 has also been listed as part of the Sêvî tribe. Lineage 1 is just said to be 'from Iran'. Several lineages do not seem to belong to any tribe, but lineages 3 and 5 have often collaborated with the Çetin lineage. I have heard one lineage called 'Filekî' in semi-jest on several occasions, 'file' referring to the Armenians who used to live in Van province.[13] The implication is that this lineage is made up of converted Armenian Christians.

The Çetin lineage is the only one in Gundême claiming to be Müküsî, but there are families in other villages of Muradiye district defining themselves as members of that tribe, too. Aydin Bey, a prominent leader of the Müküsî from a Muradiye village,[14] recently deceased, was the central figurehead for this tribe, but he was not a feudal landlord from a long-established family of such aghas. Rather, he was an entrepreneurial individual who managed to first raise the status of his family in his own village, and then extended his power base among the scattered Müküsî and their allies in other villages through both careful political planning and force. Aydin Bey made his brother mayor of the district town and later Member of Parliament, while he continued to act in the background. It is due to its associations with Aydin Bey that the Çetin lineage, although small in size, was able to maintain an influential position in Gundême. Haci Fahrettin, who has been living in Van for many years, still enjoys considerable status among Gundî and villagers from the district.

Speaking with interlocutors from neighbouring villages, I have come to the conclusion that it is typical of the area that villages contain a mixture of lineages and have no feudal landlords (who feature in mainstream clichés about Kurds). One reason for the lack of feudal landlords is perhaps the mountainous land in Van province, which lends itself mostly to animal husbandry, rather than large-scale field and plantation work. According to Beşikçi, the percentage of land-less families in the east of Anatolia was 38 per cent in 1970, but this rate was higher—45 per cent—in the southeastern provinces of Urfa, Mardin, Gaziantep, and Diyarbakır (1970: 140). In the area of Gundême, some families have more and some less land, depending on when they arrived in the village, yet there is no completely landless class that works for a feudal landlord.

Another explanation for the dispersion of tribal lineages may be found in the events of the First World War, which resulted in a total upheaval of the region. First of all, local men were recruited as soldiers. The Russian front was very close by; for instance, tens of thousands of Ottoman soldiers died in the disastrous battle of Sarıkamış[15] in the winter of 1914. The war meant that villagers were deprived of their male workforce, and the older people today still speak of a time of famine that their parents remembered. Many villagers were dispersed from Van, either fleeing from the Russians or leaving to avoid star-vation. In her work in the neighbouring province of Hakkâri, Yalçın also points to the upheavals of the 20th century as a reason for village settlement that is 'less homogeneous in terms of tribal membership' (1986: 191).

Not only were local Kurds dispersed, but the war also brought an end to the existence of a very considerable Armenian population in the area. In April 1915, according to Kieser, the systematic massacre of Armenian villagers in Van province had started, Muslims being for-bidden on penalty of death to help them. Similar to events in 1896, the Armenians in Van city were armed and prepared for conflict, whereas those in villages who could not flee to the city were killed. Up to 10,000 Armenian villagers fled into Van city, seeking refuge with fel-low Armenians or Western missionaries, who were running schools in Van at the time. When the Russians entered Van in May 1915, the Armenians turned from being the victims into perpetrators them-selves. When the Russian army left Van in July, most Armenians left with the Russians, knowing full well what would lie in store for them otherwise (Kieser 2000: 449). All in all, Van would be occupied by the Russians three times (Ter Minassian 2000: 172), and in the end, there were no Armenians and very few Muslims left. The area was gradually repopulated, either by returning Muslims or by newcomers. The villages emptied of Armenians were later appropriated by Kurds, either nomads up to that time or in search for a new home after the ravages of war. Many former Armenian villages were occupied by members of the Burukî tribe when they returned to Turkey from Iran and the Caucasus (Özer 2003: 78, Bruinessen 1978: 65).

According to Haci Fahrettin Çetin, his ancestors were the first to arrive in Gundême around 200 years ago, prior to many of these events. Other lineages are said to have arrived later. It should not come as a surprise that the households in Gundême often formed neighbouring clusters according to patrilineage. For the patrilineages, postmarital residence was patrilocal, and the land was usually divided only among the sons of a family, thus, over time, creating smaller parcels of adjacent land where separated agnatic households settled. A sketch of the village (Figure 1) shows the clusters of patrilineal households with numbers; there were only very few households that were not at least adjacent to one or two other households of the same lineage. This

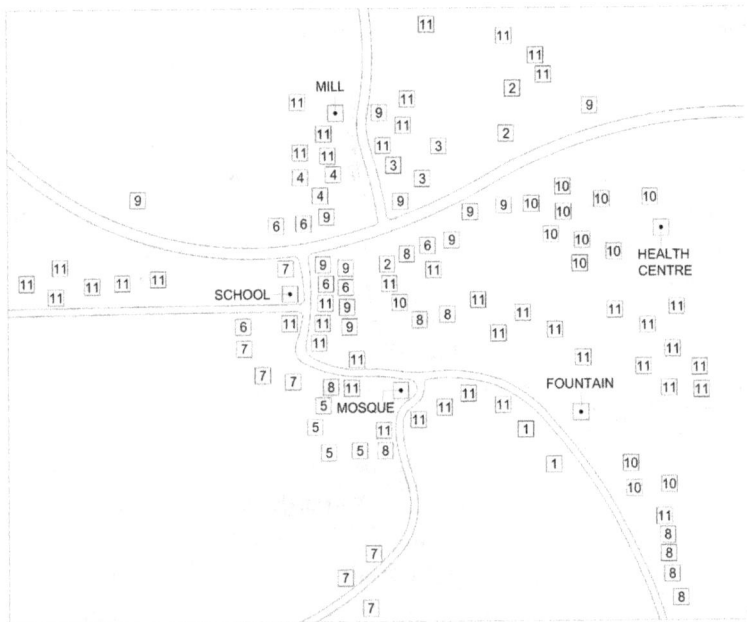

Figure 1: Lineage Household Clusters in Gundême

means of course, that there were multiplex relations between these households, based on residence in the same village, membership of the same lineage, and neighbourhood, and often, as is discussed in Chapter 7, intermarriage. This multiplexity increased the likelihood of collaboration in agricultural tasks; women would work together to wash wool, collect herbs and spring onions for the cheese, or to host and serve large numbers of guests. Men would collaborate during harvest time or when carrying out repairs on the houses.

Gundême—'Our Village' as a Key Symbol

As pointed out at the beginning of the chapter, the pseudonym for my village of research is deliberately generic since the village and rural life I have described were constantly referred to by my Kurdish Vanlı interlocutors in Van city, in Tepelik, and in Istanbul. 'The village' or 'our village' played an important role in everyday conversations among migrants, and I have suggested that it represents a summarising key symbol in Ortner's sense.

Often 'the village' is used without elaboration and often in the classic dichotomy of rural-urban, with a second key symbol of urbanity/ modernity offered in explicit or implicit contrast. As Rapport and Overing note, the rural-urban distinction is often associated with ideas about progress and 'modernity' (2000: 320). While I have found this to be very true among my interlocutors, one should beware of reducing each key symbol to one fixed meaning only. Ortner points to the multitude of ideas contained in key symbols, and Ferguson reminds us of Raymond Williams' observation that meanings attached to the rural or the urban are historically specific. In his discussion of the rural and urban in the Zambian Copperbelt, Ferguson noted that in Zambia, over time, the metaphors used for rural and urban life changed. He describes a nostalgic attitude of rural-urban Zambian migrants towards village life from the 1920s onwards, and also points out that many ethnographies of the 1950s found a similar idealisation of the rural, a 'moral contrast' to urban selfishness and depravity. However, not all depictions of city life were negative, and urbanity was also associated with development (1992: 80–2).

During fieldwork in the 1980s, Ferguson found that the symbolic dichotomy of rural and urban had to a great extent collapsed and other ways of talking about Zambian society had taken over—both rural and urban Zambians were often described as innately selfish (1992: 85–8). This is a point I will discuss later. For now, I would like to draw attention to two different associations with the key symbol of rural life among Vanlı Kurds. Since migration from the villages has been relatively recent (i.e. the last 25 years) compared to the Zambian migration, it is perhaps not surprising that these associations resemble the earlier attitudes towards rural and city life in Zambia in the first half of the 20th century.

As Smith points out, migration can be analysed in terms of different social spaces, one of them being discursive (2002: xii);[16] the physical act of removing oneself to a different place is thus accompanied by ways of talking about this removal. When discussing discourses, as I repeatedly do in this book, I make use of a very common-sense definition offered by Link, 'an institutionally solidified way of speaking, insofar as such a way of speaking determines and solidifies action and thus also exerts power' (Jäger 2001: 81, author's translation).[17] According to Jäger, *discourse strands* (*Diskursstränge*) are a collection of discourses that share the same theme, that is, a strand represents all the things that are said or thought about a certain theme. Discourse *fragments* are smaller units within each strand, and represent different discursive positions on the same theme (Jäger 2001). To refer back to Ortner, one may thus liken a discourse strand to a key symbol. Since, as Ferguson pointed out and as I have found in my fieldwork, attitudes to the key symbol of rural life are ambiguous, it is useful to try to untangle these attitudes by representing them as separate discourse fragments on a theme. This framework is useful since it reflects the reality of different actors participating in the interaction with and production of discourse fragments; these discourse fragments revolve around one issue, but allow for the fact that there is difference in attitude, too:

> The active individual is thus fully involved in the realisation of
> power relations (praxis). He thinks, plans, constructs, interacts,
> and fabricates. And as an individual he also faces the problem

of survival, that is, of asserting himself and finding a place in society. However, he does this within a sprawling network of discursive relations and contentions, within 'living discourses', in the sense that he brings them to life and, entangled in them, lives them and contributes to their transformation.

(Jäger 2001: 87, author's translation)

As pointed out earlier, discussion of village life is very common among migrants. Since mass migration from Kurdish Vanlı villages has been relatively recent, most of my interlocutors are familiar with village life. In Istanbul, most of the Vanlı in the Tepelik estate have a rural background; their migration to Istanbul took place over 30 years ago,[18] when villagers from Van province had not yet moved to the city of Van in great numbers. They thus came to Tepelik directly from their villages. While all of the families living in Tepelik now have relatives who have left villages for Van city, the older generation and many of the second generation women (who migrated with their husbands or came to Istanbul in marriage) experienced childhood, and perhaps also adulthood, in a village. Most of the young adults and children who were born in Istanbul know their parents' villages through visits to Van, visits from relatives to Tepelik, and through the narratives of their parents.

In Gundême, Haci Fahrettin was one of the first to leave the village permanently with his nuclear family around 25 years ago. Other families from the village following later have had varied experiences of village life, some remaining there until 2007. In any case, Gundî families living in Van continue to visit Gundême for funerals, weddings, and other occasions.

Migrants use narratives about village life to make sense of their current lives. Their present situation in Van city or Istanbul is removed from the village in several ways; for one, time has passed. Just as adults everywhere may reminisce about their childhood and youth, Gundî reminisce about village life, with memories of an untroubled childhood with unlimited physical freedom but perhaps also poverty. These conditions of the past are made the more remote due to the physical distance that has come between the migrant and the village.

Depending on the level of happiness a migrant Vanlı feels at a certain point in life and also depending on the type of interactions people within the translocational migratory social field engage in, these memories of village life are tinged by nostalgia or contempt. In short, discursive constructions of rural life differ situationally, a point taken up in the discussion of Kurdish ethnicity later on.

Nostalgia and Contempt

A common discursive position when talking about village life is nostalgia. In Levitt and Glick Schiller's terms, this discursive fragment is a 'way of belonging' (2004: 1010), an explicit identification with and remembrance of a 'community'. Nostalgia for village life is particularly strong for a woman if many of her relatives remain in the village and she does not see them often. She may also fondly recall a carefree childhood; often the girls of the house did not need to work very hard as their mothers and the *bûks* were available to do housework. Patrilocal residence after marriage means that many women have married into other villages and have lost touch with their friends from childhood and adolescence.

Nostalgia is also embodied knowledge, as contrasts are made between village life and urban discomforts. This contrast was expressed to me in a much stronger manner in Istanbul than in Van as migrants to the latter city mostly lived in quieter neighbourhoods with at least a small garden. However, Istanbul's toxic smell of burning coal in the winter and the sickly-sweet smell of uncollected rubbish in the summer, particularly in less well-off neighbourhoods, was contrasted with the fresh rural mountain air; the chlorinated undrinkable tap water in the city with the clear cold streams in the village; the mass-produced bread loaves of the city with the flat bread baked in the *tendûr* ovens of the village; the anonymity and coldness of urban relations with the crowded, happy gatherings in the village; the dangers of urban life for children and teenagers compared with the freedom to roam in the village; and the weddings in stuffy wedding halls with cheap cake and lemonade were compared to outdoor dancing and homemade food at village weddings. In short, a rural idyll (cf. Rapport and Overing

Illustration 2: A Rural Idyll

2000: 315) was evoked, very similar to the depiction of a moral universe that Ferguson described.

This perceived idyll has become particularly poignant as a return to the village is unlikely for most. On the contrary, through the process of chain migration, more and more relatives have moved to Van or western Turkish cities like Istanbul in an effort to increase their economic and social opportunities. The lack of profitability of animal husbandry in Van's rural areas has forced many young men to work on construction sites in and outside of Van, and the lack of schooling opportunities in the countryside has led many of them to bring their families to Van or to western Turkey, in the hope that their children will one day do better.

Thus another discourse fragment sees village life in a much more critical light. All the women I spoke to were grateful for living in the city as they said the living conditions were better. Many women spoke of the hard work involved in having to carry water from a central village fountain to their homes, as well as constantly baking bread for big families, looking after the animals, and living through the harsh

winters. Additionally, women who now live in the city were aware of
the inherent power they had obtained with the allocation of household
budgets. In the village, by contrast, it was usually the men who went
to town to do the shopping unless enterprising travelling salesmen
came to the village. Furthermore, in Istanbul many of the women
even earned their own money with their sewing and embroidery skills,
working for piece-making workshops. Many women also participated
in money and gold collection days with neighbours and relatives;
women who trusted each other through neighbourhood, friendship,
or family ties came together at regular intervals and contributed a
fixed amount of money or gold to the group. The lump sum was then
handed to a different woman each time, following a pre-arranged
order. This allowed the women to make larger purchases without having to use credit cards or making debts. When I asked whether their
relatives in the villages also practised this custom, one woman replied,
'The women [there] can't lay their hands on a penny!'

Here one has to be careful to point out that my interlocutors have
been more or less voluntary migrants who have been able to establish
a relatively safe economic base. A study of internally displaced people
in Diyarbakır city shows that women remembered the ease with which
they had access to (homemade and homegrown) resources to make food
in the village, whereas they had to beg money from their underpaid
husbands for each meal in the city (Şen 2005: 120–2). Clearly, urban
poverty would show up more instances of a nostalgic discourse on the
village.

Access to money means that women can purchase more things. In
the past, a woman was given a dowry on marriage, which consisted
of bedroom furniture and household goods. It would be the last time
her natal family spent money on her, and it was tacitly considered a
premortem inheritance, thus excluding women from inheriting land
and property later on, despite the Turkish civil code prescribing equal
distribution. As more young men have started bringing home cash,
both in the villages and cities, couples have been able to buy more
goods throughout their marriage. If the woman additionally earns
money from home, as many did in Tepelik, then she can buy items
of her choice. Migrant women were very proud of the decorative items

and household goods they had bought. To a certain extent, these items epitomised urban living for them. This was particularly striking in homes where the families had bought beds for the children, dining tables and chairs, desks for their children to do homework at, and computers, all items not to be found in their village homes in the past.

In addition, the women in Istanbul and Van city were able to make use of health services for themselves and their children more easily. At the health centres, women could also obtain information about and access to birth control methods. Although health circuits now extend to villages and many women there now have fewer children, village life can still mean too many pregnancies, stillbirths, and even infant deaths. Finally, many women hoped that the city could offer their children better educational opportunities.

This ambivalent attitude towards village life, nostalgia coupled with a sense of necessity to leave the place in order to do well, is also described in Gardner's study of Sylhetis in Britain and Bangladesh; *desh* (home) stands both for economic insecurity and a spiritual identity, while *bidesh* (foreign contexts) symbolises opportunity as well as a threat to this spiritual identity (Gardner 1995, Vertovec 2007b: 154). For most of my Vanlı interlocutors, the city represented the future, where most villagers would soon end up living. 'Modernity' was, they believed, unavoidable, at least for their children. Indeed, the hurried manner in which many villagers abandoned their homes and fields in the village spoke of an intention never to return.

The migrants I talked to were used to accommodating the apparently contradictory attitudes of nostalgia for village life and a simultaneous devaluation of village life as an unsuitable occupation for 'these modern times'. While these two discourse fragments on 'the village' by migrants were by no means the only ones expressed by Vanlı Kurds, they were the ones most frequently produced, both by migrants from Gundême and other Kurdish villages. They represent the 'ebb' and 'flow' (Levitt and Glick Schiller 2004: 1012) of attachment to the sending community in the mind of individual migrants at different times as they position themselves in practices and discourses in the translocational social field. This fluidity has been recognised as a typical migration experience; rather than being attached to only one place, migrants and non-migrants can orient themselves towards different locations at different stages of their lives (Uehling 2002: 388–9).

As discussed above, Gundême, with its mountainous location, the architecture of the buildings, and the activities carried out by men and women, was very similar to the description of other Kurdish villages by Vanlı migrants. The next chapter is about the reasons why Gundî have left the village, about their dispersal and increasing social differentiation. Here again, the village Gundême stands for the more widespread rural-urban migration within and from Van province.

3

GUNDÊME AS A SENDING COMMUNITY: DISPERSAL AND DIFFERENTIATION

Mücahit and Süleyman Amca: Different Generational Interests

Although rural-urban labour migration has taken place in Turkey for a long time, and Kurdish villagers have been leaving for the cities since the 1950s when agriculture started to be mechanised (McDowall 1997: 401, Robinson 1958), it took longer for migration to become a phenomenon in Gundême. Around 25 years ago, Mücahit Çetin, a son of Haci Memo now in his late forties, was one of the first young men to leave the village of Gundême and work on building sites. He first worked in Van and then in Istanbul. At the time, it was unheard of for a young man to work for someone other than his father and anywhere but on the land of the family; Mücahit was considered by some to be acting shamefully. However, it did not take long for other young men, both from his lineage and from the village in general, to follow in his footsteps, attracted by the promise of independence and cash in hand. Dramatically, by 2006, 98 per cent of households in Gundême had at least one male working away from the village in the construction industry.

This labour migration of the young, which took place throughout the province of Van, was initially seasonal, as reflected in Table 2.

Table 2: Vanlı Male and Female Employment in Agriculture and Other Sectors

Sector	Year and Percentage of Male and Female Employment					
	1985		1990		2000	
	Men	Women	Men	Women	Men	Women
Agriculture	65.4%	97.2%	57.6%	94.9%	46.7%	94.9%
Other	34.6%	2.8%	42.4%	5.1%	53.3%	5.1%

Source: Tarım ve Köyişleri Bakanlığı 2005

The statistics clearly show that there has been an increase in the number of male seasonal labour migrants, whose wives and children have
remained in the villages. Thus, the number of Vanlı men employed
in agriculture went down from 65.4 per cent to 46.7 per cent between
1985 and 2000 as they sought work elsewhere, whereas the percentage
of women working as unpaid family workers on farms remained stable,
at least until the year 2000.

It is likely that the percentage of both women and men working in
agriculture has gone down quite dramatically since then, judging from
my observations in Gundême and conversations with permanent migrants
in Istanbul from different villages in Van province. Seasonal migration
has often been followed by complete migration away from the village. In
Gundême, there has been a rapid increase in young families leaving the
village completely, with or without members of the older generation. My
interlocutors in Tepelik, Istanbul, also spoke of both seasonal and complete migration in their families; there is a definite sense that it is now
considered desirable among younger couples to migrate together permanently in order to live together throughout the year. However, the process
of deciding to leave the village is not an easy one and may cause intergenerational conflict, as the following example of Süleyman Amca[1] shows.

Summer 2008: It has been half a year since Süleyman Çetin and
his wife Melek left the village of Gundême to settle in the province
capital of Van. Süleyman Amca is a small wiry man with countless
wrinkles and bowed legs, his age estimated at between 75 and 80.
He was always seen out and about in the village, often with a gnarly
walking stick, and always with his flat cap on his head. He was infamous for getting up early and forcing others to do so, too, by visiting
their houses after his morning prayers. As he has been fairly deaf since

childhood, everyone is used to him shouting at family, animals, and other villagers. For Süleyman Amca, his land and his animals were precious. The thought of giving up village life was unthinkable, but a combination of circumstances made it inevitable.

After marriage, Süleyman Amca had soon asked for his portion of land to be separated. According to custom, but contrary to Turkish Law, the land was divided among the four sons, ignoring the daughter; as the separating son, Süleyman Amca received a quarter of the estate, while the other three brothers stayed together. One brother later died in his early twenties, and his share was only divided between the two other brothers. Although Süleyman Amca had the least land, he embraced animal husbandry with more passion than either of his two brothers ever did.

Like his two younger brothers, Süleyman Amca had 11 children, partly in an attempt to improve the relatively weak position of the family in the village at a time when fights over land were common.[2] However, by the time his children had grown up, the economic, and thus also symbolic, value of land had decreased, as had the importance of male muscle to earn respect. While four of his five daughters married men from other villages and live there, his sons started working in the building trade in urban centres, predominantly in the southern holiday resort of Alanya. This meant seasonal migration for the sons, who, if already married, left their wives and children to live with Süleyman Amca and Melek in Gundême.

By all accounts, Süleyman Amca was not an easy man to live with. In the village he had created a niche for himself as a village joker. His 'mad' behaviour meant that he had license to make jokes that would in other cases have led to bloody fights. No one but Süleyman Amca could suggest, for instance, that his interlocutor should give him a go with his wife ('and you hold my jacket then'). His swearing and excentricity might have been entertaining for a general audience, but cohabitation must sometimes have been trying.

When I got to know Süleyman Amca's family over 12 years ago, his sons were building an apartment with four flats in Van, one for each of the married sons. The four daughters-in-law had previously stayed in the village with their parents-in-law when their husbands were away in Alanya building summer apartments for foreign and native tourists;

however, this was changing. The eldest son, Abdullah, who today has nine children, moved his family to Van first. His wife and some of their children used to go back in the summer months to help with the household or herding animals. Then Hayrullah's wife and four children moved to Van, too, and later Cengiz's wife with four children. Only Mehmet's wife and their three children remained in the village. The two youngest single sons also worked with their brothers in Alanya. The youngest unmarried sister cared for her niece and nephews in the village, leaving Mehmet's wife to do the bread baking and care for the animals. Süleyman Amca and Melek were getting older and were ailing, particularly the wife.

The sons' moves to Van brought a dilemma; the men did not want to leave their nuclear families in Van without some male support when they were working in Alanya. In addition, continuing the farm meant that male labour was required during harvest time and when the animals gave birth. The brothers had to take turns spending time in Van and the village, thus losing out on potential earnings in Alanya.

Süleyman's youngest daughter and one of his single sons were due to get married in the autumn of 2008. Süleyman and his wife would have been deprived of a caretaker when their youngest daughter moved away, and their son had no interest in living in the village after marriage. Indeed, his older brothers had already started adding a third floor to the apartment in Van city, and his wedding was to coincide with the completion of the flat. Süleyman's sons increased pressure on him and Melek to move to Van.

When Süleyman Amca finally sold his animals and moved away from Gundême with Melek in late autumn 2007, other villagers felt the loss of an institution, however infamous. Many predicted that Süleyman Amca would not live long after leaving behind his world, in which he had had agency, power, friends, and, for him, meaningful activity. However, he and his wife are well, now living in a flat with Cengiz's family in Van. Even if it is not said explicitly, they have been demoted from land owners, whose control of family assets gave them power over their dependents, to dependents themselves. Nevertheless, it is perhaps now easier for sons and *bûks* to pay the elderly couple the respect the elderly expect as other aspects of the younger generation's lives are more satisfactory.

Hayrullah, who is the financial organiser of the extended family, has moved his nuclear family even further, to Alanya, in order to put an end to the constant separations. As Hayrullah has been working in the building trade for a long time, he has been able to barter his work for a flat in one of the buildings he worked on. He works together with his brothers, who now live in a separate flat in Alanya when they work; they continue to see their own families only for a few months of the year when they return to Van. It is perhaps only a matter of time until other brothers follow his example and move their families to the place where they earn money.

In this extended family, within one generation, their home in the village has turned from the only place they have ever known to an unprofitable and uncared-for piece of land. It will not be long before the house there, a relatively small and unstable building anyway, collapses. As it does not have a slanted roof, heavy snow fall in the coming winter may well cause the flat roof to cave in.

Süleyman Amca's family is not the only one to have left the village for good. In the summer of 2006, there were 106 households in the village; the village health centre manager estimates that, had it not been for migration, there would have been double that number. Many households have left Gundême for Van city or other cities in the west or south of Turkey. A recount in the summer of 2008 showed that another four households had left in the intervening two years, and that other households have become reduced in size as some adults have left permanently.

The reasons for migration are similar for different Gundî families. From observations, conversations, and literature (as discussed below), I have come to the conclusion that migration from Van province, if not from the whole region, is due to a limited number of reasons. Just as interlocutors' narratives about 'the village' were very similar, so were the reasons given for 'the migration' by different Vanlı in Van city and in Istanbul.

Before Deciding: Expected Net Returns and Social Capital

My interlocutors from Gundême did or do not leave their village because of the armed conflict between the Turkish army and the PKK. Rather, their decision about whether to leave the village or to stay is taken by considering the financial consequences of either decision, often called the 'expected net return' of migration (Palloni et al. 2001). A move to the city can only be contemplated if a family has bought a plot of land and has built a house there. To pay rent would be inconceivable for the families, most of whom cannot even afford to pay social security contributions.[3] If there are several married brothers living together in the village, they may want to move into separate apartments in the city and thus have to spend more money and time on building the separate flats. It can take years for families to complete the flats as they add to the construction every time there is some spare cash available. Often the men do the building work themselves when they are back from working outside of Van. Thus, driving around certain fast-growing neighbourhoods of Van,[4] one sees that the majority of houses are incomplete in some way—families may move in when the brick walls are finished, waiting with the plastering until they have money again. Painting the house is considered a luxury few can afford immediately and others never spend money on. Since there is likelihood that other flats will be added later, many houses do not have a roof. Rather, one sees the flat tops of apartments with rusty ends of iron poles sticking out, left in anticipation of columns for the next storey.

In addition to the cost of housing, families must consider the immediate loss of foodstuff and fuel they would face in the city. Villagers complain that animal husbandry no longer makes a profit as raising the animals costs more than what they can make on the sale of the animals on the meat market. However, villagers have always practised subsistence animal husbandry and consumed the animal produce: milk, yoghurt, butter, cheese, eggs, and meat— all foods that would have to be bought in the city—as well as *sergîn*, dried cow dung used as fuel. In addition, it may be easier to plant a vegetable garden in the village than in the city, and it may also be difficult to build a *xanî* for baking bread and cooking on the smaller plots of land in the city. Families moving to Van or other cities thus have to purchase coal for their stoves and gas cylinders to cook on kitchen stoves, as well as having to buy bread, a basic food, every day. In short, a family wanting to leave the village must be sure that they can earn enough money to meet such basic expenditure.

Some of the families who still remain in Gundême thus do so because of their relative poverty. A move to a city would not only mean an immediate increase in expenses, but also the loss of a social network that offers support to the needy through an exchange of labour for goods. In Gundême, men from families with little or no land can work as shepherds or cowherds in the summer, daily herding the animals to higher-up meadows and bringing them down again for milking. They receive a fixed number of animals at the end of the herding season in return for their labour. Women from poorer families may clean the cowsheds of others in the summer and prepare the *sergîn*, of which they then receive a share. Young unmarried women may help out in the households of relatives or neighbours that lack young female labour, serving food to a large group of guests, washing carpets or wool, or collecting herbs for the regional cheese; these services may be repaid by better-off families in goods, such as cheese, meat, and *sergîn*. As this bartering of services for goods is impossible in Van city, let alone further afield, these families have remained in Gundême. The expected net returns of migration are not high enough.

Interestingly, however, many of the families who are still in the village full-time seem to be relatively well-off. Many have diversified their income, either through sons working on building sites and sending remittances home or through income generated in the village. The health centre manager, for instance, is a civil servant, which means that he receives a regular monthly wage to supplement any agricultural activities he may pursue. There are three small grocery stores operating in Gundême and as long as there are other villagers buying there, their owners have no reason to move. Several men own and drive minibuses between the village and Van or between other villages. The extra cash income allows these families to make a living in the village. For the last three years, the health centre has employed a female cleaner, and the primary school has also begun to use a man to clean the school and heat it in winter; this means that two more families living in the village are receiving a regular wage.

Families who have a lot of land also tend to leave at least some members in the village. Animal husbandry has become particularly expensive for those with few meadows to make hay from in summer as they have to buy additional feed for their animals in winter. If a family has enough land, however, they may save on these costs. For these wealthier families, then, the net returns in the village are high enough to continue living there.

Finally, there are also some people who love living in the village and do not let financial considerations sway them. Süleyman Amca was forced to leave since his sons gradually withdrew their support for his life there, but others remain. Muhammed Çetin, for example, a man in his late forties, gets restless when he leaves the village. His face is burned a dark brown because he is out with the animals or on the fields most of the time. Two of his older brothers have moved to Van, but Muhammed Amca loves his sheep and his daily routines. His extended family is also one of the very few who have invested in village life by buying a share of a tractor and a share in the mill.

Researchers studying transnational Mexican migration into the USA have emphasised the relationship between the likelihood of migration and network relations with people who have migrated already. They argue:

> Everyday ties of friendship and kinship provide few advantages, in and of themselves, to people seeking to migrate abroad. Once someone in a person's network migrates, however, the ties are transformed into a resource to gain access to foreign employment and the money that it brings. Each act of migration creates social capital among people to whom the new migrant is related, thereby raising their own odds of out-migration.
>
> **(Palloni et al. 2001: 1264)**

Indeed, their study found that having an older sibling who had migrated to the USA made the likelihood of a person's out-migration from Mexico thrice as high. They also suggest that even weaker friendship ties with migrants increase the likelihood of out-migration (2001: 1295–6).

This should be kept in mind during the following discussion of reasons for leaving villages in Van. When villagers from Van province have migrated to cities because of the earthquake or forced village clearances, it is likely that they did so in bigger kinship clusters. In this case, the social capital theory does not apply to the *decision* to leave; however, social network ties may have determined *where* a family that was forced to leave decided to settle. When people leave in search of a wage or better education opportunities for their children, however, it is highly likely that they are emulated by younger siblings and others in their kin and village network, unless attachment to village life is extremely high or remittances sent back make village life sufficiently comfortable.

Lack of Viable Income and Dissatisfaction

If one looks at Van province from a wider perspective, there have been four main reasons for the migratory move from villages to Van city and/or other cities in the south and west of the country. The most commonly cited reason is financial, and this was also one of the reasons why Süleyman Amca's sons were reluctant to stay in the village any longer.

All my Gundî interlocutors have mentioned the impossibility of getting by purely with animal husbandry and a little bit of agriculture, as was indicated in the example of Süleyman Amca. To begin with, Van as a province is a difficult terrain anyway, with mountains making up 53 per cent of the land (Tarım ve Köyişleri Bakanlığı (TKB) 2005: 21). This explains why much of the land, 67 per cent, is used as grazing meadows for animals, whereas only 17 per cent can be used as fields or gardens (TKB 2005: 25).

According to the Turkish Ministry of Agriculture and Village Affairs, one problem with animal husbandry in Van is that the meadows are grazed too early in the year or too intensively. This is of course in order to save money on animal feed, but, together with erosion, it creates a vicious circle of increasingly less grazing land, which forces villagers to buy more feed. This in turn makes the cost of raising each animal higher (TKB 2005: 108, 114). Villagers have told me that the expenditure involved in animal husbandry hardly makes the sale of animals worthwhile. Celebratory feasts apart, villagers themselves often only slaughter and eat their animals when they show signs of ill-health. Too frequent consumption of meat would mean depriving oneself of one's income.

According to data from 2000, 67 per cent of Van's population worked in the category agriculture/hunting/fishing, which in Van can be read as animal husbandry and limited agriculture (TKB 2005: 29). The province has over 40,000 farms, virtually all of which are small and family-run. Their small size and the lack of processing plants in wider Van mean that families mostly produce for subsistence rather than for profit. Food produced beyond subsistence quantities, such as herbal cheese, butter and yoghurt, is not sold at local markets due to lack of cooperatives and packaging facilities; rather, a lot of this produce is sent to relatives in Van or other cities for private consumption (TKB 2005: 45).

Once when in Gundême, I witnessed a young boy begging for a piece of homemade herbal cheese from his mother. It was not, as I first thought, for eating, but for bartering with in the village shop. The shopkeeper thus collected pieces of cheese from different producers, probably under questionable hygienic conditions, and then sold the cheese on to Van. Sometimes a middleman would come to the village and buy cheese off women in larger quantities, then making a profit in Van. There have been few efforts made by villagers or by the government to standardise and improve the local dairy produce industry. Rather, it is left to a few enterprising individuals to collect and sell produce at a small profit. There are two milk and dairy produce plants in all of Van province, and in 2004, they were only working at 50 per cent capacity (*ibid.*).

Two reasons for the inefficiency in animal husbandry and farming are a lack of education and a lack of capital to invest. The Ministry of Agriculture's master plan is particularly critical of the lack of training for women, who are responsible for looking after the animals in Van (TKB 2005: 113). In addition, the generally low income level in Van, at $1,053 annual income per capita in 1997, compared to a national average of $3,021 (*ibid.*), means that planting trees, paying for vets, artificial insemination or better breeds of animal, buying tractors, or building watering canals are all beyond the means of most villagers. As Turkey is trying to align itself with the Common Agricultural Policy of the EU, it is foreseeable that many of the small-scale family farms will not meet the criteria of hygiene and standardisation of animal husbandry in the future.

While animal husbandry is becoming more expensive and quality soil more rare, there is another factor adding to the need for migration.

Large families have been the norm in rural Van, and even if young women move to their husband's home after marriage and do not inherit parental plots,[5] the land still has to be shared among the sons. Plots of land have thus become smaller, which makes economic survival even less viable. Young men in particular have thus been pushed into unskilled labour away from the village.

On the other hand, it has also been the attraction of wages that has made some villagers dissatisfied with their lot in the village and unwilling to invest time and energy in the remaining land. Dissatisfaction with village life has become self-perpetuating. Families in Van city, even if migrants from villages themselves, have always been reluctant to let their daughters marry (back) into villages, and increasingly, families in villages also desire their daughters to move to the city in marriage. There are several reasons for this preference. First of all, there is a kind of snobbery that makes people quickly forget their own recent arrivals in the city. Villagers are sometimes portrayed as less sophisticated and as less hygienic (for instance smelling of the animals they look after) than their urban relatives. Coming to the city may force the villagers, especially the elderly and middle-aged women, to use the Turkish language they are not very familiar with, which may expose them to ridicule. Indeed, people of different ages have recounted to me the humiliation they suffered at the hands of what turned out to be fellow Kurds when they had just arrived from the village, being mocked for their accent and lack of Turkish. Villagers are thus not necessarily considered desirable in-laws.

A second reason for preferring daughters to marry in the city is that the workload for women in the village is still considerable. Not only do they have children and care for them, but they also make food, bake bread, milk the cows, sheep, and goats, turn the milk into yoghurt, cheese, and butter, collect herbs on the mountainsides, tend gardens, make bedding, knit clothing, often still wash clothes by hand, and wash woollen bedding and carpets in the mountain streams. For girls from the village, a move to the city represents an escape from some of this work, while women from the city do not have the experience or inclination to carry out the domestic and farm duties expected of a villager wife.

A third reason for preferring marriage in the city is that the younger generation is less dependent on the elders. For young men, labour migration offers more independence from the father, who, as we saw in the example of Süleyman Amca, turns from being the patriarch controlling the land and the income into a merely symbolic figurehead of the family. Although young men are often required to send their earnings home to their parents, they may insist on a separation of wealth upon marriage or a bit later, creating a new *mal*. This kind of set-up in turn makes the young men more attractive for potential female marriage partners as it means that there will be no competition between parents (-in-law) and siblings (-in-law) for one income and also less control over the labour and fertility of the inmarrying woman.

Investing in the Future Generation

Another reason for migration, the education of children, is related to the first and is indeed often the factor pushing families from seasonal migration to a complete move away from the village. The village of Gundême offers only five years of schooling, despite the fact that compulsory education in Turkey has been raised to eight years; many villagers in their twenties and even some in their late teens only went to school for those five years, if that.

However, my observation has been that there have been radical changes within families; it is arguably seasonal labour migration that has brought a change in attitude and commitment towards education. Seasonal work on the construction sites in different cities is hard. Often several villagers work together on a site, sleeping in a semi-finished room of the building and collaborating in the cooking and washing of clothes at the end of a tiring work day. They have to bear long separations from their wives and miss out on their children growing up. The construction workers may also face discrimination in the city due to their ethnic background or due to their dishevelled appearance after a hard day of physical and dirty labour. They are insecure financially as their employers often refuse to pay their (compulsory) health care and pension contributions. This means that they and their families are not insured and that they will not receive a pension when they are too worn-out to work any longer. Work is sometimes difficult to find, and their employers may sometimes be unable or unwilling to pay on time. Construction work also brings hazards; villagers have been involved in accidents likely to happen all over the country, considering that security precautions on sites are minimal. Two young Gundî men reported that in their work on the facades of high buildings they have witnessed others falling off the scaffolding, either dying or being paralysed.

The workers see alternative lives around them and desire their own sons to do better than themselves on the labour market. As for their daughters, the workers know that without education they will eventually be married to someone very similar to themselves, thus condemned to a life of long separations when the husband goes to work. If the girls are sent to school, however, they can improve their marriage prospects or even work themselves. Education of both boys and girls thus represents the hope for a better future for the next generation.

Financial hardship and traditional gender expectations have prevented many children, but particularly girls, from going to school in the past. Indeed, the literacy rate of Van was cited as 52 per cent as late as 2005 (TKB 2005: 128). There has been a dramatic change in attitudes towards the education of girls within the last five years, something I was able to witness personally in Gundême. Families who in the past were not financially able or willing to send their daughters to school are now doing so. One of the reasons for this change of heart has been a campaign spearheaded by Unicef and the Turkish Ministry of Education, simply called 'Off to School, Girls!' ('Haydi Kızlar Okula!'). Van province was one of ten provinces in Turkey (out of 81) with the greatest gender gap in education; these ten provinces were initially targeted in 2003, with the media, teachers, health workers, meles, muhtars (Turkish for neighbourhood officials), and other volunteers involved in convincing parents to send their daughters to school. Poorer families were supported with a Conditional Cash Transfer from the Turkish Social Solidarity Fund (SYDTF) in order to finance the education of their children; they were paid 20 per cent more for each girl sent to school (Unicef 2005).

In Van province, this campaign led to the identification of 54,400 school-age girls and boys who were not going to school, and by 2007,

43,513 of them were registered for school, 28,585 of them girls ('Van'da Haydi Kızlar...'). Arguably, the campaign has made it easier for young families to defy traditional values and educate their children, and the experiences of the young wage-earning seasonal migrants have made families receptive to the campaign.

It is clear that the drive to educate Kurdish children while refusing to allow mother language education is based on an assimilationist agenda (Wedel 2000: 114, Skubsch 2001); this is an issue that will be discussed further in Chapter 4. However, reasons given to me by Vanlı interlocutors for why they had not been sent to school or had not sent their children were always concerned with money or 'traditional values' rather than an aversion to homogenising state propaganda. Similarly, when families now send their children to school, they emphasise their desire for the children to better themselves and do not seem to dwell much on the assimilation their children undergo.

In Beyazlı, a village across the plain on which Gundême borders, a regional boarding school has been operating since 2007. It offers children in the area eight years of schooling and a place to stay. They only return to their villages at the weekend. In 2007, over 50 pupils from Gundême attended this school, with a relatively even gender balance. In 2008, the number is said to have risen to around 70. This boarding school may offer a temporary solution to the educational needs of young families, but any children wanting to continue their education up to high school, that is, another four years, still have to leave the village.

If families are hoping for their children to go on to university, they will in most cases pay several thousand Turkish Liras a year (over a thousand Euros) for special weekend classes to prepare them for the annual central university entrance exam, a highly competitive event. These classes are only available at private courses in the city of Van, or in other cities around Turkey.

Indeed, if a family is really ambitious for their children, they will soon realise that children going to school in Van have a lower success rate in the university exam than children in other provinces. It is a known fact that the level of education outside of the big metropoles is lower, making it more difficult for the students to pass the exam.

The Ministry of Education openly acknowledges that Van province lacks over 2,000 teachers. In the Muradiye district, where Gundême is located, for instance, there are 265 teachers, but another 184 are needed. This lack of teachers means that the pupil ratio is high; there are 57.6 students per teacher in primary schools in Van province (TKB 2005: 33–4). Village schools may still be forced to teach several classes in one room, and the lack of teachers also means that some subjects can only be taught in an amateur manner. Villagers who work in large cities in the west of Turkey may thus decide to move their families even further away from Van to improve their children's chances of getting into university and studying the subject of their choice.

The first two types of migration discussed above are voluntary and can be described in terms of capital. Rural-urban migrants may move for the sake of economic capital or for the sake of human capital, that is, the education of children, which in turn can be converted into economic capital in the future. The next two types of migration from Van province have been involuntary; many Kurdish villagers in Van and other provinces have been forced to move because of armed conflict, whereas yet others have had to leave their homes because of natural disaster.

Forced Village Evacuations

Although Gundême and other villages in the Muradiye district have not been directly affected by village evacuations, the migration of Gundî must be seen in the context of the general migration landscape of the province and of Turkey as a whole. In Van city, forced evacuations have affected the job and housing market, as well as the ethnic and political landscape of the city. Turkey-wide, the continuing silence on this issue means that discourses on rural-to-urban migration tend to denigrate Kurdish migrants as a threat to urban culture, disregarding the reason for much of the displacement.

Parts of Van, just like other eastern and southeastern provinces, have suffered from forced village evacuations at the hands of the army or the PKK. As this is a controversial topic, any statistics, be they from the government or from NGOs, are bound to be biased. Çelik quotes a parliamentary report of 1997 that counts 378,335 internally

displaced persons; however, 'many human rights organizations estimate the number of forced migrants to be around 2–4 million' (2005:
140). This disparity is explained by sociologist Yükseker:

> The government says that 355,000 people have migrated due
> to villages emptying. Human rights organisations and NGOs
> say that this number is inaccurate. It is clear that the number
> given by the government is too low because the government is
> only counting the villages it emptied itself. And even then, the
> government does not say 'we emptied them', but 'they were emp-
> tied'. And it does not include in this number the people who
> were forced to leave their villages and district towns because
> the fighting made them fear for their safety. NGOs rightly say,
> 'Whoever had to leave the place where they lived due to the con-
> flict is a victim of forced migration.' We estimate that a million
> people are in this situation.
>
> (Düzel 2005, author's translation)

Moore and Shellman point to the fact that for people deciding to leave
their homes without compensation, a certain threshold has to be overcome first. The fear of persecution by government troops, dissident
groups, or an interaction of both must be greater than the fear of leaving for an uncertain future (2004: 726). As such a decision is not made
lightly, forced migration should thus include both victims of village
clearances and people who left out of fear for their lives.

Any evaluation of forced migration is further complicated by the
fact that migration organisations in Turkey have listed the evacuated villages with their old names, whereas available maps only
show new names.[6] Furthermore, it is not clear whether counts of
currently existing villages include any of the evacuated villages. The
discrepancy in counts by the government and human rights associations suggests that some villages, although evacuated, have not
been counted as empty. The data presented can therefore only point
to general trends.

Table 3 shows the number of villages/hamlets per district in Van
(as counted by the Van Province Governorship) and to their right the

Table 3: Settlements Evacuated in Van Province

District	No. of Villages/ Hamlets in 2000	No. of Settlements Evacuated pre-2000	Percentage of Settlements Evacuated
Van *merkez* (central Van)	124	–	0
Bahçesaray	62	1	0.2
Başkale	124	27	18
Çaldıran	91	–	0
Çatak	116	113	49
Edremit	13	–	0
Erciş	124	–	0
Gevaş	48	21	30
Gürpınar	152	90	37
Muradiye	50	–	0
Özalp	72	–	0
Saray	34	–	0

number of villages evacuated (as claimed by Göç-Der, a pro-Kurdish migration association campaigning for the acknowledgement of evacuations and the hardship of migrants, the abolition of the village guard system, and realistic return programmes to the villages). Since the governorship's population data are from 2000 and most village evacuations happened earlier, I am assuming for the purposes of this comparison that the governor's cited number of villages does not include any evacuated villages. I have then calculated what percentage of villages/hamlets has been evacuated.

It is clear that some districts have been affected much more than others. One reason is their geographic location. The districts of Van *merkez* (central Van, i.e. the province capital), Edremit, and Erciş are on the shore of Lake Van and served by tarred main roads. Frequent army road blocks and easy access by the army have thus made it hard for the PKK to establish a base in those areas. The district of Muradiye, where the village of my study is, has also been relatively unaffected by clashes between the army and the PKK.

On the other hand, Başkale, Çatak, Gevaş, and Gürpınar are all southern districts of Van, bordering the provinces of Şırnak and Hakkâri,[7] and, in the case of Başkale, also bordering Iran. This area is much more mountainous and there has been much more fighting between PKK and army.

Another reason given for the different number of village evacuations is that the population in certain districts is more 'assimilated' than in others. The argument is that there are more ethnic Turks living in districts such as Van *merkez* and Erciş. This is supported by Andrews' summary of an unpublished village survey carried out in the early 1960s. According to the survey, of the 546 villages counted in Van, 34 were Turkish and the others Kurdish. In Van *merkez*, for instance, six out of 23 villages were Turkish, and in Erciş 12 out of 82, whereas other districts, such as Başkale, Çatak, Gevaş, Gürpınar, Muradiye, and Özalp, had none (Andrews 1989: 197). Local Kurds in the districts that have Turkish populations are said to be less supportive of the PKK. I would suggest that whatever the initial attitude towards the army or the PKK, fighting between the PKK and the army has offered villagers in the affected areas no choice but to take sides. However, the PKK is likely to have entered areas that promised some support as well as geographical security.

In popular telling, village evacuations happened as follows: PKK fighters visited villages in mountainous areas in order to command provisions or to recruit new members. Villagers would comply, either because they supported the PKK or because they were given no choice. The army would become aware of PKK activity and tell villagers that they would have to provide village guards (Turkish: *köy korucu*) to support the army in its fight against the PKK. These village guards would be based in the village, receive a regular salary from the state, and be armed.[8] They would be required to join military operations in the area with the army. If villagers refused, either because they supported the PKK ideologically and did not want to fight against them or because they did not trust the army to protect them from PKK attacks once they had started working for the state, the army forced the villagers to empty the villages. Leaving the village of course meant leaving behind unsellable land and the property of the family.

Some of the villagers migrated to big Turkish cities. The Kurdish Rights Commission of the Human Rights Foundation published a report in 1995, in which they speak of an estimated 2,500 villages that were completely emptied. Talking to around 340 families, they noted that most of them came from villages or hamlets (67.3 per cent) and that most of them had come as a result of the fighting (58 per cent), while some also cited 'security' (16.7 per cent) or 'economic reasons' (12.6 per cent). 90.9 per cent claimed they had experienced some oppression before leaving, such as torture (24.6 per cent), pressure to become a village guard (20.5 per cent), or villages/fields/forests burnt or bombed, or animals killed (48.6 per cent). The interviewers noted that the interviewees were often nervous and that many of them felt discriminated against in the city for being Kurdish. The vast majority of respondents claimed they had problems finding housing and jobs (Türkiye İnsan Hakları Vakfı n.d.).

While there is a general migratory move to the West, most families who were forced to leave their villages settled in nearby cities (İflazoğlu 2006). Diyarbakır, a Kurdish-majority city in the southeast, for example, is bursting at its seams with migrants from the countryside. Similarly, Van city has received many migrants from villages, both from Van province and neighbouring provinces, particularly Hakkâri, where a lot of villages were emptied, too. The village of Sisin in Hakkâri, where anthropologist Yalçın-Heckmann conducted fieldwork in the early 1980s, exemplifies these clearances: the village of her study simply does not exist anymore (Strohmeier und Yalçın-Heckmann 2000: 221–7). A 2004 study from the Faculty of Education at Van University also notes that since 1990 Van has received many migrants from the neighbouring provinces of Hakkâri, Siirt, Muş, Ağrı, and Bitlis (Tunç 2004: 3).

While the district in which Gundême lies has not been affected directly by this forced migration, Gundî labour migrants are competing for work and accommodation in Van city and other cities. In addition, they are affected by the prejudices that western urbanites may harbour against villagers in general and Kurds in particular.

Earthquakes

A more specific reason for migration from the area where Gundême lies was an earthquake in the region around 30 years ago. In fact, this earthquake was the reason for the migration of the Vanlı whom I met in Tepelik, Istanbul.

On 24 November 1976, Van province experienced an earthquake measuring 7.6 on the Richter scale. The epicentre was Çaldıran, a northeastern district of Van. Although the area was sparsely populated, over 4,000 people died. Özer describes the neighbouring district town of Muradiye, which he came back to the day after the earthquake:

> The road had opened up. A fault line had split buildings and homes and then continued through the road, finally disappearing in the stream [...]. Buildings had collapsed, trees were uprooted, and the metal electricity poles had turned into piles of scrap. Big cement buildings had cracked, some of them collapsing to the side, and there was no trace of the stone and mud brick houses. The ground and the asphalt had been cleaved so dramatically that we could only jump over the cracks. [...] It was as if a monster had passed underneath the town and then shaken itself.
>
> **(2008: 261–2, author's translation)**

According to Özer and interlocutors who experienced the earthquake, there was no real emergency relief or long-term support for the victims of the earthquake. Bruinessen reports:

> Thus most of the victims in Muradiye died after the quake. They were forced to remain outside, as the sent tents did not reach their destination, and many froze to death. Food and other aid 'disappeared' before reaching the earthquake area. Villagers were forced to sell their animals because they could not feed them, so many survivors of the catastrophe were financially ruined.
>
> **(1978: 26)**

It has been estimated that in an area of 2,000 square kilometres, 80 per cent of the buildings, that is, around 10,000 homes, were destroyed (Işık 1992: 107). It is not documented how much of the migration out of the area has been due to the earthquake, but the destruction of houses and the lack of government support must have aggravated poverty and accelerated labour migration. According to Ammann's study of Kurdish migrants in Europe, earthquakes have been one reason for migration abroad (2000: 121). Referring to earthquakes in Muradiye and other cities, she says:

> These natural catastrophes and the bureaucratic treatment of the victims caused many migratory movements, since the distribution of aid and donations by the bureaucracy was clearly marked by politically motivated anti-Kurdish irregularities.
>
> (2000: 131, author's translation)

In the case of the Vanlı migrants who moved to Tepelik after the earthquake, their move from the area has started a chain migration that is still continuing.

At the time of writing, Vanlı is still reeling from the effects of two major earthquakes in October and November 2011. People have left the area in their thousands, many of them relying on a network of relatives in other cities. It remains to be seen whether Vanlı will return to the city when winter has passed. It is likely that these last earthquakes will push some people who already considered migrating to do so earlier. On the other hand, the eventual reconstruction of the city may also provide work for others.

To summarise, villagers from Van province leave for Van city or other large cities in Turkey for one or more of the following reasons. For some, the farm does not earn enough money for the whole family or wage labour seems more attractive. Other families want to improve the educational opportunities of their children. Involuntary migration happened because of the conflict between the PKK and the Turkish army or because of a natural disaster, such as the earthquake of 1976 and the more recent ones in 2011.

A Village Emptying...

Migrants of each lineage in Gundême have followed their own pioneers and pathways, having to make decisions about the financial viability of complete versus seasonal migration, as well as attachment to village life versus the education of children.

All lineages that still have family members in the village have had members settling somewhere else permanently; seasonal migrant work outside of the village also continues and, through remittances, makes it possible for these lineages to remain in Gundême. As discussed above, some Gundî have also found ways of earning money without having to leave the village either seasonally or permanently (Table 4).

Very few Gundî have actually invested any money into bringing more advanced technology to the village, perhaps an indication that they are waiting for the right time to leave themselves. Those families who have a steady income from inter-village transport or a shop do not (all) need to leave the village, unless the population declines so far as to make these enterprises unviable.

Since the initial household count in 2005, four more households have left the village completely, and others have been reduced in size.

Table 4: Migration of Gundême Lineages

Lineage	Destinations for Permanent migration	Continuing Seasonal Labour Migration?	Supplementary Income in Gundême
1	Bursa	yes	
2	Bursa	yes	cleaning the health centre
3	Sweden	yes	
4	Van, Istanbul	yes	lorry driving, petrol trade
5	Bursa	yes	hiring out tractor
6	Van	yes	inter-village buses
(7) Çetin	Istanbul, Alanya, USA	yes	health centre manager, renting out tractor, renting out mill
8	Van	yes	
9	Van, Mersin, Bursa	yes	village shop, gas cylinder sales, driving, petrol trade
10	Van, Mersin	yes	village shop, inter-village bus
11	Izmir	yes	inter-village buses, tractor, village shop, lorry driving, *muhtar*, grain mill.

As pointed out earlier, the migration of other kin, or even friends, makes migration of others more likely. One young seasonal labourer from Gundême put it like this:

'If the older siblings have moved to Van and they are doing well there, then the wife of the man remaining in the village will start pestering him about a move to the city. Then it becomes impossible for them to stay in the village.'

This young man has chosen to cloak the pull-factor of successful siblings in the guise of a nagging wife. Whoever the initiator, it is a well-accepted fact that many people in Gundême are getting ready to move. Indeed, the situation has become similar to a Mexican study that Levitt and Glick Schiller cite, where migration had become a (male) rite of passage (2004: 1018). When I spoke to interlocutors at the Tepelik housing blocks in Istanbul, I could then see the other end of the migration chain: many were making arrangements for their parents or siblings to join them, seeing it as desirable or inevitable that they would eventually leave the village, too.

For the Gundême lineages, migration has brought socio-economic differentiation. Today there are university graduates, brick layers, and self-employed tradespeople to be found among them (cf. Just 2000: 91–2). This can be exemplified by a more detailed account of the Çetin lineage.

The Çetin Lineage: Coming to and Leaving Gundême

Like all the other lineages in the village, the Çetin lineage consists of smallholders; a typical household in the lineage owns around 75 acres of land. In the past, disputed land borders could cause fights between lineages, but not today. There also used to be fights with the neighbouring village about the exact borders of the grazing grounds on the mountain between the villages.

Between 2005 and 2008, four of seven households from the Çetin lineage left the village completely. The other two households shrank in size, so that there are today only 12 adults remaining in the village instead of 27. The average number of adults per household is roughly the same (four instead of 3.9) since two of the remaining households are a fraternal joint and a paternal joint household respectively.[9]

Haci Fahrettin was considered the authority on the origin and gene-alogy of the patrilineal descent group, but he, too, did not know the reason for the lineage's move northwards to the village of Gundême two centuries ago. What Haci Fahrettin remembered was a bare skel-eton of male ancestors:

> 'We came to Gundême from Cizre, a district of Şırnak, via Bahçesaray [a district of Van]. They call us *Müküsî*, after the old name for Bahçesaray, Müküs. We are also sometimes called '*Berjerî*', '*jeri*' being the Kurdish for 'below'. Our lineage is called '*Mala Axa Sor*', that is, the House of the Red Agha. The Agha is said to have been a great landlord with a castle and land reach-ing to Syria.'

Haci Fahrettin was able to recite the male ancestors in biblical fashion, recalling that it was Cihangir who settled in the village. Most mem-bers of the lineage cannot remember that far back; rather, they refer to Cihangir's great-grandson Osman as a common ancestor. The lineage is thus commonly referred to as '*Mala Ose*' in Kurdish, the 'House of Ose' (short for Osman).

Three of Osman's grandsons, all deceased, are well-remembered ancestors of three extended families from Gundême who consider themselves part of the Çetin lineage. Felit and Haci Kasım were half-brothers, sharing a father. When their father died, his widow was mar-ried to her brother-in-law. Their son Mahir was thus Haci Kasım's half-brother and Felit's cousin.

Another of Osman's descendants, his granddaughter Meryem, had a daughter called Ayşe, who married Haci Memo, a man today in his eighties. His extended family is also considered part of the lineage, des-pite having a different surname. In this book, he is also referred to by the Çetin surname in order to minimise confusion and emphasise the sense of relatedness he and the other Çetin members feel. This sense of relatedness is not purely a case of matrilateral reckoning; rather, Haci

Memo's father is said to be a patrilineal relative in ways they cannot figure out anymore.

When I first visited Gundême in 1998, the Çetin lineage in Gundême consisted of the extended families of Felit's three sons, of Haci Kasım's four sons, of Mahir's three sons, and Haci Memo and his six sons. Felit's three sons all used to live together in the village, but the oldest, Süleyman Amca, separated very early. However, the older children of Felit's other sons, Haci Fahrettin and Tacit Amca, still remember living together with their cousins, some of them also being milk siblings.[10] Haci Fahrettin left the village around 25 years ago, but the families remained close, with some of Haci Fahrettin's sons working on the farm in Gundême and some of Tacit's sons living in Haci Fahrettin's house in Van city in order to go to school.

At the same time that Süleyman Amca finally gave up his household in Gundême in late 2007, Tacit Amca also left for Van city. Two of Tacit Amca's sons had long gone to university in different cities, and one had completed high school in Istanbul. The three were working in Istanbul, while another son had left for the USA after having lived in Istanbul for several years. Another daughter and two sons moved to join their brothers in Istanbul after the family moved to Van.

Haci Kasım's four sons all lived together in the village until 2006, when the older two left for Van with their wives and children. Now Muhammed Amca and Nedret Amca remain there, the latter working as the village's health centre manager.

As for Mahir's three sons, the two older ones have also left the village within the last two years, building separate houses in the same neighbourhood in Van. The oldest son, Alaaddin, has been able to 'retire' as three of his sons (the oldest of whom is married) are working in construction and thus supporting the family. The second son, Tacettin, still has to work himself as the older five of his seven children are all daughters. The family of Mahir's youngest son, Feyzettin, remains in the village while he works on building sites. He has, however, purchased a plot of land in Van and is planning to move there eventually.

Haci Memo is still living in the village. Four of his sons have long left the village. The oldest son, Haci Şako lives in Van and for a long time worked as a lorry driver, until the employment of his sons meant that he could semi-retire. His next two brothers, Mücahit and Ali, spent many years working on building sites in Istanbul, living there with their families before moving back to the city of Van. The second-youngest son, Hüseyin, is working as a carpenter in Istanbul. The fourth-oldest son, Onur, left for Van with his family two years ago as one of his sons is disabled and needs special physiotherapy. Now, only the youngest son Mehmet, with his wife and three children, remains with Haci Memo in Gundême.

It is perhaps surprising to see how quickly land and a whole lifestyle have been abandoned for the city. However, apart from the factors outlined above, one should also consider that the attachment to the land was based on its importance for the subsistence of the *mal* (here: lineage), which Yalçın calls the 'smallest tribally recognized social unit' (1986: 187). Prior to the 'retribalisation' of Kurds in urban settings as a means of acquiring political and economic influence (Bruinessen 1999a, 2003), tribal entities throughout rural Kurdish regions had become ever smaller; confederations have long been dissolved and tribes partitioned (cf. Bruinessen 2003, Yalçın 1986).

In Gundême, not just the Çetin lineage but also the ten other lineages represent small splinters of tribes, so that the lineage rather than tribal membership has been relevant. The patrilineages arrived in the village at different times, and none of them ever achieved dominance over the others. Lineages sometimes banded together, for example in quite brutal physical fights when villagers argued over land boundaries or other issues. However, these alliances were based on a sense of neighbourhood or friendship and perhaps sometimes relations of alliance through marriage rather than shared tribal membership.

Gundême and other villages on the plain have thus not experienced the feudal structure often associated with Kurds. Although some lineages in the village own more land and some less, there has never been a ruling lineage with subject peasants, all members of the same tribe (cf. McDowall 1997: 17, 419).[11] The fact that no tribe, and no *one* lineage has ever 'owned' the village has arguably made it easier for Gundî to leave their land behind. The symbolic value of land was higher even a generation ago, when it represented the means of survival. It was also relevant in intergenerational relations as fathers could exert power over their sons until they inherited land. When the sons opted out of the system by entering the wage market, the value of land declined rapidly, both in financial and in symbolic terms.

Increasing Dispersal and Socio-Economic Differentiation

Rural-urban migration among Kurdish Vanlı villagers has led to heightened differences in socio-economic standing. This becomes obvious even within one lineage, as I show with the example of the Çetin lineage.

Members of this lineage are fond of each other. They visit each other on religious holidays and they might help each other in myriad ways, both in the same location and from a distance: sharing work in the fields and other farm work, preparing items for trousseaus, handing on children's clothes, doing building work at a reduced price, finding employment for someone, lending money, finding a lawyer for someone in difficulty, taking someone to the doctor's, etc. Over time, they have become more dispersed, some remaining in the village, some in different neighbourhoods in Van, some in Alanya, some in Istanbul, and one even in the USA, but they keep in contact by mobile phone, Internet chat and social network sites, visits, and news passed on by others. Many of the lineage's middle-aged members can look back on a shared childhood in the village and delight in recalling anecdotes of that time.

It is in memories of the past and of village life that the lineage finds unity; migration has brought out differences, not only in the lives of families belonging to the same lineage, but also within families. Particularly those between the ages of 20 and 40 show incredible differences in their lifestyles, depending on the decisions their parents made and make related to migration. These decisions have affected marriage choices (see Chapter 7), access to education, and work opportunities (see also Chapter 8).

Take the sons of Felit, the Gundî who died young in the 1940s; their lives, and as a result the lives of their children, have turned out very differently. Felit's second-oldest son, Haci Fahrettin, was one of the pioneering villagers who left Gundême around 25 years ago. His sense of entrepreneurship can be traced back to his childhood, when, aged four, he lost his father. Haci Fahrettin's older brother Süleyman is said to have been unable to take on any real responsibility at that time. There was a sister older than Fahrettin, a younger brother (who would later die in his early twenties) and his mother was pregnant with Tacit. Her determination to stay with her children meant that she was married to Mahir, Felit's paternal uncle's son. Fahrettin's mother was by all accounts a formidable woman who resisted Felit's male relatives' efforts to get rid of her—she would have had to leave the children with the patrilineage. Several members of the lineage have quoted her as having said, 'If you send me out of the door, I will come back through the chimney.' For her son Fahrettin, life became serious very early:

'I became the head of the household when I was seven or eight. People brought goods over the border from Iran and I used our ox to distribute these goods to villages in the area, making a profit in the sales.'

As a young adult, he brought a bus to the village, using it to earn money by transporting other villagers to Van at a time when transport opportunities were scarce. When Haci Fahrettin came to Van, he invested in an intercity bus together with an affinal villager from lineage 9. Haci Fahrettin built a house in an established residential neighbourhood of Van, where people own two-storey houses and considerable plots of garden, thus giving the area a lush, green feel. Today, Haci, as many just call him, feels great pride in the fruit trees he planted years ago; they yield apricots, apples, pears, and cherries every year. If one compares Haci's Fahrettin's extended family to that of many others, the most remarkable difference is that all of his sons have remained and work in Van. This represents a considerable achievement in the light of the very high unemployment rate in Van.

Haci Fahrettin's early success as a pioneering migrant has translated into job opportunities for his sons, opportunities later arrivals have not had. His oldest son Mehmet, married with three children, has managed to become a government employee, the epitome of job stability in Turkey. Most of Haci's other sons have been or are bus drivers working for the family business. Son Ali, married with four children, drives an intercity bus belonging to the family between Van and other cities, as far as Istanbul. Sons Erhan and Fikret drive buses that transport personnel in Van from one place to another. Erhan has recently married and has just had a child, whereas Fikret is still unmarried. Son Ahmet, married with two children, has retired from driving himself and now organises the bids for municipal contracts for transportation. For these bids, the family buys the vehicles and then hires drivers.

Apart from Mehmet, there is only one son who is not a bus driver: Ömer, the youngest son, has gone to university and has become a teacher, working in Van. The fact that he, as well as two younger sisters, Gülay and Şengül, have been able to study is a sign of the relative wealth of the family. The family has been able to forego the earnings of a male family member (Ömer), as well as investing money in the university preparatory courses and then education of three siblings. Gülay also works as a teacher in Van, whereas Şengül has just begun her studies in Ankara. Haci Fahrettin's oldest daughter, Nurdan, was married early and lives in a district town in Van province. She has five children and lives in the same house as her parents-in-law. Another daughter, Dilan, in her late twenties, has taken over much of the running of the household from her mother.

Because of his pioneering and dominant character, Haci Fahrettin has managed to retain the pivotal role in the extended family. He cares for all the family members but also expects them to pay back into the system. His son Mehmet spent a few years living in the same small flat as his large natal family with his own wife and children and later had to share a flat with his brother Ali and his family for a considerable time. It was only a few years ago that the two brothers, now in their late thirties, were able to move to separate flats, albeit still close to Haci. Across the yard from the two-storey house in which Haci and his unmarried children occupy the top floor, Haci has built a three-storey house with apartments for Mehmet, Ali, and Erhan. While the teacher will earn his own salary and find independent lodgings on marriage, son Fikret can expect to move into the flat below Haci on marriage. Son Ahmet moved to a separate flat on marriage as his wife's family, which is Turkish, insisted on neolocal residence.

When Haci Fahrettin sits in his garden, he is surrounded by the trees he planted so many years ago and many of his children and grandchildren. The garden, flanked by the two buildings that house many of his family members, represents his achievement as a family patriarch. His association with the local Müküsî leader Aydin Bey, mentioned in Chapter 2, as well as his entrepreneurial skills and early arrival in Van have secured prestige and employment for his sons. Haci is straddling two worlds successfully. On the one hand, he has been able to keep his sons with him, which means both a guarantee that he and his wife will be looked after in old age and a way of showing strength at other times. On the other hand, he has also 'gone with the times' by letting his younger daughters enter university and the job market, one even leaving home to stay in a dormitory in Ankara. It is unlikely that a Turkish Vanlı family with a longer history of urbanity would have consented to their daughter marrying his son Ahmet if his family had not appeared sufficiently well-off, as well as urban and 'modern'.

In Haci's brother Süleyman Amca's family, all the young men work away from Van and only return for a short time every year. In the case of Hayrullah, the nuclear family has even moved to Alanya for good. However, Süleyman and Melek still have their other daughters-in-law, the *bûks,* and the grandchildren around them to make them feel valued and important. Even if all the families decided to move to Alanya eventually, the parents would move with them. Süleyman's relatively higher age, his long stay in the village, and his long insistence on the importance of village life all mean that none of his children attended high school, let alone university. His daughters have all married into villages, something that would be inconceivable for the three unmarried daughters of Haci Fahrettin. His sons are all employed in physical labour, whereas the sons of Haci Fahrettin are employed in less gruelling work. On the whole, then, this family is less well-off financially, while at the same time being much better off than many other Vanlı villagers moving to Van city.

Tacit Amca's family is different yet again. When he was still in the village and Haci Fahrettin had moved to Van, Tacit married his oldest daughter to a Gundî from lineage 11. He also sent several sons to live with his older brother in Van in order to allow them to continue their education. Indeed, the first son, Ramazan, managed to go to university and then moved to Istanbul. As in Süleyman's family, the role of head of household has fallen to one of Tacit's sons. Ramazan today employs four siblings (three brothers and a sister) and a cousin in his service provision company, and another brother, also a university graduate, has followed to Istanbul to work independently as a civil engineer. The sister in Istanbul is also taking a distance learning university course. Another brother has moved to the USA, making a living as a shop owner. This further migration away from Van has meant that there are now only three unmarried children at home with Tacit, two of them daughters. None of his older sons is likely to move back to Van even if they marry, thus depriving Tacit Amca of the moral support and prestige acquired by having one's extended family surround one. Tacit Amca's children are an example of socio-economic upward mobility in the 'new' capitalist system. While this brings its own prestige, it also means that the proximity of the sons, still cherished by the older generation, has had to be foregone.

These examples show two different forces at work. The likelihood of socio-economic success in the capitalist market increases with a move away from the village to Van and even more with a move from Van to other cities. On the other hand, the older generation, many of whom are economically reliant on their children, desire their children, particularly their sons, to live close to them. Even if the sons have to work elsewhere, as is the case with Süleyman's children, it is desirable (for the older generation) to keep the rest of the extended family together by leaving wives and children with the parents. This scenario becomes less likely, however, when children become socially upwardly mobile and economically independent from their parents. An increase in education and income can often only be achieved and maintained outside of Van and is likely to result in marriages with spouses from a similarly upwardly mobile background. In Van province itself, even young village women, with a relatively narrower choice of marriage candidates, are increasingly less willing to acquiesce to postmarital residence with their parents-in-law or long absences of their husbands.

It is thus foreseeable that as migration offers the younger generation wage labour and more access to education, young couples will push for neolocal residence after marriage, even in other cities. While this may lead to a dispersal of siblings, it is highly unlikely that elderly parents will be left to live completely alone. Sons, even if they have migrated to a different city, will be expected to have their parents live with them.

Return Migration?

This chapter has described unilineal migration away from the village or the provincial city. Gmelch points out that returns to a sending community were largely ignored in the past, due to the dominance of the rural-urban paradigm and the short-term study of communities in anthropology (1980: 135–6). This is a valid point; indeed, the Turkish State Planning Organisation noted in 2008 that although rural-urban migration is often considered the most common type, this is actually not the case. In Turkey between 1995 and 2000, many more people migrated from city to city (57.8 per cent), and also more from city to village (20.1 per cent) than from village to city (17.5 per cent) (Devlet Planlama Teşkilatı 2008: 19). That said, however, migration from city to city has often been preceded by migration from village to city, as can be seen in several families from Gundême, who moved first to Van city and then on to Istanbul or Alanya. As for city-village migration, one has to distinguish between counter-urbanisation (Rapport and Dawson 1998: 23), that is, the move from city centres to rural quasi-suburbs of the urban wealthy trying to escape city stress, and the return of former villagers to their villages.

Migration from Gundême and other Vanlı villages to cities in large numbers is still relatively recent and indeed still mostly unidirectional. The desire for economic and human capital can currently not be satisfied in the village, internally displaced villagers have not had sufficient support for a permanent return to the village, and the earthquake victims have no homes to return to.

However, as studies on (transnational) migration remind us, people may move back to where they came from, or at least to a town or city near their village of origin. Migrants themselves may subscribe to a paradigm of unidirectional rural-urban migration, but the reality is that there is an increasing flexibility in the way people move. In 1980, Gmelch already pointed out that it may be difficult to determine whether a person is 'home' on an extended visit, for a seasonal return, or for a permanent return (1980: 163). As a migrant's situation changes, a move that previously seemed inconceivable suddenly becomes feasible or even necessary. Thus, Ferguson shows that people in Zambia may need to move back to their village of origin for financial reasons even if they never intended to (1992: 89). Cliggett describes for the same country how migrants 'hedge their bets'; despite financial restrictions, they send remittances to the sending community so that they have a network of support to fall back on if the volatile economic situation necessitates a return (2003). In other cases, a return to the sending community will be carried out not by the original migrants but by their descendants, sometimes because of economic factors and sometimes because of a continuing emotional attachment to the area of origin (Tsuda 2009).

Thus, it is conceivable that Vanlı migrants may move back to their villages or to Van province at a later stage. One reason might be positive or negative changes in the Turkish economy; thus, a decrease in jobs in other regions of the country may push people to rely more on networks of non-migrant family members back in the village and the province. On the other hand, the beginnings of a construction boom in Van city since the recession of 2008 led to further employment of previous migrants in their home province. The destruction of many buildings in the most recent earthquakes may also result in work offers. Other villagers may return in old age or because they feel more comfortable in a Kurdish environment.

Whether or not individual Gundî will move back to Gundême thus remains to be seen. For now, the move away from village life, which was ethnically homogeneous, has led to changes in the way that migrants are conceptualising what it means to be Kurdish. This is discussed in the next chapter.

4

KURDISHNESS AFTER MIGRATION

An Unequal Relationship: Policies of Assimilation

In a family home in Van, I was sitting with relatives of different ages when Ahmet, a young boy of around nine years old, stood up in a position of mock-attention, simulating the position students have to take in school for their oath. Much to the amusement of other children and adults, he started reciting in Turkish: 'I am Kurdish, I am wrong,[1] I am lazy...'

What he was mocking was the recital of a weekly pledge in primary schools in Turkey, which adults, years later, can still recall word-perfect:

I am Turkish, I am honest, I am hard-working.

My principle is to protect those younger than me, to respect those older than me, and to love my country and my people more than myself.

My ideal is to improve and to develop.

Oh, great Atatürk! I swear that I will walk on the path that you created, towards the goals that you showed us.

May my existence be sacrificed to the existence of the Turks.

Happy are those who call themselves Turkish!

With a few moderations, this pledge has been sworn in primary schools since 1933. It represents a direct disciplining of bodies and minds. At least twice a week, the children stand up, and in a chorus, led by their teacher, declare their allegiance to Atatürk and the Turkish state.

Ahmet's mocking performance, his cheeky questioning of an all-pervasive, mostly unreflected disciplining of the body and mind, was received with laughter from all his Kurdish relatives. However, the light-hearted mockery should not disguise the fact that ethnic assimilation policies have been carried out in anything but a playful manner in Turkey.

In Turkey, there has often been denial of the existence of Kurds (Haig 2004), who have been labelled 'mountain Turks' by some (Ammann 2000: 79), as well as attempts by a nationalist academia to prove that Kurds are really Turks (Andrews 1989: 114). It is only recently that this denial has been openly acknowledged in mainstream discourses and the media, as, for instance, in an article by the editor-in-chief of a mainstream newspaper:

> At one time it was claimed that there was actually no such thing as a Kurdish people in this country; rather that they were Turks who lived in the mountains and whose name came from the 'kart kurt' sound they made when walking on the snow (in contrast the other Turks presumably either made a different sound or no sound at all when walking on snow . . .).
>
> **(Berkan 2005, author's translation)**

Assimilation through the education system, the military service, and the mainstream media means that it has often been difficult to express any ethnic identification other than Turkishness. Houston aptly sums up the situation when he writes about the

> [. . .] full repertoire of the Turkish nation-state's techniques for producing an homogeneous citizenry: a standardized and nationalist school curriculum; a calendar year punctuated by national holidays like October 29th; the colonization of public space by monuments and memorials honouring the nation's founding heroes; the encouragement of a collective remembering and forgetting; the endless repetition of the narrative of the

nation's birth, including the important genre of battle-accounts; the censorship—often by the proprietors—of the mass media in the name of national self-interest; the registration of residential permits by state-appointed functionaries; the omnipresence of police stations, gendarmeries, and military zones; the formalization of the 'cultural' sphere (particularly in the areas of folk-dance and music); the naming and renaming of streets, suburbs, public buildings, parks; even the permissibility of children's names, etc.
(2001a: 9)

The pledge at school described above is thus only one of many practices that have infiltrated daily life and ensure that non-Turkish ethnic entities do not express difference. Just as urban spaces are Turkified through the use of certain street, square, and neighbourhood names, rural areas have been Turkified by deleting Armenian, Greek, and Kurdish village names from the map.[2] A total of 12,211 village names have been changed in Turkey since the 1940s; in Van province alone, 415 villages have lost their old names (Tunçel 2000: 28). Although, as in the case of Gundême and many of the surrounding villages, middle-aged and elderly people still refer to the villages by their old names, on official maps they no longer exist. Thus, for instance, a middle-aged Vanlı teacher told me of how he was given a teaching duty in a village he had never heard of. It took someone to 'translate' the name for him to realise that it was a familiar village nearby. Recent discussions on solving the Kurdish question have included the suggestion that old toponyms be reinstated, a suggestion both the Prime Minister and the Minister of the Interior seem amenable to ('Adı Değiştirilmiş...').

Turkish political supremacy has been marked not only in the mapped but also in the real landscape, with large Turkish nationalist slogans carved, planted, or painted onto the bare mountainsides, particularly so in the Kurdish regions (Ammann 2000: 84). Driving around Van province, I saw several such slogans, some in spots that must have been extremely difficult to access. Obvious efforts are thus made to remind citizens of their 'Turkishness'.

The current Turkish constitution, passed by a military junta two years after a military coup in 1980, states that 'Everyone bound to the

Turkish state through the bond of citizenship is a Turk' (Article 66). The claim is thus that 'Turk' is a non-ethnic label that encompasses all citizens of the country. However, according to Çağaptay, this does not reflect the discursive realities in Turkey. He posits the existence of three 'concentric zones of Turkishness' in the state discourse on citizenship; the most inclusive zone, based on territory, defines everyone within the borders of the Turkish Republic as a 'Turk' (or Turkish citizen). The second zone, less encompassing than the first, is based on the religious identity of the former Muslim *millet*,[3] equating only Muslims with 'Turks' but excluding non-Muslim citizens. Although Kemalism officially stood and stands for laicism, a reformed Islamic identity was and still is inherent in the system. A third zone adds Turkish ethnicity as a criterion and is thus the most exclusionary; it means that neither non-Muslims nor non-Turkish Muslims are part of this core-definition of 'Turkishness' (2006: 159–60).[4]

The expectation is that non-Turkish Muslims, in this case Kurds, will eventually assimilate (cf. Gürbey 1997: 10), particularly as demands for cultural or linguistic rights and expressions of a different ethnic identity have been harshly prosecuted in the past. Indeed, I often heard Kurdish Vanlı lament themselves that they had become 'assimilated' (*asimile* in Turkish), especially in comparison to Kurds in the provinces of Hakkâri, Şırnak, Mardin, or Diyarbakır. Interlocutors sometimes made fun of the enthusiasm with which Kurdish Vanlı have allegedly embraced the discourse of homogeneity, quoting them as saying, 'We am Turkish' ('*Biz Türk'üm*') in faulty Turkish pronounced with a strong Kurdish accent.

The expectation of the eventual assimilation of Kurds has encouraged the denial of the existence of this ethnic group by the state and most political parties. However, a parallel awareness of the 'not-quite Turkishness' of Kurds has been translated into a discourse that camouflages Kurdishness as something else. Thus, argues Yeğen, the Turkish state has used 'terms of reactionary politics, tribal resistance or regional backwardness' when speaking about Kurds. By representing Kurds as backward Muslims, as members of tribes, as bandits or smugglers, as victims of feudal landlords, and as economically and culturally underdeveloped, this discourse produced by the establishment has created its own justification for oppressing them (1996: 216–7).[5] As will be discussed in

Chapter 5, the political establishment has not hesitated to encourage and manipulate tribal allegiances for party benefits while at the same time loudly condemning such 'anachronistic' social structures.

In Gundême, like in many other villages, the state's assimilation policies were represented by the teachers sent to the five-year village primary school. These teachers were mostly Turks and were often neither willing nor able to communicate in Kurdish with their young charges. Of course, the official state policy of denying the existence of a Kurdish ethnic group precluded any training of teachers in second language teaching techniques before they were sent to Kurdish areas. Many Kurds, not only those from Gundême or Van province, remember being beaten by teachers for speaking Kurdish at school, the only language they knew at the time (Ammann 2000: 188). A Turkish writer describes his experiences of teaching in Hakkâri, a province to the southeast of Van, which, due to its mountainous geography and proximity to the Iranian border, has always been more isolated and 'Kurdish' than Van. In a chapter entitled 'First Lesson', he describes how he painstakingly collected 50 words the children knew in Turkish (Edgü 2002: 67–9). Children had to learn Turkish before they could even start to tackle the normal syllabus. A similar experience of a young teacher from the west of Turkey coming to a Kurdish village in Urfa is shown in the documentary *İki Dil Bir Bavul* ('Two Languages, One Suitcase'). It is a sign of gradual changes in the political climate in Turkey that this film has been awarded several prizes in Turkey in recognition of its poignancy.

Adult villagers in Gundême, too, recall going to school for several years before understanding anything the teachers said, and they continued to speak Kurdish at home. As is discussed below, however, linguistic assimilation policies have had very powerful effects on language acquisition among many middle-aged and younger Kurds, particularly among migrants.

Who is a Kurd?

As Moerman points out, it is virtually impossible to delineate 'ethnic entities' through specific linguistic or cultural boundaries as there is invariably variation within alleged groups as well as commonality across alleged boundaries (1965: 1215–6). This is certainly true for Kurds, among whom there has always been a very diverse population and a range of social relations.

The majority of the Kurdish population lives in the neighbouring states of Turkey, Iran, Iraq, and Syria. After the First World War and the dissolution of the Ottoman Empire, Kurds were initially promised a referendum on self-rule in the Sèvres Treaty of 1920. However, in 1923, the Treaty of Sèvres was superseded by the Treaty of Lausanne, which recognised the borders of the Turkish state, approximately as we know them today. Kurdish autonomy or independence quickly became unthinkable as the building of a Turkish nation out of a multicultural imperial polity required the suppression of alternative identities (Yeğen 2005: 105, Zürcher 1997: 178).

Apart from the different state cultures that Kurds have interacted with in Turkey, Iran, Iraq, and Syria since the 1920s, there are also inevitable tensions within Kurdish societies, 'based on wide gaps in development, different orientations of the leading classes, and the conflict between still-existing tribal structures and attempts at civil society' (Strohmeier and Yalçın-Heckmann 2000: 14–5, author's translation).

In addition, writes Bruinessen, there are different religious affiliations that cut across ethnic lines, so that, for instance, a Kurdish Alevi is more likely to marry a Turkish Alevi than a Sunni Kurd and vice versa, and Yezidis are much more likely to marry endogamously. Indeed, Bruinessen argues, it might be 'more apt to consider the Kurds not as one, but as a set of ethnic groups' (1989b: 614).[6]

The degree to which people see themselves as Kurds may also differ. Identification as Kurdish is often more politicised among those in the cities whose families were forcibly displaced in village clearances carried out by the state in the 1980s and the 1990s. This is both due to the fact that those who were forcibly displaced feel victimised because of their ethnicity and that they have often had to settle in urban ghettos with fellow Kurds (Çelik 2005: 143, 148).

In short, Kurdish Vanlı, and people who describe themselves as Kurds in general, may lead considerably different lives in villages or in urban centres. There are differences in social class and religious beliefs, and finally, there is also disagreement over whether one's Kurdishness should be confined to everyday practices or should result in political activism. Just as Moerman found over 40 years ago, then, it is impossible to delineate a group of 'Kurds' based on fixed criteria.

It follows then that ethnic identification is a matter of much more subjective boundary-setting. Speaking about the Lue of Thailand, Moerman concluded, 'Someone is a Lue by virtue of believing and calling himself Lue and of acting in ways that validate his Lueness' (1965: 1222, cf. Eriksen 1993: 11). This sense of voluntary self-identification has been reiterated in studies of ethnicity ever since. Barth's seminal essay (1969) also pointed to the importance of constantly redrawn boundaries rather than objective characteristics differentiating groups from each other. This is not to say, however, that Kurds (and Turks) do not engage in primordialist discourses to justify the ethnic boundaries they draw, a point that will be discussed below.[7]

Eriksen argues that ethnicity is 'essentially an aspect of a relationship, not a property of a group' (1993: 12). It is thus impossible to discuss the 'Kurdishness' of Kurds in Turkey without also discussing 'Turkishness'. As the anecdote at the beginning of the chapter shows, children who may have identified as Kurds at home are told that they are Turkish as soon as they attend school. The relationship between Kurdishness and Turkishness has thus been marked by imbalances in power, so that other-identifications have often had more influence than self-identifications (cf. Brubaker and Cooper 2000).

Linguistic Assimilation

Given the assimilation projects of regional nation-states, there is not a straightforward relationship between Kurdish language and ethnicity. For instance, the KONDA survey carried out in Turkey in 2007 showed that 4.08 per cent of those who defined themselves as 'Turkish' spoke Kurdish as their mother tongue, and that 8.82 per cent of those who defined themselves as 'Kurdish' or 'Zaza' spoke Turkish as their mother tongue, showing that ethnic self-definition is not always predictable ('Biz Kimiz?').

Nevertheless, among my interlocutors language was considered an important factor in their construction of themselves as Kurdish.

This is presumably due to the fact that they or their families all had a relatively recent rural background and were thus either fluent Kurdish speakers or had at least some passive knowledge of the language. When 89 per cent of my questionnaire respondents concurred with the statement 'The loss of Kurdish means the loss of a culture', they were echoing Gudykunst and Schmidt, who say:

> The language or dialect speakers use provides cues that allow others to determine if speakers are members of an ingroup or an outgroup. Research indicates that ethnic group members iden-tify more closely with those who share their language than with those who share their cultural background.
>
> (1988: 1)

For many of my interlocutors, who had left behind a village life where Kurdishness was constructed less explicitly, the knowledge of Kurdish was seen as a vital marker of ethnicity in the city; indeed, it could be argued that it was only the use of Kurdish that made them any differ-ent from the many rural-urban migrants from all around Turkey.

For the elder and middle-aged generations of today, their village was a relatively homogeneous linguistic community. Children learnt Kurdish as their first language at home and, before the arrival of tel-evision in the late 1980s, did not speak Turkish before they went to school. Many of their mothers never learnt much Turkish. Most men learnt the language as they left the village to do military service and, in the last 20 years, to work on construction sites. However, Kurdish continued to be the language spoken at home, between couples and between parents and children.

Migration has brought a drastic change in linguistic behaviour. First of all, men working for long periods of time in Turkish-speaking areas of the country (no matter how Kurdish-dominated parts of the building sector are) interact with Turkish workers, shopkeepers, doc-tors, and others. They start to code switch, sometimes out of a reluc-tance to speak Kurdish in front of others (a reluctance very common in western Turkey until a few years ago) and sometimes also because talking about non-village matters is easier in Turkish.

If families remained in the village for a longer time or if several generations have lived together in one household in the city, the younger children will today still be able to speak Kurdish with ease. They are used to speaking to their grandparents, other elders, and their parents in Kurdish. However, all children today will also pick up Turkish before they start school as the ubiquitous television teaches them.

In cases where whole families have migrated to Van or other cities, Kurdish gets lost as a shared language very rapidly. I would concur with Andrews, who notes that language attrition is faster in urban centres than in rural areas (1989: 38); this is true both in terms of the total number of Kurdish speakers and the degree of linguistic competence of individual speakers.

Van city has a larger Turkish population than other cities in Kurdish-majority provinces. Data from the 1960s shows that 50 per cent of the population in Van province was Turkish-speaking, compared to 22 per cent in some of Diyarbakır province (Nestmann 1989: 547). Although this percentage has gone down with rural-urban migration, Van province is known to be more 'assimilated' than other Kurdish-majority provinces and has always had a larger Turkish presence. Migration to the province capital from villages has resulted in a rapid loss of Kurdish.

Haci Fahrettin's family can be used to exemplify the change in language use. His older children grew up in the village for at least five to ten years, and his wife Melek is not very comfortable speaking Turkish. The younger children (now all over 20 years old), who were born and grew up in Van, still understand Kurdish very well and may also speak it, but much less comfortably than their older siblings. It might be said about them, as many Kurds say when people have more passive than active knowledge of the language, 'their tongue does not turn' ('zimani wan na zivire'). Because there have always been many visitors from the village at the house, Haci Fahrettin's children are nevertheless all able to speak the language. However, among Haci Fahrettin's grandchildren, none use Kurdish as a language of communication. Their parents have always spoken to them in Turkish, and their extensive exposure to Turkish in school means that Kurdish for them is now only the language spoken between their parents. Even the children of Haci Fahrettin's daughter Nurdan, who lives in the smaller district town of Muradiye, are not really able to speak the language any longer.

This loss of the mother tongue within just one generation is even more dramatic in cities in the west of Turkey. Kurdish parents have largely internalised the denigratory attitude towards their mother tongue or fear that their children will grow up with too much of an accent if they learn Kurdish first. In Bourdieu's terms, they have been exposed to 'symbolic violence', which through both objective power structures and subjective ways of thinking (1998: 40) has made them accept as 'natural' the attitude that Kurdish is an inferior language, if a language at all. At the same time, adults may harbour a sense of loss at not passing on their mother tongue, exemplified by the following anecdote in Istanbul recounted by Kurdish writer Muhsin Kızılkaya:

> The other day, when I was taking my daughter Lian to her crèche, we took a taxi. As we were talking Kurdish to each other, the taxi driver said, greatly surprised, 'She speaks Kurdish.' He was from Mardin. He stopped the taxi at the side of the road and started to cry, saying, 'She speaks Kurdish.' He tried to refuse our fare as we got off. You cannot describe this to people. Only people whose language has suffered so much unfairness, only a people who has been hurt can understand.
>
> **(Örer 2008, author's translation)**

Among all of my Kurdish acquaintances and interlocutors in Istanbul, I have only met one (non-Vanlı) couple who consciously teach their children Kurdish and Turkish at home. Because of the restrictive linguistic policies of the Turkish state, they themselves do not know how to write Kurdish and have had to make do with passing on the spoken language. There are virtually no Kurdish children's books available; this makes it difficult to teach vocabulary beyond that used in everyday interactions. There are no educational Kurdish audio tapes or videos for children that would allow for a broadening of vocabulary, although some Kurdish associations in Europe have begun putting educational material onto their websites that could be accessed by families in Turkey if they so wished. The private regional Kurdish TV stations that have been allowed to broadcast a few hours of Kurdish a week were forbidden to target children with educational programmes. The spoken language passed on has thus always been limited to certain topics, and children naturally revert to Turkish when talking about school, computers, TV programmes, sports, or books.

In Tepelik, married housewives may still talk to their spouses and each other in Kurdish when discussing certain issues where the vocabulary is familiar, while their children may not. In several families, the parents noted that the girls still understood more Kurdish as they were encouraged to spend more time at home than their brothers in order to help with chores. In several families, both in Van city and in Istanbul, I have witnessed middle-aged mothers with very little Turkish and children with very little Kurdish living together and overcoming hurdles when communicating more complex matters to each other. Lacking the determination or education to raise their children bilingually, many parents I spoke to have regretfully accepted that their children will not speak the language anymore.

Among the respondents to my questionnaire, all of them Vanlı migrants to Istanbul, the majority considered themselves as Kurds (85%). Asked whether it was important for them to speak Kurdish well, 93 per cent of all the respondents replied in the affirmative. Nearly as many wanted their children to speak both Turkish and Kurdish well (91%). From my observations in other migrant families, however, I would guess that no active steps are taken to promote bilingualism within the family. Rather, children pick up some passive knowledge of the language from their parents' conversations.

It remains to be seen what effect the Turkish state TRT 6 channel, which has been broadcasting in Kurdish since January 2009, will have on Kurdish language attrition or acquisition. Watching it with Kurdish Vanlı, I have come across a variety of responses. One was frustration at the lack of comprehension of programmes completely in Kurdish. Another was a nostalgic remembrance of elder relatives who had used certain words that had been forgotten by the younger generation. Yet another reaction was the eagerness to learn obvious neologisms (often created in exile by a more politicised and more educated elite) or loan words from other Kurdish dialects. All viewers, however, exulted in the fact that with this channel, Kurdish was implicitly acknowledged as a real language that could be used for a variety of registers, ranging from serious news programmes and theological discussions to football league coverage and live music shows. There is hope that this step will be followed by more explicit acknowledgement of the value of the Kurdish language.

The situation of Kurds and Kurdish in Turkey can be described using the succinct analysis of Bourdieu:

> Cultural and linguistic unification is accompanied by the imposition of the dominant language and culture as legitimate and by the rejection of all other languages into indignity (thus demoted as patois or local dialects). By rising to universality, a particular culture or language causes all others to fall into particularity. What is more, given that the universalization of requirements thus officially instituted does not come with an universalization of access to the means to fulfill them, this fosters both the monopolization of the universal by the few and the dispossession of all others, who are, in a way, thereby mutilated in their humanity.
>
> (1998: 46–7)

This 'mutilated humanity' can be seen in the dilemma that many Kurdish Vanlı and other Kurds face in relation to the state. On the one hand, Kurdish village life is considered to represent 'pure' Kurdishness. This is particularly true for village women, who are often illiterate and, at least in the past, only spoke Kurdish. Their isolation and lack of education resulted in the next generation of children being brought up as 'Kurds' (Yalçın-Heckmann and Gelder 2000: 79, Wedel 2000: 106). However, young Kurdish women in Van, too, have realised that education in the Turkish school system offers them more life choices later on and leads to different treatment by others. More and more young women are going to school for longer, which leads to an accelerated Turkification of Kurds.

The attempts by the state to make the new generation literate and more educated cannot just be read as a well-meaning attempt at developing the region (although there are certainly well-meaning individuals and associations involved in this educational mobilisation). As a Kurdish lawyer argues, the campaign 'Off to School, Girls!' (see Chapter 3) has been an effective means of rapid Turkification as girls educated in Turkish will turn into mothers who will not teach their children Kurdish any more (Tugan 2009).

Tugan recounts going to Hakkâri, the province south of Van, and meeting school girls who had come home from a regional boarding school for the weekend. The children did not speak Kurdish very well, and they were unhappy to be home from the school:

> It was very clear that rather than be with their family crowded into a two-room mud-plastered house, the girls would rather stay hungry most of the time in the girls' boarding school, where their mothers' language was forbidden and its existence denied, but which was a place made of cement and had bathrooms, where girls were some-times put in rows and had their hair shaved off. They had learned the language of power and had said farewell to their mother tongue. They wanted to study, go to university, and leave this place behind as fast as possible. [...] I wanted to tell my little sisters in Çukurca that Kurdish is not at all a language to be ashamed of. But I did not have the heart to let their poor parents know that their children were ashamed of them. I remained silent.
>
> (*ibid.*, author's translation)

As Bourdieu points out, the dominant language and culture is not eas-ily accessed by everyone. For Kurds in Turkey, it still comes at the price of giving up or at the least severely neglecting one's mother tongue. As the example of the young school girls above shows, and as I found countless times among Kurdish Vanlı interlocutors, the denigration of the Kurdish language has been internalised to a great extent, making its preservation even more difficult.

Language loss among migrants, which entails an even greater dearth of cultural characteristics that are purely Kurdish, can have one of two effects. On the one hand, a lack of Kurdish language proficiency can accelerate assimilation; on the other hand, individuals may emphasise their Kurdish ethnicity more as a reaction to assimilation policies and migration. These two attitudes can often be observed to be coexisting within one individual. The contradictory discourses of nostalgia for and contempt of village life (see Chapter 2) are often also applied to Kurdishness and the Kurdish language. Thus, migrants may denigrate themselves, their ethnic group, and their language, criticising their own perceived 'ignorance' and lack of modernity. At other times, however, they may revel in the use of Kurdish with others, reminiscing about songs, stories, and other experiences that the use of the language immediately brings to mind.

Assimiliation versus Politicisation

Eriksen delineates Handelman's typology of ethnic entities, according to which the salience of ethnic identity increases through different stages: ethnic category, ethnic network, ethnic association, and ethnic community (Eriksen 1993: 41–3). The ethnic category is a way of delineating oneself, while the ethnic network also involves frequent interaction between people from the same ethnic category. When these people mobilise in organisations, one can speak of ethnic associations. An ethnic group, finally, writes Eriksen, has the 'highest degree of ethnic incorporation': 'This kind of collectivity has, in addition to ethnic networks and shared political organisation, a territory with more or less permanent physical boundaries' (1993: 43).

These stages of ethnic salience can be considered at three levels: for one, they describe a chronological order, that is, groups may go through a development where a corporate ethnic identity becomes increasingly important. Second, the stages can also be considered as a typology, categorising synchronously existing groups. Finally, the salience of ethnic identification also varies situationally, so that individuals may feel part of a different type of ethnic entity at different times (*ibid.*).

Ethnic identification is situational not only in the sense that a person may feel more or less Kurdish in different situations, but also in the sense that expressing such an identification is not always wise. Secor perceptively describes her Kurdish interlocutors as being aware of 'spaces that demand particular identity performances', oscillating between 'spaces of anonymity' and 'spaces of Kurdish solidarity' (2004: 360–1), pragmatically hiding or communicating their ethnicity. I have observed countless times how people gingerly avoided a direct reference to Kurdish ethnicity by either side-stepping the issue or making use of euphemisms.

Despite individual and situational variety, I would argue that migration has, generally speaking, led to a development of increasing corporateness of Kurdish identity. In pre-migration village life, Kurdish identity was inextricably linked with religious, village, and perhaps also lineage or tribal identity. Because of the relative ethnic homogeneity of village life before mass labour migration, Kurdish ethnicity was an everyday experience based on shared experiences of language, religiosity, solidarity, and conventions of modesty and respect, with little need for explicit identity politics.

Today, there is more contact with the Turkish world, primarily because of labour migration, which in turn has also led to more children entering the education system and remaining in it for longer. It is through the necessity of re-negotiating boundaries that Kurdish identification has become more salient for many (and less so for others).

Indeed, the very formation of the militant PKK, which began its armed struggle against the Turkish army and establishment in 1984, can be said to be due to migration:

> Th[e] expansion of Turkey's democracy [in the 1960s] coincided with the rise of a more educated and cosmopolitan Kurdish population. The first generation born after the Kurdish rebellions had come of age, and they did not carry with them the same fears and memories of the army's harsh put-down of the uprisings that helped silence their parents. More Kurds were attending university, where they were exposed both to new ideas and other Kurdish youth. At the same time, Kurdish peasants seeking a way out of economic hardship were moving to the cities, where they were more likely to hear grumbling about economic inequality between Kurds and Turks and whispers of a new Kurdish political agitation at home and in Iraq.
>
> **(Marcus 2007: 19)**

The PKK of course epitomises a drive to first push people towards self-identification as Kurds, that is, consideration of themselves as an ethnic category, and then towards identification as an ethnic community with political claims.

Among my Vanlı interlocutors I often observed ambivalence towards the PKK. For a long time, it represented the only voice insisting on the reality of a Kurdish identity. The presence of a pro-Kurdish party in parliament today is said to be due to the pressure that the PKK has exerted on the government, and party links to the militant organisation are openly acknowledged. Many interlocutors have voted for a succession of pro-Kurdish parties, many of which were closed down, as a matter of course. On the other hand, families in Van and Tepelik voiced very real fears that their children, especially their sons, would become involved in militant activities. People spoke in hushed tones of children from other families said to have been forced to join the PKK or have run away 'to the mountains'. If sons were out too late in Van city, there was great worry that they were getting involved with 'the wrong crowd', that is, with groups that were too extreme in the eyes of the parents. In Van and in other cities, forcibly displaced Kurdish migrants or those whose relatives have disappeared are much less ambiguous in their support for the PKK (cf. Çağlayan 2007, Çelik 2005: 149).

The politicisation of a Kurdish identity has also got transnational dimensions. The Kurdish diaspora in Europe, with many politically motivated migrants, has been particularly influential in furthering a discourse of a 'Kurdish community' or even a nation. Through associations, culture centres, political organisations (legal or illegal), and media channels, they have countered the Turkish mainstream discourse that silences or denigrates Kurdishness. For one, when watching the many Kurdish TV channels available to Kurds via satellite, Kurds in Turkey (both in villages and in cities) are presented with images of Kurds different from the often negatively loaded stereotypes portrayed in the Turkish mainstream media (Grabolle-Çeliker 2009). Second, language courses, language research (e.g. the electronic NGO Kurdish Academy of Language, KAL, founded in 1992), online Kurdish news websites, and literature written in Kurdish (e.g. by Kurdish migrant writer Mehmed Uzun in Sweden) have all contributed to the development and standardisation of the Kurdish language, at least for an intellectual elite, both in Europe and in cities in Turkey. In addition, membership in organisations explicitly founded by Kurds has also reinforced the concept of an ethnic group. Finally, the 'Kurdish community' has also been given increasing legitimacy through journalistic and academic analyses (e.g. Chaliand 1980, Deschner 2003, Gunter 1997, Kirişçi and Winrow 1997, Olson 1989, 1996a, 1996b) and the foundation of Kurdology centres abroad (e.g. Europäisches Zentrum für kurdische Studien Berlin, Institut Kurde de Paris, Centre for Kurdish Studies at the University of Exeter). Partly because of domestic pressures and partly because of this precedence, Turkey is now also considering the foundation of Kurdology departments at existing and new universities, a dramatic step towards a reversal of the assimilation policies practised so far.

All of this has led to the discursive creation, in transnational space, of a Kurdish ethnic community, that is, an ethnic entity with political organisation and a territory (Eriksen 1993: 43). The controversy around the term 'Kurdistan' has to be understood in this context: while the use of the term (which was applied during the Ottoman Empire) is more or less illegal in Turkey today, it has become revitalised as a proto-national (cf. Eriksen 1993: 14) reference to a country, which, in defiance of actual state borders, is used to talk about, for example, 'Northern Kurdistan' (the Kurdish-majority region in Turkey) and 'Southern Kurdistan' (in Iraq). Thus, the experiences of discrimination and exile among many migrants to western Turkish or European cities have led to an 'imagined community' (Anderson 1991). This heightened sense of ethnic identification is one that Vanlı migrants and non-migrants with less traumatic experiences can also draw on if they so wish. That many do so is obvious from the rise in support of pro-Kurdish parties in Van province in local and parliamentary elections (see Chapter 5).

Self-Descriptions: Nostalgic Idealisation and the Tradition of Victimhood

Keeping in mind that Kurdish Vanlı may deny, ignore, denigrate, embrace, or advertise Kurdish ethnicity in different situations, the following offers a look at how Kurdish Vanlı interlocutors themselves have spoken about Kurds.

One frequently-heard discourse fragment was that of nostalgic idealisation, by which I mean the citation of primordialist characteristics to evoke a sense of ethnic unity. A small Kurdish intellectual elite may evoke a long history of existence in a certain territory and list continual Kurdish revolts against oppressive regimes in order to support the notion of a Kurdish community. Most ordinary Kurds, however, are not so concerned with an exact historical narrative of independence struggles; rather, they make use of potent symbols of the mountains and village life as 'typically Kurdish'. They recall plants, animals, and activities of rural life and also place great importance on material cultural items, such as ceramic storage pots, scythes, mill stones, and handmade clothing and carpets. Ironically, these items are often not used anymore, or are anyhow not exclusively Kurdish (Ammann 2000: 100).

A striking example of this use of rural symbols is the production and dissemination of VCDs with amateur actors from various Kurdish-majority provinces performing sketches. The sketches are in Kurdish, yet simple enough for younger migrants with little command of the language to follow. They contain slapstick-style comedy with a backdrop of rural landscapes and material culture. These sketches have proven to be extremely popular, both in villages and in cities in eastern and western Turkey. They are sold by street CD vendors and can also be found in Van city and in Istanbul. With echoes of the Kurdish rural tradition of bards (dengbêjen) (Kızılkaya 2000: 14, Bruinessen 1989a: 106) and Anatolian mummery plays (And 1987: 86), the actors act out comical situations. 'The villager' is then portrayed as a buffoon or a shrewd trickster, both representations of 'the Kurds' that the viewers recognise as 'typically Kurdish' (Grabolle-Çeliker 2009).

Apart from the sketches, the use of the Kurdish language is often also inextricably linked to the evocation of rural material culture as Kurds who grew up in the village may only know the Kurdish names of certain plants, tools, and other items related to rural life. In addition, speaking Kurdish amongst each other, Kurdish migrants often seemed to re-enact a different 'self' in their communication (cf. Koven 1998), being wittier, more confident, more intimate, or wiser. Even Kurdish migrants with little or no Kurdish may feel nostalgic associations with Kurdish music and may remember some of the lyrics and find out what they mean. Indeed, Yalçın-Heckmann critically described a Kurdish participant at a conference who accused Turks of 'stealing' Kurdish songs (1989). Clearly, the urge for a 'pure' Kurdish heritage had caused the participant to ignore centuries of coexistence and cultural diffusion between Kurds, Turks, and many others, and he felt the urge to claim the existence of a pure Kurdish musical heritage.

An underlying primordial assumption of the ethnic group as an extended kin group can be found in the claims of many Kurds that they recognise each other as such (cf. Ammann 2000: 181–5). Despite the fact that Kurds display a variety of physiognomic features that do not distinguish them from other ethnic groups in the region (McDowall 1997: 9), I have watched countless exchanges between strangers in Istanbul where an initial 'hunch' was proven to be correct. While this may of course be due to accent, clothing, or other subconsciously perceived information, Kurdish Vanlı interlocutors have interpreted these encounters as a case of 'blood boiling' ('xun dîkele'), implying a consanguineous connection with other Kurds.

Another unifying belief has been the concept of the Kurds as a suffering people, a 'victim tradition' that has also been noted as one possible discursive construction of diasporas, particularly the Jewish and Armenian ones (Cohen 2002: §2). This Kurdish construction of victimhood is centrally rooted in the lack of a nation-state and is echoed in studies about the Kurds as 'a nation/a people without a state/country' (e.g. Chaliand 1980, Deschner 2003). According to a story I was told by several Vanlı independently, the Kurds are only little better off than the *mirtip*, the Roma they mostly look down on, because of the involvement of the two peoples in the attempted murder of a prophet:

In Urfa the prophet Abraham (*İbrahim*) was supposed to be burnt on a pyre for preaching monotheism. The fire was burning and he was meant to be thrown onto the pyre, but no one was able to approach it because of the heat. A *mirtip* came forward and suggested using a catapult to throw him onto the fire. It turned out that this machine resisted being used to kill Abraham and could only be made to obey if adultery (*zina*) was committed underneath it. In one version of the story, it was the Kurds who, upon the suggestion of the *mirtip*, carried out the shameful act of adultery. The machine could then be used to throw Abraham into the fire, but the fire and the wood turned into a lake with fish, today a tourist attraction in Urfa.

As a result of this legendary attack on the prophet Abraham, the Roma and the Kurds are said to have been cursed, the curse being that they have nowhere to live.

Of course the Kurds *do* have somewhere to live, but they have faced discrimination because of their ethnicity. The discourse of victimhood that Kurds sometimes engage in can thus also take the form of lamenting their own 'backwardness' in terms of their socio-economic, educational, and political status. An often-heard refrain is that of 'ignorance' (*cahillik* in Turkish). Aware that, according to official rhetoric, they are meant to be part of the country, but that they are economically underdeveloped,[8] educationally underserviced, and often represent the 'Other' for a more established (Turkish) elite, Kurdish villagers and migrants often resort to a defiant stance as the underclass, by, for instance, reappropriating words such as '*kıro*', which are used in a denigratory manner by others (see Chapter 1).

What all these approaches have in common is that they conceptualise a 'we', an ethnic 'group' or 'community'. As argued above, migration has led to a more selfconscious identification as Kurdish by Kurdish Vanlı in all locations. Divisions that used to be highly salient, like those between quarreling factions in a village or between villages, have diminished in importance, similar to the Pakistanis of different origin who meet in Norway, described by Barth (1995: 4). As is discussed below, however, this discourse of an increasingly corporate ethnic identity is paralleled and contradicted by a discourse of differentiation and tensions.

Social Differentiation: *'Beyaz Kürtler'* and *'Kırolar'*

When analysing rural-urban migration in the Zambian Copperbelt, Ferguson describes the use of 'ruralist themes', both by what he calls 'localists', migrants with strong links to their home village, and by social reformers who try to purge the country of colonial influences by 'constructing an authentic "Zambian-ness"' (1992: 83). I have argued that Kurds, too, have used rural symbols, both to contextualise their migration and to construct Kurdishness.

The Vanlı migration I have charted began later than that in the Copperbelt, but a second discourse that Ferguson describes in Zambia in the 1980s and 1990s can also increasingly be found among Kurdish Vanlı in Turkey. He writes about an 'inwardly directed moral critique', critical both of urban life, the conditions of which have become worse, and of rural populations, which are accused of selfishness. As some migrants who never dreamed of going 'back' have had to contemplate a return to the village, and as rural dependants make increasing demands on urban migrants, tensions have increased. Thus, says Ferguson, it has become common to hear sweeping, negative statements about 'us' (1992: 85–8).

Similar to the idealising and disparaging discourse fragments on the village among Kurdish Vanlı, there were countless statements about 'us', 'the Kurds'. Very similar to Ferguson's findings, the focus has just as often been on selfishness or other negative features as on an idealised Kurdish community, and, like Ferguson, I would argue that the reason behind this discursive variety is economic.

Rural-urban migration has caused much more socio-economic differentiation among Kurdish Vanlı than would have been possible in the village before. Although there were differences in wealth in Gundême (and in other villages of the region), these were rooted in land ownership or the number of animals one had. Both types of property nevertheless required hard physical work and neither could be easily converted into 'ready cash', particularly not the land. Migration and financial remittances have allowed many people who have remained in the village, and also people in Van city, to improve their dwellings and clothing, buy vehicles, go further for medical care, and have more leisure time. The pursuit of education has meant that some young people in the new generation will diverge from the options of farming or construction site labour (for men) and early marriage (for women) to seek more professional work.

In the cities where villagers have migrated to, there is also greater socio-economic differentiation. As will be discussed in Chapter 6, migrants vary in the kinds of networks they participate in and thus in the type of social capital they accumulate. In the light of the difficulties of urban life, the gap between migrants is likely to widen ever more. Rents and living costs are high compared to the low minimum wage. Familial, hometown, tribal, regional, or ethnic solidarity is likely to decline when people find it hard even to feed and educate their own children or look after their parents.

It is in such a climate of economic difficulty and socio-economic differentiation that tensions become apparent in the way that Vanlı speak about each other or about 'themselves' as Kurds. A realisation of the decline in generalised solidarity may lead to statements such as: 'We are a selfish people.' Kurdish Vanlı who have difficulties getting by may talk disparagingly about 'white Kurds' ('*beyaz Kürtler*' in Turkish), an adaption from the term 'white Turks' that has become a popular label for an urban bourgeois elite. On the other hand, these 'white Kurds' may talk in a denigratory manner about those who have not 'made it'; they refer to the villagers' or migrants' perceived laziness or uncouthness, the latter expressed with the term '*kıro*'. Finally, I have also heard Kurdish Vanlı seasonal migrant workers complain about the greed of villagers, often their own family members, who may demand that they stay in the city, away from wife and children, to work more and to send more money.

Of course these tensions are not expressed or felt continuously; rather, they are one of the many coexisting discourse fragments on Kurdishness. In everyday life, individuals may gladly help one another, while at other times grumbling about a particularly demanding relative or fellow villager. In business, a shared Kurdishness can lead to particular trust and friendship or to bad experiences that make a Kurdish person swear 'never to do business with a Kurd again'. A Kurdish Vanlı migrant may indulge in nostalgia about Kurdish village life and yet refuse to go back to the village even for visits because it is 'too dirty', 'too boring', or the people are 'too lazy'. The ideal of generalised solidarity among Kurds, fellow Vanlı, fellow villagers, or lineage members may be espoused, but people do set realistic limits on how much money they lend and how much time they spend on the problems of others.

What many Vanlı migrants attempt to achieve is a balance of solidarity and support with the protection of their individual and nuclear family interests. People try not to lose symbolic and social capital by refusing support, while at the same time protecting their economic capital so that they can ensure the lifestyle they envisage for their immediate family.

Migration has meant that Kurdish villagers have created more self-conscious discourses about Kurdishness than used to exist in the village. Migrants, and through continuing interactions with migrants also Vanlı who have continued to live in villages, today oscillate between identification as Kurds and assimilation, between fervour and nostalgia for and contempt of a Kurdish 'community', between solidarity based on generalised reciprocity among networks based on culturally salient commonalities and a concern for the material well-being of an ever-smaller unit of the kinship group.

An identification as Kurd can be pushed to the background to make way for other identifications. Thus, as is discussed in the next chapter, a corporate tribal identity may be evoked for political purposes, particularly in Van city. At other times, migrants to large cities feel more solidarity with fellow Vanlı or villagers than a complete Kurdish 'community'.

5

SOCIO-POLITICAL CHANGES AND NETWORKS

Ethnic Make-Up of Van Province

This chapter discusses three changes in socio-political organisation among Vanlı Kurds caused by large-scale rural-urban migration in recent decades: for one, the changing population of Van city has caused a partial 'retribalisation' of Kurdish society. Second, migration of Vanlı to other cities in Turkey has led to involvement in hometown organisations. Third, I discuss how Vanlı have created networks of transaction among migrants and between sending and receiving 'communities'. A discussion of these phenomena needs to be prefaced with a look at the ethnic make-up of Van, which has changed with the move of many rural Vanlı to the city.

During the First World War, the city of Van was razed to the ground, and today only a few ruins of the old city remain. The many Armenians in the area fled to Armenia, converted, or were killed. Other non-Muslims, such as Jews, Yezidis, and Nestorians[1] have mostly been forced into leaving the area, even the country. There is no collective memory of the once so varied ethnic make-up of the city (cf. Wießner 1997).

It has been difficult to analyse the Turkish-Kurdish population ratio in Van. Ottoman censuses only differentiated between Muslims and non-Muslims and thus not between the Muslim Turks and Kurds. In the Republican period after 1923, it gradually became undesirable to ask about the ethnic origin of Turkish citizens.[2] From oral accounts of interlocutors of different ages and ethnicity, it seems that after the First World War, Van city (Van *merkez*) was predominantly Turkish. Even if there were many Kurds living in the city, the administrative and merchant classes were Turkish or assimilated Kurds. In conversations, Turkish Vanlı would repeatedly emphasise their *'merkez'* (centre) or *'yerli'* (local) identity in order to distinguish themselves from Kurdish Vanlı, whom they consider villagers and late-comers. A Kurdish Vanlı said that before the 1950s there were hardly any Kurds to be seen in Van. He also recounted being made fun of by neighbours as his Turkish was not good enough. Even in the 1980s, village Kurdish primary school pupils joining school in Van were teased for their accents and for being 'Kurdish', the term being used as abuse. It only dawned on them later that those teasing them were often Kurds themselves. Van *merkez* thus either had a majority of Turks living in it, or the Kurds were particularly 'assimilated'.[3]

Illustration 3: Van City Today

Particularly before the term 'Kurdish' became a self-conscious badge of ethnic identity politics, labelling someone as 'Kurdish' was a way of showing contempt for rural life. It seems that people in Van city felt the need to prove their urbanity by denigrating rurality, either because they had only arrived recently themselves or because they felt that their provincial urbanity was under threat by an increase in rural-urban migration.

As discussed earlier, since the second half of the 20th century Van city has received a lot of migrants, from villages within Van province, from villages in other eastern provinces, and even from Iran and Iraq. In the city, the major ethnic groups are now Kurds, Turkish *yerli*, Azeri Turks from Iran (*Acem*), and Roma (called *mirtip* by the Kurds). Although no official numbers are available, it is safe to say that the Kurds now make up the majority of the population. In the country-side, most villages are populated by Kurds. An official Turkish source (in English) blithely writes about Van:

> Migrations have changed the demographic structure of the city as well. A century ago, the population of Van was 56 per cent Muslim and 41 per cent Christian, the remainder being Jews, Yezidis and Romanies. Today the population of Van is almost entirely Muslim. Instead of the mosaic formed by different ethnic groups in the past there is now only a mosaic created by regional differences.
>
> **(Turkish Ministry of Culture 2000)**

As well as not offering any explanations for the disappearance of virtually all the Christians, Jews[4] and Yezidis in Van, the Ministry website avoids using the ethnonyms 'Turk' and 'Kurd', euphemistically speaking of 'regional differences'.

Tribes and 'Neopatriarchy'

As discussed earlier, many Vanlı Kurds belong to tribes, while the Vanlı Turks do not. The influx of Kurds into Van city with rural-urban migration has meant that the political landscape has changed.

While members of the army, security forces, and province administration are still mainly Turkish and dispatched to the region by the central government, the Kurds have taken over in local government. Tribal membership has become one means of creating 'social capital' with which to fight local elections. Once candidates get elected as mayor or councillors, they are in a position to award municipal contracts and employ people, so, just like anywhere else, supporting a candidate is also a means of looking out for oneself.

The influx of Kurds from villages of Van province and other provinces has meant that within the Kurdish 'community'[5] in Van city, tribal balances have changed. It has to be said, of course, that many Kurds now find tribal membership irrelevant and do not know many tribal names. Nevertheless, because of migration to Van province there are now also tribes that did not exist there previously, and this sometimes leads to friction and mistrust. One tribe considered a latecomer by many of my Kurdish interlocutors is the Burukhan tribe. Originally from the Diyarbakır area, the tribe split and migrated to Iran and the Caucasus in the 17th century. It was only in the 1920s that tribal members came back to Turkey. Reasons cited for their return are the Russian revolution and the fact that there were villages left empty after the Armenians of the area had fled. Today, there are around 75 Burukhan villages in Van province (Özer 2003: 73–9), and their villagers have of course also taken part in the rural-urban migration to the province centre. In Van, one gets a sense that the Burukî, as they are known, are somewhat resented by many other Kurds. At other times, my interlocutors spoke disparagingly of tribes from Hakkarî that have become more prominent in the city.

Generally, tribal connections have long been exploited in Van province not only for local but also parliamentary elections. In Turkey as a whole, personal connections in politics, euphemistically called 'a maternal uncle in Ankara' (Ankara'da bir dayı), are valued in order to overcome bureaucratic hurdles and forge useful networks. Despite their public denouncement of tribal politics as backwards (cf. Yeğen 1996), many mainstream parties have been heavily involved in the bargaining for the bloc votes some tribal leaders still promise to deliver (cf. Bruinessen 1999a, McDowall 1997: 397, Yalçın 1986: 222).[6] The bloc votes are of course not based on blind loyalty but on pragmatic expectations of later repayment of some kind.

The mutual exploitation of the central national government and dominant regional personages has been called 'retribalisation' by Bruinessen (1999a and 2003),[7] a similar process to what happened in Northern Iraq, where the competition for power by Barzani and Talabani in the 1990s was labelled 'neo-tribalism' by McDowall (1997: 385–6). In her book on Kurdish women in Diyarbakır, Çağlayan also notes that 'there is collaboration between the rural organisation of central bureaucracy, tribes, and local party branches' (2007: 43, author's translation). The same phenomenon has been described as 'neopatriarchy' in Arab countries by Sharabi; he argues that traditionalist society is exploited by an absolute regime crippling any emerging civil society (Sharabi 1988, cf. Frisch 1997: 343). Sharabi describes kinship, tribal, and religious affiliations as 'primordial forms' that 'remain the ultimate ground of loyalty and allegiance, stronger than abstract ideology' (1988: 28–9). While Sharabi posits loyalty of the individual to the tribe and tribal 'collective responsibility' for the individual, I would argue that tribal membership today is used pragmatically by most Vanlı as it offers an idiom in which to cloak patronage. Sharabi rightly points out the importance of mediation (*wasta* in Arabic) in society; every person involved in the system benefits, 'the supplicant, the bestower of favour and the go-between as well' (1988: 46), and this is of course what makes it so durable. Thus, he laments, 'Neopatriarchal patronage, as it displaces legality and renders public institutions superfluous, takes away the individual's claim to autonomous right' (*ibid.*).

In local elections in Turkey in March 2009, the importance of the position of 'go-between' became evident even at the lowest level. The elected neighbourhood officials, *muhtars*, earn around 300 Turkish Liras a month (around 150 Euros), much less than the minimum wage; they also have to pay their own insurance contribution, which amounts to nearly their total wage. Although they charge fees for the services they provide (issuing documents of residence), they also have to pay the bills of the *muhtar* office with this money. Many *muhtars* are the first port of call for poor or unemployed people and act as go-betweens between them and the state and also between the poor and the rich, who may offer to pay for the schooling of a child in the neighbourhood or give other support. The importance of this broker function seems far to outweigh the fact that the job does not pay well. Thus, the 2009 local elections witnessed fights in many villages around Turkey on account of *muhtar* elections, leaving 19 dead and around 150 injured. In Van province, there were fights in at least two villages: In the Ilıkkaynak village attached to the town of Erçek, one person died and five people were wounded in a fight about the *muhtar* office. In the village of Dibekli in the Özalp district, three people were injured after two families started a stone and sticks fight over the same issue ('Muhtarlık Seçimlerinde...', 'Seçim Bilançosu...').

At the parliamentary level, it is easy to give concrete examples of neopatriarchy by looking at electoral lists in Van province. Indeed, the names of past MPs and parliamentary candidates from Van evoke a sense that seats in parliament have been hereditary. Educated or wealthy leaders, often with a base in the city, have been able to encourage and exploit latent tribal connections with both the rural population and migrants to Van city.

For instance, the Burukhan tribe has fielded a number of candidates over the years. Kinyas Kartal (1900–88), the acknowledged leader of the tribe, was MP for the Justice Party (AP) for five terms. His nephew Remzi Kartal became MP for the pro-Kurdish Democracy Party (DEP) in 1991, but fled to Germany in 1994 when the party was disbanded. Kinyas' son Nadir Kartal has been an MP in the True Path Party (DYP) and then stood, unsuccessfully, for the Young Party (GP) in the 2007 elections. Mehmet Kartal from the same family has been an MP for the Republican People's Party (CHP) but was not placed on the list in the last general election in 2007. Another Kartal, Saim, stood as an independent candidate supported by the pro-Kurdish Democratic Society Party (DTP) in 2007, but failed to get in.

Another prominent family of the Burukhan tribe, the Kurşunluoğlu family, has also been active in parliament politics: Mirza Kurşunluoğlu is a former MP for the Motherland Party (ANAP). Paşa Kurşunluoğlu is a former candidate for the True Path Party (DYP) and stood, again unsuccessfully, for the CHP in the 2007 elections. The Berjerî tribe has had a father, İhsan Bedirhanoğlu, and then a son, Şerif, in parliament.

The former was an MP for the CHP and ANAP, whereas the latter has been an MP for ANAP and then stood, unsuccessfully, for the CHP in 2007. It is easy to notice that important families have been at ease with switching parties in order to ensure their placement on candidate lists, and that political parties have had no qualms in accepting candidates switching allegiance from other parties as both sides benefit.

While tribal leaders may switch parties for different elections, tribes have also had several candidates standing concurrently. So, for instance, the Burukhan tribe had three candidates in three different parties standing in the 2002 general election, while the Ertuşî tribe fielded two candidates in two parties (Sevinç 2002).[8] This phenomenon can be interpreted as the attempt by political parties to ensure success in the province by offering a variety of tribal candidates; tribes also tried to make sure that at least one of 'their men' would enter parliament. On the other hand, it could also point to the weakening of the bloc vote system as not all tribal members could be united behind one candidate.

In Tepelik in Istanbul, I met Ahmet Bey, a descendant of a tribal leader who had been MP for Van in the first Turkish parliament. Ahmet Bey's father had changed his surname to the name of the tribe, and Ahmet Bey was very proud to carry it. He hinted that he had been approached several times by political parties who were interested in the symbolic capital of his name. Regretfully he explained that the former wealth of the family had been lost and that it was impossible to go into politics without money.

During the 2007 general election in Van, members of the Berjerî tribe pulled together behind their candidate and toured all the villages in the province that had significant numbers of tribal members living there. Thus, rather than relying on the appeal or programme of the party he stood for, the candidate asked for votes on the basis of shared tribal membership. While he ultimately failed to enter parliament, the party's votes were clearly boosted through its association with the tribal personage.

This shows that tribal allegiance has been exploited by political parties, by tribal leaders, and by tribal members. It is important, however, to remember that this 'tribal allegiance' is not a never-changing, 'traditional' loyalty. Rather, the 'tribe' has been found an effective idiom to base patronage relations on; 'tribal membership' is mostly a self-ascribed category that has become revived as people have migrated to the city of Van.

However, there is some indication that people are no longer so easily convinced to vote in blocs. To put it in Sharabi's terms, the 'supplicants', that is, the voters, have not felt that the 'go-betweens', that is, the MPs, have paid back enough. In addition, the parties the candidates chose were unsuccessful. In the 2007 general election, for instance, the Burukhan tribe had three candidates in three different parties, but none of them managed to enter parliament. Of the parties they had chosen, the Young Party (GP) did not pass the national election threshold of 10 per cent, and the CHP put most voters off with a Turkish nationalist and anti-religious discourse—fatal in a Kurdish-majority, religiously conservative area.

Another reason was that the governing Justice and Development Party (AKP) had appealed to many voters, particular women, with child benefits and coal donations for needy families. The payments for needy families who send their children to school are actually handed out by the Foundation for Social Assistance and Solidarity (SYDV), established in 1986. As for the coal, the AKP has been caricaturised extensively for the manner in which many needy families, who are of course also potential voters, have been wooed by coal donations. In 2007, the AKP won five of the seven parliamentary seats in Van, the other two going to two independent candidates supported by the pro-Kurdish DTP.

The pro-Kurdish DTP was successful in the 2009 local elections, taking over local government, an indication that Kurdish identity politics was becoming more important. The 2011 general election showed that votes in Van are now mostly divided between the pro-Kurdish movement (re-formed as the Peace and Democracy Party, BDP) and the AKP. The independent candidates supported by the BDP received 49.6 per cent of the votes, translating into four MPs, and the AKP won 40 per cent, also sending four MPs to Ankara ('2011 Van Genel Seçim...'). The results represent a 17 per cent increase for the pro-Kurdish movement and a 13 per cent decline for the AKP since the 2007 elections ('2011 Genel Seçim...').

There is some indication that the AKP, which is currently the only party in Van province able to compete with the pro-Kurdish movement, has realised the continuing profitability of tribal negotiations. While the party did not have any clear tribal candidate in the 2002 general election, the Ezdinan tribe was said to be supporting them, which could amount to 12,000 votes. This was not an inconsiderable number in Van (Sevinç 2002).[9] Prior to the 2011 general election, a local Van newspaper reported that the prominent Mehmet Kartal, a former MP for the CHP, had lent his support to the AKP by appearing at a district party election office opening and expressing, 'as a family', support for the party. In a later statement, Kartal claimed that he had even been asked to stand as a candidate for the AKP, but that he had handed in his application too late ('Kartal'dan AK Parti...'). Several comments on the Internet page of the newspaper reacted angrily to this support of the AKP and revealed a continuing rhetoric of a corporate tribal identity. Thus, one commentator discussed where 'our votes' would be going, while another one said:

'The Kartals have been breaking up the Burukhan tribe for years. In one election, three brothers were candidates in different parties. Just imagine such a mentality!'

('AK Parti'ye...')

Thus, in the political landscape of Van province there now exist two concurrent discourses on tribal membership. The pro-Kurdish movement emphasises an ethnic identity that renders tribal membership irrelevant and condemns it as divisive. On the other hand, the AKP, as the only national party receiving substantial votes in the province, has to some extent continued the cooperation between mainstream parties and influential tribal leaders in order to strengthen its position.

In addition to political lobbying, some tribes and their leaders have also been involved in economic activities (Bruinessen 2003: 6), some of them illegal. Allegedly, there has been an increase in crimes such as smuggling, people trafficking, and prostitution in Van, often blamed by my interlocutors on members of tribes that have migrated to Van from Hakkâri. Smuggling—of animals, consumer goods, petrol, and heroin—is made easier in Hakkâri due to the proximity to the Iranian and Iraqi borders, the mountainous landscape and the fact that kin and tribespeople live across these borders (cf. Beşikçi 1970: 26, Yalçın 1986: 57). This is not to say, of course, that there is no smuggling carried out by Vanlı.

One infamous example is a former MP of Van, Mustafa Bayram, who was in parliament for the ANAP party in 1995 and then the religious Fazilet Partisi in 1999. He is a prominent member of the Gevdan, who are considered by some to be an independent tribe (e.g. Wießner 1997: 71) and by some a sub-tribe (in Kurdish *qabile*) of the Ertuşî (e.g. Müküs 1970). His name has been linked to the heroin trade in the media (Tayman 2004, Toprak and Ateş 2004). Names of other tribes and tribal leaders were sometimes mentioned in relation with racketeering, drug and petrol smuggling, and corruption in local government in Van. As a news feature on Vanlı tribes said, 'The broken tribal moulds that mostly become evident in political elections currently only work perfectly in illegal activities' (Tayman 2004, author's translation).

Even if one ignores the illegal goings-on in Van, tribal connections may still foster cooperation and accumulation of wealth. Legal business, too, is often organised along tribal lines in Van:

> Nearly every business in Van is either run by a tribal member or is under the protection of a tribe. The best-known way of being protected is to take the son, nephew or brother of a well-known tribal leader on as a partner.
>
> **(Tayman 2004, author's translation)**

Indeed, my Kurdish Vanlı interlocutors often discussed which tribe prominent business men belonged to. Their own tribal identity emerged in a more corporate manner in these discussions as they talked about other tribes favourably or unfavourably. Such inter-tribe relations were largely irrelevant in the village but have become more important in the political and economic landscape of Van city. A process of 'retribalisation' has taken place in the city, by means of which more educated, wealthier migrants have forged connections to the 'centre' (political parties, security forces, municipal officials, and the business world) because of a provincial rural and urban power base. They either have this powerbase as a result of their families' influence in a tribe, or they have become influential in a tribe due to their wealth, education, or charisma. They have become 'go-betweens', or in Burt's terms, 'brokers' (1992), using the principle of *wasta* that Sharabi describes (1988: 46).

These 'neopatriarchs' are prominent personages and would be recognised by Vanlı wherever they go; I have met Vanlı in Istanbul who are keen to emphasise their relations to a certain MP, local politician, or tribal leader, showing that their influence is translocational. However, many migrants outside of Van city do not have the possibility to foster such connections, or the neopatriarchs are too far removed from daily life in other cities to be relied on continuously. Vanlı migrants thus also resort to another identification, that of common province origin, to form smaller social fields in hometown organisations. This is also the case in Istanbul.

Vanlı Hometown Organisations in Istanbul

Hometown organisations (HTOs) are by no means the reserve of Vanlı; indeed, all over Turkey, 'the scope of hometown associations has grown incessantly since the 1990s' (Hersant and Toumarkine 2005: §1). They have mushroomed in large cities in Turkey since the military coup of 1980, after which civil activity in political parties and trade unions was suppressed to a large extent (Narı 1999).[10] The suppression of organisations based on certain ideologies and principles has thus favoured the emergence of networks based on a shared region of origin. People who had migrated to cities from the same region formed associations or, rarer, foundations.

As the setting up of a foundation requires much more capital, Hersant and Toumarkine predict that associations and foundations have very different clienteles, the latter having more 'members of the middle classes, graduates, the liberal professions, and hardly an inconsequential female presence' (2005: §23). I have found this to be true in the case of Vanlı in Istanbul. There exists one Vanlı foundation (*vakıf*), but there are at least five associations (*dernek*); they indeed have a different member profile, reflecting the different types of Vanlı that also still live in Van city.

First of all, there is a difference in ethnicity and attitude to religion. The foundation has predominantly Turkish members, and its Kurdish members do not emphasise their Kurdish identity in public. As a result, at events organised by the foundation witnessed by me, Turkish was used exclusively, also by musicians singing folk songs. The founder and former head of the foundation is a retired governor (*vali*), and in a booklet of the foundation he writes:

> We Vanlı are rational, enlightened, and modern people who believe in positive science. We are really patriotic people who have always supported unity and togetherness in our activities and have never got embroiled in ethnic, ideological, or political speculations.
>
> **(Van Vakfı Genel Başkanlığı 2004: 12, author's translation)**

From conversations with several members of the foundation, I got the impression that they viewed both pro-Kurdish lobbying and the rise of religious groups with distaste and fear, and the above quote seems to hit back at both perceived threats, too. Three elderly members were staunch Kemalists (laicists), and they combined this with a moderate religiosity. One man, while performing daily *namaz*, did not believe in the covering of women, and he and his wife lamented the increase in covered women in Van since the 1980s. Indeed, at a fundraising lunch of the foundation, most of the women present wore 'modern'[11] clothes and were not covered. At the lunch, members sat in families rather than in the gender-segregated manner that Kurdish Vanlı of rural origin often adopt at events.

On the other hand, the Vanlı hometown associations (HTAs) in Istanbul, some of which unite people from districts rather than the whole province, have mostly Kurdish members. Even if the Kurdish identity is not always salient on public occasions, the association events feature Kurdish as well as Turkish music, and some of the dignitaries may use some Kurdish in their address. Tribal membership fades into the background; rather, the focus is on shared province or district origin and shared Kurdishness. While HTAs are obliged to have a non-political agenda, some of the prominent members of the Vanlı HTAs are politically active, mostly on the left or with pro-Kurdish parties.

In the Vanlı HTA in Tepelik, I sensed an uneasy coexistence of a traditional age-gender hierarchy adhered to by many members and a discourse on civil rights perpetuated by the association. At the fund-raising dinner of an HTA that I attended, most women were covered and there were more men than women present. Some women of my acquaintance had not come to the dinner as they never went to public halls, so their husbands came on their own.

Another difference between the foundation and the associations is the socio-economic status of the members. Although not officially measured, there seems to be a correlation between ethnic origin and socio-economic status, particularly since ethnic origin in the Van con-text also shows whether a person has grown up in the city or in a village. The poor educational infrastructure in villages, the handicap of education in a second language, less concern with education in the past, and perhaps also lower incomes in villages have all meant that Kurdish Vanlı villagers on the whole have lower education levels and have been less likely to enter a profession or start businesses. To give an example, three of the Turkish Vanlı I talked to were over 70 years old and had grown up in Van *merkez*. In the early decades of the 20th century their fathers had all been civil servants in Van and had sent them, one of them a woman, to school; a comparable level of education has still to be achieved by many Kurdish migrants to Van or other cities many decades later. The member list of the Turkish Vanlı foun-dation sports a lot of university graduates and business people. The above-mentioned booklet published by the Van Foundation in 2004 contains a directory of members boasting '24 building contractors, 21 doctors, 27 lawyers, 101 retired people and 310 [...] business people' (Van Vakfı Genel Başkanlığı 2004: 9, author's translation).

The (mostly Kurdish) association I observed in Tepelik was very dif-ferent in make-up; among the male members, and indeed there were only male members, there were very few university graduates, and only a few had completed high school. Many of their wives or female relatives over the age of 40 never went to school at all. In Tepelik, as opposed to the village, schools were close-by; however, some families still lacked the money or the inclination to educate their children beyond the first eight years. Many Vanlı Kurds live in clusters in less desirable parts of Istanbul, and it is near these clusters that the HTAs have been formed.

As far as organised activities go, there are some similarities between the foundation and the associations. The foundation and the association I visited both had 'centres', which really were men's tea houses (*kahve*). In both cases it was only men who frequented these places daily, drinking tea, smoking cigarettes, chatting, or playing card games. Both types of organisation have fixed events during the year; in the case of the foundation, there is a yearly ayran soup and fish lunch in May, a fundraising *iftar* (breaking of the fast) during the month of Ramazan, and a 'Vanlı Night' in a luxury hotel, to which Vanlı MPs and other politicians are also invited. In 2005, the Minister of Education, himself from Van, came, as well as the Prime Minister. In 2006, two Vanlı MPs and a government consultant attended. The foundation also takes part in a festival of HTOs in Istanbul, organised by the women members, who also arrange collections of clothes and books to be sent to Van. The associations, too, have regular events: every association has a yearly fundraising dinner. Members and friends pay for tickets and are also encouraged to participate in a raffle during the evening. The Vanlı associations all collaborate in the organisation of a Vanlı picnic; in 2006, this took place for the third time. This kind of picnic is commonly organised by HTAs from all regions in Turkey (Hersant and Toumarkine 2005: §8), and local politicians may be invited to the picnic.

Since the foundation has more capital, it is able to offer a further service; there is a dormitory for male Vanlı university students, housing 58 students in 2006. In the same year, the foundation also opened a dormitory for female students. The *vakıf* was able to pay for these services through donations from Vanlı business people. The Vanlı associations, on the other hand, had a vision of increased cooperation. They wanted to buy a building in order to establish headquarters for all the Vanlı HTAs there. In addition, they came together with the HTAs of other

Kurdish-majority provinces and formed the 'Southeastern Platform', aiming to influence government policy on the Kurdish question. The platform formed a delegation that travelled to several eastern and southeastern provinces, interviewing ordinary people as well as governors and compiling a report with recommendations for the government.

What both types of hometown organisation have in common is that they represent a discursive construction of a 'community of Vanlı'. They obviously differ in membership profile and self-image, but they offer a 'way of belonging' to migrants in an explicit and institutionalised manner (cf. Levitt and Glick Schiller 2004: 2010). However, as the discussion below shows, this idealised 'community' of Vanlı is also a pragmatic way of surviving in the city. For migrants, they represent a possible port of call where one can appeal to shared regional origin.

Solidarity or Network Brokerage?

The few yearly events of the HTOs hardly seemed to warrant the effort that some members put into these organisations. It has to be asked then why people invest time, energy, and money in HTOs. Although the 'official' vocabulary of the HTOs is non-political and emphasises attachment to the region of origin and its people, as well as the buzzword of 'civil society', many of the unpublicised activities of HTOs are embedded in the social, economic, and political networks of Istanbul or other cities.

I argue that the networks formed by political parties, MPs from Van city with tribal backgrounds, and their power bases, discussed above, are repeated at a local level in networks formed by local government, leaders of HTOs, and HTO members in cities around Turkey, and that the three functions discussed below thus apply to both the national policy of creating neopatriarchs and the national/local policy of encouraging HTOs; both types of network replace the involvement of working class and lower middle class citizens in trade unions, political parties, or human rights groups.

Çaymaz, in his study on HTAs of migrants from the central Anatolian city of Niğde in Istanbul, points to three functions of HTAs, the first being their use as ports of call for local politicians aiming to collect votes before elections (2005: §8), which is also what political parties expect when recruiting tribal leaders as parliamentary candidates. Both instances show that politics in Turkey is often based less on the representation of citizens who have rights and duties than on the representation of voters who know that they will not get far without *torpil* (connections), a point made by Sharabi when he speaks about the displacement of legality and the lack of access that individuals have to what should rightfully be theirs (1988: 46). As Çaymaz points out, however, members of the HTAs are by no means naive victims in this game. One HTA leader told him that he worked according to the principle of 'using politics for the *dernek* without letting the *dernek* be used by politics' (2005: §8, author's translation). The presence of MPs at the Vanlı Foundation night and the invitations to local dignitaries issued by both *vakıf* and *derneks* show how intermeshed with politics the HTOs are. Doğan Bey, the leader of the Vanlı *dernek* in Tepelik, was keen to invite local politicians to the Vanlı picnic, which, he predicted, would draw a crowd of thousands; he said this would show the 'voter potential' of the Vanlı. As Sharabi points out, in patronage relations the broker, the supplicant, and the favour-giver all benefit (1988: 46).

Indeed, the second function of HTOs that Çaymaz points out is the benefit to leading members. An article on HTOs in Nigeria optimistically speaks of 'the likelihood of a more pluralistic and democratic political order' by 'expanding the sphere of "civil society"' (Barkan, McNulty and Ayeni 1991: 458); however, much of what goes on in the name of 'civil society', at least in Turkey, seems more self-serving. Interactions between HTOs and local government politicians in migrant-receiving cities such as Istanbul are indeed often cloaked in an idiom of 'civil society' and service provision, but they are just as much relations of mutual interest. While local politicians and officials, such as *muhtars*, municipal district councillors, and district mayors, mostly do not share a region of origin with the Vanlı, the two sides act as brokers (Burt 1992) that connect two networks, that of a bureaucratic structure and that of a migrant population respectively.

HTO members who act as brokers accumulate social capital,[12] which Bourdieu, together with Wacquant, defined thus:

Social capital is the sum of the resources, actual or virtual, that accrue to an individual or a group by virtue of possessing a durable network of more or less institutionalized relationships of mutual acquaintance and recognition.

(Palloni et al. 2001: 1263)

Social capital, in Bourdieu's sense, thus refers to the potential accrued by individuals based on their social relations, or, as Lin formulates it, to 'investment in social relations for expected returns in the market place' (2001: 19). It is important to remember that social capital can be converted into other kinds of capital (Palloni et al. 2001: 1263), which is what makes it so desirable. Friendships, acquaintances, and exchanges of favours in certain networks can lead to concrete improvements in socio-economic status for those most active in the role of broker. Baumann points to the same benefits for 'community leaders' who are able to access more desirable networks in Southall, London. They also receive respect and gratitude (1996: 66), which can arguably be translated as 'social capital'.

To give one example from Tepelik, Doğan Bey had invested a lot in his position as HTA leader. First, his position meant a real loss of income. He was a retired civil servant with a limited pension, but he had a young family with two pre-school children to support. He bought a car after retirement and earned money as a driver for official food inspectors. His involvement in the *dernek*, particularly in preparation for the fundraising night and the picnic, meant paying a driver in his stead. Second, extensive HTA activities cost him money in petrol, bus fares, and phone bills. Third, his position meant that he was invited to weddings and circumcision celebrations of many fellow Vanlı and was expected to give presents of gold and money. Fourth, when there were unexpected expenditures at the *dernek*, such as a higher-than-average bill or an urgent loan to a member, it was the leading members who collected among themselves.

Another sacrifice was made in terms of time spent away from the family. During the Vanlı HTA picnic season, several families from Tepelik commented on the time their husbands and fathers had spent on organising it, coming home very late and spending all their free time at the *dernek*. Çaymaz witnessed similar complaints: 'The *dernek* leaders we talked to stated that they were "sacrificing themselves" for the unpopular job of associationism [*dernekçilik*] that required the devotion of time and money' (2005: §14, author's translation). The willingness to sacrifice can only partially be explained with idealism; there is also the knowledge that long-term benefits in terms of social capital are accruing. As Szreter points out, '[p]eople voluntarily engaging in networked activities with others almost always do so to attain specific personal benefits' (2002: 575). And indeed, when talking to men in Tepelik, many of them proudly referred to former or present involvement in *dernek* leadership, happy in the belief that connections with 'the system' thus established would be useful in the future.

Such self-interested behaviour has to be contextualised with the real fight for survival that everyday urban life means for Istanbul's inhabitants. Typical expressions by working class or lower middle class urban dwellers exemplify this. When asked how they are, many people will reply '*uğraşıyoruz*', that is, 'we are doing our best' or 'we are getting by'. A typical phrase for earning a living in the city is '*ekmek kavgası*', that is, 'the struggle for bread'.

While leading members of HTOs do of course benefit themselves, others are also able to use their contacts to make life slightly easier for themselves; Putnam speaks of ' "externalities" that affect the wider community, so that not all the costs and benefits of social connections accrue to the person making the contact' (2000: 20). Thus, a third function of HTOs is that of bridging the gap between 'the system' and migrants with less social capital from the same province, so-called *hemşehri*:

> In some cases the problems people face when trying to benefit from basic public services like health and education in cities that attract migration [...] can be overcome with the help of *hemşehrilik* relations. In Turkey, the *derneks* have mobilised according to the commonly-accepted principle of 'finding a man and getting the job done' and have turned into founders of a specific network and active agents. With the opportunities that this network offers, the *dernek* forms a bridge between those who provide a service and those who would normally find it hard to access the service.

[...] In other words, where citizenship is impotent [*tıkandı*], the *hemşehrilik* solution appears as a productive form of identity [*aidiyet*].

(Çaymaz 2005: §13, author's translation)

A similar function of 'community leaders' was found by Baumann, who noted that those people 'unable to secure the resources due to them on the basis of citizenship alone' make use of the community idiom and the brokerage offered by 'community leaders' (1996: 66).

Another bridging function of HTOs is a movement of resources from the better-connected to the less well-off; in the *vakıf*, the most obvious example is the support given to university students coming from Van province, or books and clothes sent to needy families there. The *derneks* too, with less economic capital, are nevertheless able to procure some advantages for their members. When there is municipal support for the poor, the Tepelik Vanlı *dernek* has acted as a go-between, identifying needy families who then receive coal in the winter or food packages during the month of Ramazan. Members of the *derneks* may also collaborate in providing employment, money, or small loans to other members or *hemşehris*. This kind of support is provided without an expectation of immediate reciprocity as the concept of *hemşehrilik*, as a 'way of belonging', provides a framework for generalised reciprocity (cf. Putnam 2000: 20–1, Szreter 2002: 575).

To summarise, both neopatriarchy at the national level and HTOs at the local level embody the paradox of enabling people access to state resources while at the same time crippling civil society, which would make such access the right of every individual. The former system is more applicable in the rural provinces, whereas people have quickly realised the benefits of HTOs in migrant receiving cities. Both systems are arguably inevitable in a country with great disparities in income levels, continuing rural-urban migration, and relatively high levels of corruption. In 2007, Turkey ranked 64th of 180 countries in terms of the 'Corruption Perception Index' (CPI) with a CPI of 4.1—0 standing for 'highly clean' and 10 for 'highly corrupt' (Transparency International 2007). The networks described above masquerade as political party activism and hometown solidarity, yet are often a way of finding the elusive 'maternal uncle in Ankara' (or in local authorities). Both systems represent ways of managing to create networks that go beyond village acquaintances and relatives in order to meet the varied needs migrant families experience in cities. These networks are strengthened by discourses of belonging to a certain tribe or hometown.

For Vanlı and other migrants to cities like Istanbul, the degree to which they rely on such networks depends on how much social capital they have been able to accrue for themselves. As discussed in the next chapter, it is also important what *kind* of social capital they have access to. Furthermore, their reliance on networks of tribal members, *hemşehris*, and friends and family may 'ebb and flow' according to life circumstances (cf. Levitt and Glick Schiller 2004: 1012).

A third phenomenon of migration is visible at an everyday level. Vanlı migrants, seasonal and permanent, create relations of transaction (cf. Smith 2002: xii) between each other and between their rural bases and the city they live in. In the following, I consider how these networks offer pathways for goods and services, people, and ideas (cf. Werbner 1999: 33).

Remittances and Romance

Ali, the son of Haci Fahrettin, used to drive an intercity bus between Van and other cities, and has thus been witness to the movement of goods out of and into Van. He recounts how people travelling from Van carry great amounts of herbal cheese (the preserving liquid of which, so Ali complains, can make the whole baggage compartment smell for weeks if the containers leak), and freshly-cut meat, which is in danger of going off if transported in the summer months. Dairy products such as butter, yoghurt, and herbal cheese are frequently sent to relatives in cities west of Van. Honey may also be sent and even home-baked *tendûr* bread, wrapped up securely in cloths or newspaper to stop it from drying out too much. In addition, women may knit socks, woollen slippers, or baby clothes for relatives in other cities or make pillows or duvets stuffed with the wool from their own sheep. These goods embody the longings of migrants when they indulge in nostalgic reminiscences of village life. Without having to experience the difficulties in the production of these foods and goods, the migrants dwell on the romantic aspects of village life through consuming them. I have often witnessed migrant Vanlı sharing such goods as special favours, often in a large group. They may delight in the taste of the meat, which the hormone-laden products in the city cannot compare with, and they critically evaluate the quality of the herbal cheeses produced by different women, discussing whether the required variety and amount of herbs has been achieved. In such commensality, they find a 'home' within their translocational migratory social field. They can later lay their heads on a pillow stuffed with wool, the slight smell of sheep bringing back memories of farm life.

In the other direction, Vanlı migrants send remittances from seasonal labour to Van, which has increased the spending power of families, both in villages and in the city. Indeed, as I suggested earlier, the more well-off families who have remained in the village can afford to do so because of remittances. In Van city, this new wealth[13] has resulted in the arrival of major supermarket and consumer good chains. Consequently, there is now no more need for the transportation of household goods and luxury items to Van. Villagers still recall how the first migrant workers came back to the village with huge music sets that were designed to impress with their size and the number of flashing lights. As consumer goods are more readily available now, more and more families in Van province (both the city and villages) are buying washing machines, fridges, and kitchen stoves. In wealthier households in the city, there are also dish washers.

Thus, today, migrant workers send money rather than goods to Van, and here extended families have made different arrangements as to who distributes and consumes the earnings. In some families, the working sons, married or unmarried, send their money to their father, who then decides how it is spent. It is implied that a young married man who leaves his wife and children in the care of his parents or brothers should not have to worry about their needs being met. This is also true in families such as that of Süleyman Amca, where most of the brothers put their money together. Whichever brother has stayed behind in Van with the wives is morally obliged to make sure that all households are provided with what they need.

However, these arrangements are of course not without the potential for tensions, as a newly-emerging cliché shows, that of a village father who lets his sons sweat on building sites in order to buy a Ford Minibus.[14] The father then uses it to transport villagers and earn money. This image makes fun of the father, who is said to start driving the minibus without any experience and at high speed, resulting in accidents. The Ford Minibuses are thus also termed 'Kürtkıran' (literally 'Kurd killers'). Implied in this cliché is that a patriarch may pursue his own interests to the detriment of his sons' young families.

If extended families with seasonal migrants have moved to Van city, they may find that sharing one budget becomes unfeasible. City life makes more financial demands on families as children go to school and need more shoes and clothes and as families need money for transportation. It is foreseeable that financial collaboration between nuclear families will decrease in the city as individual family members are not willing to have to justify every kuruş they want to spend. As young women are less willing than before to lead a long-distance marriage and remain in the care of their parents-in-law, the trend is for nuclear families to aim to live separately and to have their own budget. That said, elderly parents will always have a claim on financial support from their male children, as well as a right to cohabitation when they are too weak to look after themselves. Most members of the older generation have never paid social security contributions, and there are thus very few elderly (Kurdish) Vanlı, be it in villages, in Van city or elsewhere in Turkey, who are entitled to a pension.

Networks of Favours, Services, and Collaboration

All over Turkey, the shared origin from a province is meaningful 'social glue' and often leads to an acceleration of close relations, of strong ties. While I have discussed hometown associations as social fields that are pragmatically used to accrue social capital that will improve the socio-economic position of individuals, households, and families, the underlying concept of hemşehrilik, of being from the same area, is a sincerely felt connection among people all around Turkey. After all, 59.47 per cent of people in Turkey still identify themselves not according to where they live but where they were born, a rate that rises to 68 per cent in Istanbul ('Biz Kimiz?'). Among my interlocutors, the term 'Vanlı' was constantly used as a label of self-identification. For my questionnaire respondents, the concept of a 'home province' was obviously relevant; 92 per cent were proud of being from Van and 82 per cent said they felt close to other Vanlı if they met them for the first time.

While hometown organisations may be an important port of call for migrants, all of my migrant interlocutors also created and made use of less institutionalised networks among migrants and between migrants and the sending community for favours, services, or collaboration. Indeed, as was indicated in Chapter 3, such networks may determine whether or not a person migrates in the first place (cf. Çelik 2005: 144).

Many Vanlı migrant workers, seasonal or permanent, only come to Istanbul or other cities once they know that work has been lined up for them by relatives, co-villagers, or friends (see Ammann 2000: 140–3 for an account of Kurdish migration to Europe according to networks of relatives or hemşehri). Working together in groups on a building site is very common as it allows men from the same family or village to collaborate in cooking, washing clothes, and any emergencies that may arise. They may stay in a part of the building they are working on or rent a flat together. For instance, Mücahit Çetin and his younger brother and their families used to share a flat in Istanbul. Currently, three sons of Alaaddin Çetin, as well as a son of Haci Şako Çetin and two of their maternal uncle's sons from the village of Pembegelin, are living together in one room of a big construction project in Istanbul. They have covered the bare floor with wall-to-wall carpet, have brought bedding from the village, and make their own meals on a camper stove. In Alanya, the sons of Süleyman Amca who have not settled there with their families, three of them married and one unmarried, have managed to buy a flat (in exchange for labour) and live in it together when working in the southern city. Such collaboration also allows some of the men to go back to Van or the village to see their families while others make sure that their employment continues.

Another area of support is in health care. As Van is in a less-developed region of Turkey, Vanlı have to come to Istanbul, Ankara, and other cities in order to deal with serious illnesses or to have operations. Doctors in Van will themselves sometimes advise patients that they should do so if they can afford the time and travel involved. Co-villagers are helped in dealing with hospital bureaucracy, and the accompanying relatives are accommodated at home, often for an extended period of time. Money may be lent or spent to help with parts of the treatment that need to be paid for. Blood donations may be collected from a wider network of relatives and fellow villagers if the patient needs transfusions. More distant relatives and co-villagers who hear that a person is in hospital may travel to the hospital from all around the city in order to offer morale or practical help.

As the education level of the new generation is rising, young people may also travel to cities outside of Van to go to high school or university. It is understood that if relatives or co-villagers live in this city, they will offer support in helping the student settle, either in dormitories or private lodgings, and continue their support in the years of study. The following example shows that this sense of *hemşehrilik* solidarity can even extend to strangers. When Şengül, the youngest daughter of Haci Fahrettin, settled down in Ankara, she found herself talking to an old man when waiting in a queue in the bank. When he found out that she was from Van, he immediately said that his neighbours were from Van and that he would give her their phone number to use if she needed anything.

People from Van may also come to Istanbul and other cities when they need to buy vehicles as the second hand markets are livelier in bigger cities, making vehicles cheaper. In the past, Kurdish villagers sometimes also felt that they were treated better at military roadblocks in the East if their cars had numberplates from a western city. People from Gundême have come to Istanbul to buy cars, trucks, and, in the case of Ali Çetin, a large Mercedes intercity bus. Co-villagers and relatives in Istanbul are better informed about local second hand car fairs and prices and offer help in going there, bargaining for a reasonable price, and dealing with the paperwork.

In short, informal networks of relatives and co-villagers (also from villagers in the proximity that people have matrilateral or affinal relations with or whom they are friends with) allow people from villages or Van to access jobs, health care, and other opportunities outside of Van province. Vanlı in the big western and southern cities are called upon to help with these issues as well as providing access to information. To put it in Granovetter's terms (1983), Gundî and Vanlı are able to exploit strong links (i.e. links between people with similar backgrounds) to access the weak links that the migrant Vanlı have established with others.

What do migrant Vanlı gain from providing such assistance? They are part of a system of generalised reciprocity, where they are not guaranteed a direct repayment for their contribution. However, for one, they may have family in Van who will benefit from their contributions at a time when they in turn need help. Another way in which they may benefit is through the sending of someone from Van to help in the household in the case of a birth or illness. Finally, giving of one's time and money is sure to increase one's social capital in the translocational network of Vanlı as deeds of support are remembered and recounted to others. News of perceived generosity and hospitality travels quickly, as does the description of behaviour deemed unsuitable or miserly by a fellow Vanlı or Gundî. Finally, the sincerely-felt self-identification as part of a 'community' of Vanlı or Gundî means that there is the trust that others would do the same. The transactions and support that travel through these networks position migrants and non-migrants in a shared social field, a 'home' that is not linked to one location.

Pathways for People

As an increasing number of Vanlı have followed pioneers to a new location and as communication and transport technology has developed, the perceived distance between the sending and receiving location has become smaller. People stay in touch with special rates on mobile phones, with the Internet, and even with webcams and free chat or social networking websites. This perceived reduction of distance leads to Vanlı being comfortable with travelling, in the case of Istanbul, over 1,600 kilometres. This journey, which takes over 20 hours by bus, can today be shortened to less than one and a half hours in one of several daily flights that are now scheduled between Van and Istanbul or Ankara. Indeed, in recent years, flights have become so reasonable that intercity bus companies, such as the one that Ali drove for, are struggling to compete on long-distance journeys.

Within Van province, the perceived distance between Gundême and Van (and indeed many other villages of the province and the capital) has also become reduced because there is easy access to frequent transport between the city and the village. Indeed, it is the Ford Minibuses paid for by remittances that travel between villages and Van every day. Roads have been improved, and the General Directorate of Roads clears these roads of snow, making transport in winter easier.

This perceived proximity has consequences for what Vanlı, in terms of dwellings, consider 'home'. In Tepelik, for instance, I came across several elderly people who chose to spend their summers in Van and their winters with sons in Istanbul, where the more temperate climate and central heating system offered more comfort. Similarly, Gundî families who have recently migrated to Van may keep up a practice of spending the summer holidays in the village, and their children grow up used to life in both the village and the city. Children of Gundî still living in the village may also be sent to Van or further afield to live with relatives during the school year, as was the case with two children of Fatma Çetin, the daughter of Tacit Çetin. In another case, Onur Çetin, who was then still living in the village, sent his son to live in Istanbul with his brother Hüseyin in order to enable him to go to school beyond the first five years. Depending on the attitudes of a husband (and often also his extended family), his wife and children may spend the summer back in Van (if she lives outside of the province) or with her migrant natal family outside of Van (if she herself lives in Van).

While many Vanlı have got used to such plurilocal homes, there is still a sense for many, particularly in the older generation, that one's ultimate resting place should be in Van. Despite the perceived lack of distance between places, many people still feel very attached to their place of origin and this is where they may want to be buried, a sentiment held by many migrant Kurds and Turks within and even outside Turkey, too. A common sight in Turkey is an extended family taking the body of a relative 'home' on the roof rack of a minibus. As flights have become cheaper, this has become a more convenient means of transporting someone's remains to Van. Whether or not someone wants to be buried in Van, or even in the village, depends very much on who else has already been buried there and what proportion of the family is sharing in the migrant life outside of Van.

As can be seen from the descriptions above, the translocational migratory social field of Vanlı involves many transactions of goods, favours, and people. My long-term involvement with Vanlı interlocutors has meant that I have seen some of the 'ebb and flow' of such transactions (Levitt and Glick Schiller 2004: 1012). Thus, a young Vanlı in Istanbul may receive more visitors from 'home' after marriage, a family from Van may travel more to visit relatives in other cities once the children are older or their financial situation is more stable, illnesses and deaths suddenly require more travel and support in both directions, and the sending of dairy products ends once a family has left the village. The pathways of transactions may lie fallow for a while, but may also be reactivated. In the following, I discuss briefly how the migratory social field also represents a network of people where ideas spread as 'social remittances'.

Social Remittances

A useful concept in the study of migration is that of 'social remittances', which Levitt describes as 'a local-level, migration-driven form of cultural diffusion' (1998: 926). In her study of Dominican migrants to Boston, USA, she points to at least three types of such remittances, two of which I am concerned with here: normative structures and systems of practice. Normative structures are ideas, which then shape systems of practice (1998: 933–4).

Because the theme of this study is migration and different aspects of migrant life affected by it, social remittances are discussed throughout the book without necessarily being called by that name. At this point, I would like to offer a summary of the kinds of remittances that I have observed.

I believe that the most important social remittance of Vanlı migration has been the diffusion of the idea of wage labour. The acceptance and increasing attraction of working for money rather than on the land of one's family means that labour migration, both seasonal and permanent, has become self-perpetuating.

Secondly, migration has led to more importance being placed on the education of children, with a particularly dramatic change in the education of girls compared to the past. The rise in educational levels among women has had consequences in cities and also in villages; women have begun to assert themselves more on certain issues. For one, they have become aware of and demand access to birth control methods and health care; the younger generation has fewer children and women are more likely to go to the doctor's with a complaint. More young women have also become aware of the possibility of deferring marriage until they themselves feel ready to get married; as education levels rise, the average marriage age is bound to rise as well. If women marry at a later age, they are less likely to acquiesce to the patriarchal bargains described in Chapter 8, particularly if they have had access to more education.

On a more macro scale, Kurdish migration from villages to cities and from Turkey and other countries to Europe has created alternative ideas about Kurdishness, which are diffused back into sending communities via Kurdish satellite TV channels, such as Roj TV, and, to a certain extent, also by the new state TRT 6 channel broadcasting in Kurdish since 2009. Migration from the village has meant that migrant Vanlı (and other Kurds) have had to reconsider what it means to be Kurdish; in the past, Kurdishness, religiosity, and rural life were inextricably linked. Kurdish media and pro-Kurdish parties have played an important role in shaping a more self-conscious ethnic Kurdish identity.

Lest it be thought that ideas and norms only flow in one direction, I would like to point out that there is also diffusion of norms from sending to receiving communities. For Kurdish migrants to Europe, Ammann argues that values are transferred in both directions (2000: 163). Historian Karpat, reviewing his classic work on rural-urban migration published in 1976, says:

I once thought that the cultural phenomenon I was witnessing consisted of the fusion of the folk culture into the urban one, but

I now realize the phenomenon was an unprecedented dialectical process that still is producing a truly national Turkish culture. In other words, it is a type of cultural, political and religious homogenization through which the local and urban cultures are interacting to produce a comprehensive national culture.

(2004: §19)

While I would question whether one 'comprehensive national culture' is ever arrived at, Karpat is right to point out the dialectic process that migration creates.

Here I would like to touch on the concept of 'tradition'. As Baumann argues, any enculturation of children involves reificiation of 'the collective heritage one wishes them to reproduce or at least learn about' (1996: 193), and this desire is perhaps stronger in migrant contexts as migrants have to negotiate more explicitly what they want to keep or discard from their 'old lives' and what they would like to appropriate or reject in the 'new life'. 'Tradition' thus means the preservation or continuous recreation of certain values that migrants have taken with them. Thus, the insistence by some families on a 'traditional' gender paradigm for their daughters means that they are not allowed to continue their schooling and marry earlier. In such families, gender ideology may still place a lot of value on certain respect behaviour of the young generation in general and *bûks* in particular.

Another 'tradition' that may be considered very important is that of religious piety. Religious enculturation can represent 'the pivot of community enculturation' for families (Baumann 1996: 181). Thus, while village life may at most leave time for individual *namaz* and some instruction for children, religiosity is taken further by many migrant women in the city, where such practice is considered part of being 'true' to one's origins, as discussed in Chapter 9.

In the study of migration, one can thus see that the transactions of goods, favours, and people in the migratory social field are accompanied by movements of discourses, which may be modified, discarded, or intensified, and which in turn affect people's behaviour.

This chapter has taken a macro-perspective on migration within and from Van province. Migrants are not mere individuals, but make

use of certain identifications to link themselves into formal and informal networks of support. Thus, the salience of tribal membership has
increased for some in Van city, while the concept of *hemşehrilik* has also
proven a useful idiom that allows Vanlı to profit from the social capital of others in cities outside of Van province. Concurrently, everyday
migrant networks of relatives and friends channel the transactions of
goods, ideas, and people. The following chapter examines a cluster of
migrants and their networks in Istanbul.

6

TEPELIK: VANLI
IN ISTANBUL

The Location

Tepelik, literally meaning 'hilly' in Turkish, is a pseudonym for a quarter in Istanbul where I found a cluster of Vanlı. I argue that just as Gundême represents 'the village', the quarter of Tepelik represents the rural-urban migratory experience of many people of a particular socio-economic standing in Turkey. The following description should thus be read as that of many of the unplanned settlements in and around established urban neighbourhoods in the cities in Turkey that receive many migrants.

Tepelik is a very hilly area, and as a visitor to the neighbourhood follows the slopes up and down, she walks through an urban neighbourhood with very few green patches to relieve the eye. The unevenly tarred roads are bordered by rows of apartment blocks, up to five storeys high, often with the storeys from the second one up jutting out an extra half metre, giving the roads an even narrower feel. The apartment blocks are not matched in size, colour, or design, but are joined together regardless. Some buildings have a decidedly unfinished appearance, still sporting the unplastered red brick walls, while others have been plastered but not painted. Squeezed in between the apartment blocks there are sometimes small, crooked one-storey houses, remnants of the first wave of shanty housing (cf. Esen 2007 37–41). Quite a few of the house walls are adorned with leftist graffiti, a sign that the—generally—more conservative Vanlı share this quarter with other communities. This impression is verified when one passes a large Alevi community centre and adjacent *cem evi*, the place of worship for Alevis.

When I first walked through this neighbourhood, it was not clear to me whether the area was residential, commercial, or even industrial. Many of the basements of the apartment blocks housed badly-lit workshops, either for carpentry or textile work. Carpenters made wooden frames for chairs, beds, and other furniture, working without mouth masks or eye protection. There was a smell of sawdust and glue fumes in the air when one passed by, and one heard the screaming sound of the circular saws and the tapping of hammers. The pavements outside these workshops were occupied by chair frames and delivery vans. People had to walk in the street and avoid the cars and vans that went by too fast. At certain times of the day, the men had a tea break and sat on the stairs or the pavement to have a cigarette, a chat, and a look at the outside world.

While the carpentry workshops were a men-only domain, the textile workshops employed both men and women. Most of the few working women and girls I met or heard about in Tepelik were employed in the textile industry, sewing with the sewing machines as *makinacı*, going from table to table supplying the *makinacı* with work, trimming the threads of the final product or ironing or packing the clothes (cf. Çelik 2005: 146). Men could be seen walking along the street carrying piles of finished clothes. Some people had also set themselves up as middlemen or women to supply housewives with clothes that needed beads or sequins sewn onto them. The more middlemen there were, the fewer earnings the housewives made, of course. In the close neighbourhood of the Vanlı blocks I came across four such places, all run by women.

Interspersed among the residential blocks and workshops were little *bakkals* (corner shops) and shops that catered for the needs of the population, offering hardware, pulses and other basic foodstuff, threads, and wool. When I approached the blocks from the other direction, I passed a lot of stores that offered goods for the newly-engaged and their families. They sold synthetic carpets, furniture, white goods and

Illustration 4: Houses near the Vanlı Blocks in Tepelik

other electrical items, duvets and bed clothes, crockery, and cutlery. It is not unusual to pay for these goods in instalments for one or two years before the wedding and to have all the items delivered to the flat that the couple rent or buy shortly before the wedding.

According to the *muhtar* of the *mahalle* (neighbourhood), Tepelik has a population of 30,000 people, forming around 7,000 households. None of the buildings in the area have title deeds (*tapu*), which is a clear indication that settlement in the area has been irregular and due to migration. Indeed, the greatest part of the Tepelik population, up to 70 per cent, comes from Giresun and Sivas, from where they started to migrate to Tepelik in the 1950s. Giresun is a province on the central Black Sea; Sivas borders it to the south. The migrants from Sivas are partly Sunni and partly Alevi. The presence of Vanlı in Tepelik started with the migration of the earthquake victims in 1976, and there has been chain migration since. According to the *muhtar's* records, there were 679 Vanlı registered in Tepelik in 2006 (roughly 2 per cent of the population), making up 168 households. It is not clear, however, how reliable these data are as many families neglect to change their registration when they move.

Coming closer to the blocks where the Vanlı live, I passed a large state primary school[1] consisting of two separate three-storey buildings in an extensive cement yard, surrounded by a high wall and fence and guarded by a man at a big metal gate. There were only a few young trees at the edge of the yard. One of the two buildings had been found to be unsafe and was awaiting demolition. In order to accommodate all its pupils in one building, the school did what many other schools in Turkey do as a matter of course: students came in shifts. They were either *sabahçı* (morning students) or *öğlenci* (lunchtime students). All the children I taught English to or met otherwise went to this primary school, and generally they and their parents seemed happy with it.

Next to the school was a large mosque. The mosque was frequented more by men than by women, but some hours were set aside for women to have prayer meetings or listen to sermons. Some women chose to perform the evening *namaz* in the mosque during the holy month of Ramazan as it is a longer, more intricate prayer. However, even if the women did not enter the mosque, the *ezan* was for many as important as a clock. Like many Gundî women, Tepelik women often referred to the times of prayer as dividers of the day. So, for example, they would set off on a communal visit to another woman's house 'after the lunchtime *namaz*'. At that time of day women would have cleaned the home and performed their prayers and then felt free to go out.

When talking to Nur, a Qur'an teacher from the blocks, I realised that she had instructed most of the girls that I taught and many more. In the summer holidays, many children went to the mosque for three to four hours in the morning. The mosque had a basement floor where these classes took place. Boys and girls were taught separately. Almost all the children I talked to went to Qur'an courses in the summer holidays, particularly the girls. When the boys could not concentrate and preferred to play football, this was met with more understanding, or at least resignation.

There was continuous coming and going in the streets of Tepelik. Children and young people went to and from school in their different uniforms. Other youngsters were clearly on errands from their workplace and hurried from and to workshops and stores. There were men in suits, in leisure wear, or in overalls. Some older men had beards and wore skullcaps, comfortable pleated trousers, and jackets, which allowed them to pray easily in the mosque. Women also varied widely in their appearance.[2] There were women and girls wearing tight-fitting tops and jeans and women with dyed hair and make-up. There were also many 'covered' women, but there were subtle differences in their appearance (cf. Özdalga 1998). Kurdish women in Van and in Istanbul often covered their heads differently at home from outside. The 'traditional', 'rural' head covering is a white or colourful thin piece of cotton material (called *tülbent/laçik* or *yazma* respectively) that has been embroidered and/or decorated with intricate bead designs at the edges. The women wrapped this head covering around their head, under their chin and then placed the remaining edge on the back of their head. This covering needs rearranging from time to time when it slips, but it is airy. Some women wore it outside, but many preferred a non-embroidered head covering. Several women said that the 'village covering' was not appropriate for the city and that they would only wear it outside if they were in the vicinity of the house. With the non-embroidered head covering there were different types and ways of tying it. One way was to cover both shoulders and throat by folding a square scarf into a triangle and pinning or knotting it under the chin. This type of head covering was often accompanied by a *pardesü*, an ankle-length coat, often with shoulder pads and a wide cut. Often the colours of the head covering and the coat were muted. Another variety, one called '*modern*' by the women themselves, was a silk or silk-like scarf that was tied tightly around the head and the neck and then tied at the back. A variety of caps or other contraptions was sometimes used to shape the scarf around the face or at the back of the head. This '*türban*' was favoured by many younger women as it looked sleeker than the larger head covering. They chose bright contrasting colours and often made sure that *türban*, handbag, and shoes matched in colour. These women sometimes wore a coat, but if they did, it was often much more fitted and made of denim, cotton, or linen rather than synthetic material. Finally, it was relatively rare to see a woman wearing a *çarşaf* (literally 'sheet', meaning the black chador) in Tepelik. Again, many women were not 'covered', and school girls or women working in public institutions were not even allowed to be.

The eight blocks that the Vanlı lived in were all five storeys high. They were built in a wide U-shape on a slope. Four blocks were in a row at the bottom of the slope, with a bit of space between each. The other four were on two sides of the slope and separated by playground and park areas in the middle, which were cleaned by a municipal worker every day. The reason for this surprising piece of greenery and for the spacious placement of the blocks was perhaps that they were intended to become police lodgings when first built. Compared to the cramped conditions of the other streets, this living space was much more restful. In the summer, many women or older siblings sat in the park minding the young ones, and other women shouted directions to their children from the balconies of the blocks, which faced the park.

Children going to or coming from school in their uniforms could be seen during the day. Women would also congregate in front of the block where there is a concrete space separated from the street by a low wall, or in the 'back garden', an area of untended grassy land.

Illustration 5: Three of the Vanlı Blocks in Tepelik

When the Vanlı were brought to Istanbul in 1976, the blocks were derelict and not much more than concrete shells (people described their state to me as *kaba inşaat*, literally meaning 'rough building'). The buildings had no windows, and one man told me that he had had to chase away dogs that were living there. Since then, a lot had been done. Most flats had double-glazing, which is highly-prized in Turkey as it reduces heating costs. Although most families still heated with a *soba* (coal stove), some had had radiators installed and heated with piped gas. Some blocks were badly in need of painting, but others were freshly painted. All families had invested in the apartments themselves, on flooring, paintwork, tiling, kitchens, and bathrooms. Some families had chosen to enclose the back balcony and add it to the living room in order to gain more living space. However, I was told that it was difficult to get all the people in one block to cooperate on improving it. There was no block manager to collect monthly payments for cleaning or renovating expenditures. Most women cleaned the stairwell themselves, taking it in turns, but in one block a woman from another block had been employed to do this.

Since the Vanlı were settled in the blocks they had not paid any rent; this, in Istanbul, was significant material support in itself as normally half to three quarters of a minimum wage is spent on rent. Additionally, the state provided food and other aid for a while. The Vanlı only started paying water and electricity bills in the 1990s, about 15–20 years after they moved in. Despite these advantages, however, the future of the blocks was uncertain, and the Tepelik Vanlı feared that any investments they had made in the blocks would be lost.

Like the other buildings in the area, they had no title deeds (*tapu*), but there was an additional problem. While the government, who after all placed the Vanlı in the blocks, may have let them live there, the land itself was not owned by the government, but by an institution called the General Directorate of Foundations (*Vakıflar Genel Müdürlüğü*). This institution sent the block residents letters asking for rent about five years ago. The Vanlı reacted by hiring a lawyer per block and arguing that they should not be paying rent. They wanted to own their flats, claiming that with the time they had lived in and improved the blocks, they had earned the right to ownership. In addition, they argued, the government had not given them help to rebuild their houses in the Van area after the earthquake, so they felt entitled to an abode.

They were willing to pay for the apartments but asked for title deeds as proof of ownership. They also expected to pay less than the current market price for the flats and demanded easy payment conditions (e.g. instalments). At the time of my research it was unclear what would happen. One rumour was that the Directorate had sold the land to a big firm that was planning to tear down the blocks and make a luxurious residential area out of the place. Another rumour was that the government was willing to sell the Vanlı the blocks and was trying to buy the land from the Directorate in order to do so. Unclear was whether everyone would be able to afford the price of the flats.

At the top of the slope, in the basement of an apartment block not part of the Vanlı blocks was the Vanlı Association centre. It consisted of a small office, a big room with tea-making facilities, chairs and tables, and a toilet. The big room was used by men to drink tea, smoke, play *Okey*,[3] or chat. In short, it was actually a men's coffee house, just like the multitude of men's *kahves* to be found in any city in Turkey. Indeed, most of the minor hometown associations serving a small area in a city are men's coffee houses. However, the run-down interior, idle chat, and games should not deceive the observer into thinking that nothing else happens here. Besides the mosque, the *kahve* is the most important gathering point for men of a *mahalle*, and it allows them to exchange information, ask for help and advice, or find work.

The Vanlı women used the building on special occasions, such as henna nights,[4] or it was used by both men and women on occasions such as circumcision celebrations or funerals. During the day however, the women I spoke to would not dream of entering the *kahve* or even walking past it. They preferred to cross to the other side of the road as part of a code of modest behaviour. Most of the men who lived in the blocks frequented the *kahve* from time to time, be it during the day or in the evenings. When I taught English, we initially used the *kahve* for the lessons; this had been suggested by the association head, who was very supportive of the project. The men would be asked to leave for the duration of the lessons, something which I felt some of them resented. Later in the summer, as student numbers began to dwindle, we had the lessons in the little adjacent office. However, my class of young teenage girls was held in their homes on a rotating basis, partly, I believe, because it was thought unsuitable for them to be in the male space of the *kahve* at all.

Tepelik: *Gecekondu, Varoş,* or Just Another *Mahalle?*

Due to migration, many cities in Turkey have experienced uncontrolled growth. In Istanbul, one can only guess at the population (12 to 15 million) since many migrants prefer to stay registered in their home-towns, where they can then use their vote, or simply do not bother to change their registration. The population explosion has led to the collapse of infrastructure and the uncontrolled building of accommo-dation. This has been possible because of a cyclical repetition of illegal construction and upcoming elections with political candidates prom-ising title deeds, electricity supplies, and running water to the settlers in return for votes.

According to Neuwirth, a researcher of shanty towns, the trend to occupy land in cities in Turkey can be traced back to a late change to privately-owned land. Up to the second half of the 19th century, land was owned by the Ottoman sultan, but people were permitted to occupy and use it. Many of the settlers in Istanbul and other cities thus settled on land that was not privately owned (2007: 3) and built *gecekondus* (literally 'put up overnight'). Somewhat misleadingly, the term *gecekondu* is still used as shorthand to refer to the many areas of later, rapid settlement of rural migrants to large cities (cf. Karpat 2004), even though the later homes took much longer to build and are often several storeys high.

Social scientists have started to study the *gecekondu* quarters in the cities (e.g. the thematic issue of the European Journal of Turkish Studies 2004, Erder 1996, Işık and Pınarcıoğlu 2001, Karpat 2004, Wedel 1996, 1997).[5] Given that the Vanlı migrants I studied were offered housing by the local council, the term does not apply to their situation. They do, however, live in an area that has many illegal build-ings. I would describe the quarter of Tepelik as generally unplanned as the area filled up rapidly in the last 30 years, with infrastructure following behind the building of houses. Tepelik was by no means an anomaly. Indeed, White quotes research that says that in the 1980s, 70 per cent of the residents of Istanbul were living in such unplanned settlements (2002: 59). Tepelik was very similar to how White describes Ümraniye, the area of her fieldwork:

> It began, as did many Istanbul neighbourhoods, as a squatter area that over the years was gradually absorbed into the city proper. Despite this bureaucratic and infrastructural incorporation, Ümraniye's residents hold a tentative position as urbanites that must be continually negotiated. This insecurity extends from the precariousness of their livelihoods to their unacceptability as 'urban types' to other city dwellers who see themselves as being modern and Westernized.
>
> (2002: 9)

Tepelik, the quarter the Vanlı of my study inhabited, was in the centre of the European side of Istanbul, unlike Ümraniye, which is on the outskirts of Istanbul.[6] However, its proximity to well-established central quarters like Taksim did not preclude it from looking 'less': less well planned, less well maintained and cleaned, and less wealthy, resulting in the 'tentative position as urbanites' for its inhabitants that White describes so well. Inhabitants themselves were aware of the disparities in service provision, quality of schools, and proximity to cultural, health, and other facilities, and they faced both existential and adaptation struggles (cf. Erman 1998b: 59).

When outsiders describe such quarters, particularly in Istanbul, the Hungarian term *varoş*, meaning 'suburb', is often used in popular speech. The term is associated with 'the population that is not part of the city, but rather is excluded from the city and watches it from the outside' (Işık and Pınarcıoğlu 2001: 192, author's translation). This exclusion is both real and at the same time perpetuated by such discourses on '*varoş*'; indeed, writer and sociologist Oya Baydar points to the coexistence of two separate cities:

> The term *varoşlar*, which has been repeated again and again over the last years [...], has come to mean settlements founded on

the outskirts of and within the city, but psychologically, socially, and culturally separate with their rural identity.

(Işık and Pınarcıoğlu 2001: 194, author's translation)

This other-identification (cf. Brubaker and Cooper 2000) often resonates with fear, pity, or disgust. Furthermore, like so many of the perspectives we offer on 'others', the concept of *varoş* also gives the impression of uniformity. I would agree with White, who urges us to see the variety in 'clothing, behaviour or attitudes' in working-class areas (2002: 65).

I doubt very much whether most of the Vanlı in Tepelik would consider themselves as living in a *varoş*. Not only *varoş* but also the *gecekondu* term is loaded with negative associations, so that people may not want to apply the term in reference to their own lives. Erder describes how people in Ümraniye could not agree on whether or not they lived in a *gecekondu* area (1996: 186–7). Indeed, migrant experiences are continuously reframed in narratives, as discussed in Chapter 2 (cf. Bora 2005, Ochs and Capps 1996, Somers 1994). This is the reason why apparently contradictory discourses on rural and urban life are (re)produced by the same people (cf. Ferguson 1992). In Tepelik, for instance, different people, or sometimes even one person, would offer a variety of comparisons of rural and urban life, depending on their perception of their current lives as an improvement in or a worsening of circumstances. As their perception could change continuously, there was thus not one, static perception of what it meant to live in an area such as Tepelik.

Tepelik Households: A Multiplex Network of Strong Links

The eight housing blocks in Tepelik represented a cluster of Vanlı, partly since many of the families moved to Istanbul at the same time, and partly because of a tendency, so common among migrants, to move to the same area as other *hemşehri*.

In 1976, the blocks in Tepelik, then empty, were offered to earthquake survivors from Van, specifically from three districts *(ilçe)*: Çaldıran (where the epicentre of the earthquake was), Muradiye (the district where Gundême is), and Erciş (a neighbouring *ilçe* to the

Table 5: Origin of Households in Tepelik

Origin of Household Head	Number of Flats
Vanlı	57
Erciş	19
Çaldıran	20
Muradiye	17
Özalp	1
Non-Vanlı	21
Empty	3
Total	81

west); today there is only one Vanlı living in the blocks who is from a different *ilçe*. Some of the original families returned to Van quite soon again. They either left the flats to relatives or 'sold' them to others, mostly non-Vanlı. Later again, some more Vanlı came and 'bought' flats in the blocks in order to be close to their relatives. These sales were of course not officially registered as the flats did not have any title deeds. However, just as in many other areas of Istanbul, even more desirable ones, people are willing to buy and sell without such documents. Most of the blocks were still inhabited by Vanlı (Table 5).

Of these 57 Vanlı households, some had been there since the beginning. As the earthquake happened 30 years ago, some of the original migrants had died. Their children, who were either born in Tepelik or grew up there from a young age, continued to live in the flats. In other households, the elders were still alive, leading to three-generation households. Some of these families had 'bought' additional flats in order to split into nuclear households. Other Vanlı families moved to Istanbul at a later stage. This information is summarised in Table 6.

Some families initially consisted of two or three generations, but the children later moved away. In those cases, only the currently cohabiting household members were considered. Generally, following local intuition, I counted the male as the household head and considered his origin first. If a son or daughter of original migrants 'bought' a flat later and settled there, I considered his or her household a split nuclear family, even if the husband of the daughter was not from Van. Similarly, if a couple that came later consisted of a non-Vanlı husband but

Table 6: Time of Arrival and Number of Generations in Vanlı Tepelik Households

Time of Arrival	Number of Generations	Number of Households
Original Migrants	1 generation	1
	2 generations	23
	3 generations	10
Split Nuclear Families	1 generation	1
	2 generations	9
Came Later	2 generations	8
	3 generations	5
Total		57

a Vanlı wife, I counted the household as a Vanlı household as the move was based on the wife's origins. In rural Van, postmarital patrilocality means that women are removed from their consanguines and men remain with their relatives. However, since migration to Istanbul is so common and any family tie means a unit of support, both patrilateral and matrilateral connections may be exploited. In some cases, when the marriage was between relatives, family clusters were linked by ties on both sides anyway.

My observations and conversations with interlocutors persuaded me that 'the Vanlı blocks' (as they were called by both people living there and others) represented a multiplex network of households and individuals, that is, a network based on multiple relationships (cf. Mitchell 1969, Scott 2000). In Granovetter's terms, the households (and individuals) formed a network of strong links (1983), as discussed below. Thus, many of the individuals were both neighbours and relatives (matrilateral, patrilateral, or affines).

The patri- or matrilateral ties between Vanlı households can be shown graphically, together with any ties of marriage since the households settled (Figure 2). This sociogram shows household interrelations based on consanguineous or affinal relations. There were only five households not related to any other household in the blocks. A further 12 households were related to one household, while the other 40 households were part of more complex clusters. Thicker lines represent first degree relations (M, F, B, Z) between households, while thinner lines represent more distant blood relations and relations through marriage.

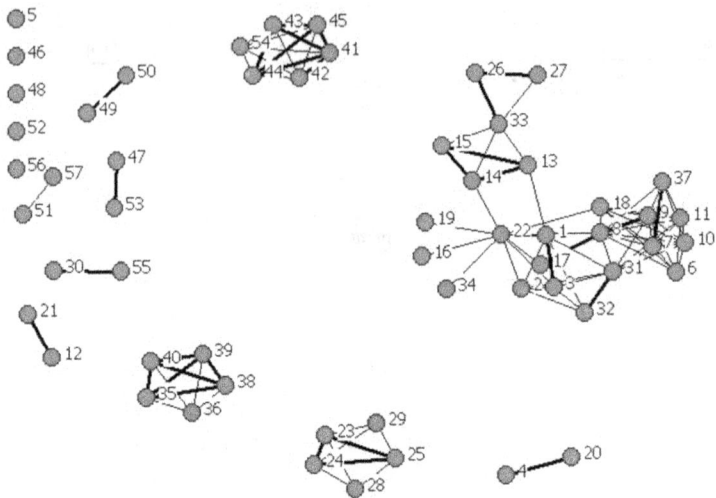

Figure 2: Tepelik Households Connected by Patri- or Matrilateral
Relations or through Marriage

The multiplexity of relations among these neighbours and relatives
was intensified through everyday interactions. Sharing Vanlı origin
immediately bound households together, and indeed many of the men
were members of the hometown association. For many marriages, cir-
cumcisions, or funerals, all the Vanlı households of the blocks were
invited to gather, either at the association building or in a rented hall.
More specifically, a shared origin from the same *ilçe* (district of Van)
had symbolic significance. Finally, families living in the same blocks
shared daily interactions, particularly the women. All households were
thus potentially connected, and a very close-knit network was formed,
close-knittedness referring to the degree to which members of a network are connected among each other (Mitchell 1969, Scott 2000:
31–2).

Shared origin from the same *ilçe* had some influence on where people lived in the blocks. There seemed to be clusters of shared origin/
relative households in each block. For instance, in block 1, there were
only households from Çaldıran and Muradiye, and most of them were
interrelated. In block 2, seven of the flats were occupied by families

from Muradiye (and the other one by a non-Vanlı). Block 6 had six
Erciş households (and was indeed referred to as the '*Erçişliler Bloku*').
However, there were also more mixed blocks, such as block 3, where
there were households from three *ilçe*. There were thus opportunities
for households to mix across *ilçe* boundaries if they so wished. The
hometown association links in particular ensured that sometimes the
block population as a whole was evoked as a network, while at other
times smaller networks of relatives, people from the same *ilçe*, or people from the same block interacted more intensely.

Bonding and Bridging Social Capital

The Vanlı block inhabitants had relations that were based on similarities in background. In Granovetter's terms, they had formed strong
links, that is, links between people who are quite similar or have a lot
in common, for instance close friends or kin. Many of the inhabitants
were linked through kin or affinal ties; they also shared origin in one
of three districts of Van, a connection that is culturally salient. In addition, most men were association members, and all of the households
were neighbours. Many of the families were working class or lower
middle class. Granovetter argues that individuals are part of a network of densely knit relations of friends who also know each other, and
that such clumps of friends are linked to others by weak ties, through
acquaintances. These weak ties are vital for the spreading of ideas or
finding jobs. (1983).

This distinction is echoed by Putnam's differentiation between
bonding and bridging social capital:

> Bonding social capital is good for undergirding specific reci-
> procity and mobilizing solidarity. Dense networks in ethnic
> enclaves, for example, provide crucial social and psychological
> support for less fortunate members of the community, while fur-
> nishing start-up financing, markets, and reliable labor for local
> entrepreneurs. Bridging networks, by contrast, are better for
> linkage to external assets and for information diffusion.
>
> (2000: 22)

As far as individuals are concerned, those with access to strong as well as weak ties, and thus with bonding and bridging social capital, are in a better position to convert social capital into economic or human capital. As discussed in the previous chapter, this was the case for people like Doğan Bey and other leading members of the Vanlı HTA, who could act as brokers between fellow Vanlı from Tepelik and local authorities, bureaucracy, other Vanlı groups, other Kurdish groups, or NGOs.

If one considers the network of Vanlı in Tepelik, the similarities between people, that is, their bonding social capital, bring both disadvantages and advantages. On the one hand, as Putnam points out, bonding social capital can provide 'crucial social and psychological support' for members of the network. However, Lin emphasises the limitations of bonding social capital. It is more advantageous for groups with high socio-economic standing as individuals maintain or further their position through other individuals with a similarly high status. However, 'when a certain group clusters at relatively disadvantaged socioeconomic positions', the individual members are disadvantageously alike. This kind of network is then poorer in resources and also has less of a variety of resources to share (2000: 786–7).

Strong links/bonding social capital and weak links/bridging social capital can be symbolised with the terms 'urban village' and 'cosmopolitanism' respectively. The first term evokes images of ethnic groups living in certain neighbourhoods of big cities, thus creating a 'Chinatown' or 'Little Italy', for instance. Transnationally, or in the case of my study, within a country, people who share origin and are maybe even kin, may cluster in certain areas as they follow each other to the city, as is the case in Tepelik. However, the strong links that offer accommodation and work initially, smoothing the way for chain migration, may also hold migrants back later. The second term, 'cosmopolitanism', was used by Hannerz in order to describe those 'willing to engage with the Other' in the city (Werbner 1999: 17). Werbner criticises Hannerz for using the term exclusively for an elite, while she points out that there may be working-class cosmopolitans as well. However, she does accept that the majority of the labour migrants she describes are 'transnationals' rather than cosmopolitans, meaning that they are 'people who move and build encapsulated worlds around them[selves]' (1999: 19).

Similar distinctions have been made in other studies on migration. Much-quoted is Mayer's study of Xhosa migration to East London (South Africa), in which he distinguished between 'Red' and 'School' Xhosa. The former were described as 'conscious traditionalists' who painted their faces with red ochre. The latter were missionary-school educated rural Xhosa. When these different Xhosa migrated to the city, Mayer argued, they formed different networks of associations. The 'Red' stuck with other 'Reds', forming a network of 'Tribesmen', while the 'School' Xhosa formed wider, and more varied associations, choosing to live as 'Townsmen' (Mayer 1971, cf. Banks 1996: 31–2, Hannerz 1980: 168–9, Ross and Weisner 1977: 360).

In her study on the Istanbul suburb of Ümraniye, Erder found that only 9.2 per cent of the households questioned had no relatives in Istanbul, and 50 per cent had relatives in the same neighbourhood, or *mahalle* (1996: 232–3). In Tepelik, too, there were constant references to other, related Vanlı households, whether in the Vanlı blocks, in Tepelik, or in wider Istanbul. Thus, while the housing blocks did not represent a complete, closed network of relations, conversations with interlocutors convinced me that many interactions in Istanbul were with relatives or other Vanlı, both from the blocks and outside of them. Among the respondents to my questionnaire, too, 71 of the 85 respondents had relatives in Istanbul (84 per cent), and out of these, 44 per cent counted between 20 and 100 relative households, while another 21 per cent noted over 100 relative households. One can assume that many of these relative households live in clusters, just like people interviewed in Ankara by Güneş-Ayata, who found that '76 per cent of the Kurdish speaking migrants claimed to have relatives living in the same quarter' (1996: 103).

In Istanbul, a city with established wealthy neighbourhoods and later central squatter districts and suburbs, the cost of living varies according to the area one lives in. Rents in the most desirable parts of town can be three times the monthly minimum wage, while in other areas, there are still people living for free on land they occupied when they migrated to the city. The prices at weekly markets, in corner shops, and in local small supermarkets vary according to the rent, too, so that, for instance, in an expensive area, a kilo of tomatoes can cost double or triple than what it costs in a cheaper *mahalle*.

When people from Van, or indeed any other part of Anatolia, migrate to Istanbul, one can predict what kind of area they will live in according to their occupation, and hence, income. An unskilled or semi-skilled worker seeking labour in the city will probably only come if others have paved the way, offering the promise of work and perhaps also initial accommodation. He[7] is likely to move to the same area with his family later as it is an area he can afford and there is a ready-made network of strong links. The area, like Tepelik, for instance, may be ethnically and regionally varied, but is likely to have clusters of people from the same villages or districts. In addition, it is relatively homogeneous in terms of socio-economic status.

Vanlı who have had more education and come to study or seek professional work in Istanbul (rarer among the Kurdish Vanlı than the Turkish Vanlı, but becoming more commonplace) are likely to settle near the relevant university or their workplace, probably in middle class residential areas where they can afford the rent. They are incorporated into a neighbourhood of people of higher socio-economic standing. Links to others at university, work, or in the neighbourhood are perhaps not as easily forged, and many of them may remain weak, yet once a network of strong and weak links is established, this kind of Vanlı migrant gains access to a greater variety of resources. Other Vanlı may only follow these Vanlı migrants to the area if they can afford to do so. However, ethnic and hometown ties tend to become secondary.

In Istanbul, this difference can be illustrated with members of the Çetin lineage living in different parts of the city as a result of their different social fields. Hüseyin Çetin, a son of Haci Memo, moved to Istanbul around six years ago, in search for better work. His two older brothers had lived in Istanbul before, but had moved back to Van. However, it was through the pathways that they had created that Hüseyin was able to find work in an area of Istanbul where he has no relatives or fellow Vanlı. Hüseyin is the only brother in the family to have learnt a trade—he is a qualified carpenter. Nevertheless, his job is physically tiring, and he works six days a week. Safety regulations at work are ignored and it is likely that his health is affected by toxic glue fumes and heavy lifting. Hüseyin and his wife Bahar have three school-aged children. They live far outside of the centre of Istanbul, in an area once separate from and now merged into Istanbul's urban sprawl. Similar to Tepelik in its lack of planning and investment in buildings, the area offers little green space. The family would like to move somewhere greener but cannot afford higher rents with Hüseyin's income. Also, they need to live near his place of work as he could not afford the time and money for a lengthy commute. There are no other relatives or fellow Vanlı living nearby this family, but Bahar socialises with other women in her apartment block and the street, both Kurdish and Turkish. These women share with her a migration experience and the worries and concerns of families with a relatively low income in the city. There is thus bonding social capital, which is of use in socialising and helping each other out on an everyday basis, but it does not change the basic living conditions for any family in this network.

Tacit Amca's children live in a different area of central Istanbul, with more green areas and proximity to central transport hubs. They too have followed each other to the city, but have had access to more education and work opportunities. First of all, Ramazan came to Istanbul to study at university in the early 1990s. His brother Serhan followed when Ramazan was still at university. Like his older brother, Serhan had finished school in Van, living with his paternal uncle Haci Fahrettin. Serhan did not want to return to the village and came to Istanbul determined to work on building sites, following the only role model he had been provided with as an alternative to farm life. However, his older brother steered him towards learning English and German at a language school, and then helped him to find employment as a receptionist at a hotel. Serhan was able to use his language skills to work his way up to positions in more luxurious hotels and later on cruise liners in the Caribbean. With the money he earned on the ships, he was then able to support his older brother, who had founded his own services company and was able to expand. Ramazan in turn helped Serhan to buy a house in the same middle class area that he lived in in Istanbul. Serhan has now settled in the USA, and he has allowed other siblings coming from Van to live in his house rent-free, thus passing on the help he himself received.

Today, four brothers and a sister, as well as a matrilateral cousin, live in the house, and all except one brother (who went to university and became an engineer) work in Ramazan's company. These siblings illustrate very clearly Lin's point about the socio-economic standing of network members: if their socio-economic standing is higher, then they can share more resources with each other. The initial bridging capital of Ramazan, his weak links, offered Serhan opportunities he had not thought of himself, and this in turn has brought more opportunities for others they have strong ties with.

When describing transnational migration of Pakistanis to Britain, Pnina Werbner picks up the distinction of Granovetter's strong and weak ties to argue that they affect the migration experience:

> Kinship ties, being by their very nature 'strong', doom migrants, if sustained in isolation to remain fixed within the social limits set by their origins and circumstances in Pakistan, prior to their migration to Britain. By contrast, new friendships and acquaintances forged by migrants locally extend their horizons and mediate processes of mobility and social transformation. They facilitate not only job searches and entrepreneurial ventures, but also the expansion of the family and the setting of novel lifestyles.
>
> (1999: 28)

A key issue in rural-urban migration is thus whether strong kin ties form the *only* links people can rely on. When some women in Tepelik voiced dissatisfaction with the neighbourhood, I sensed that they felt that these strong ties did not offer them or their children any concrete improvements.

Two women in the area expressed worries for their children's future. They felt that their children, particularly their sons, would not have any role models that would make them aspire to completing school, let alone going to university. To them, the strong ties offered in the Vanlı network were limiting the options for their families.

A third housewife and mother in her mid-thirties who wanted to work outside of the home felt that the local hometown association was incapable of offering her any support with finding childcare facilities or mobilising the women of the neighbourhood into solidarity movements that would result in more of them working outside of the home. She felt she had forged weak ties when working before, but that they would not last if she did not start working again. She was frustrated with the strong ties, which she felt were holding her back, forcing her to conform to certain behavioural patterns in order to fit in. Indeed, implied in her criticism was the accusation that weak links were often dominated by male brokers, who used them to further the interests of male rather than female Vanlı.

In contrast, I had a sense that those young women in their twenties who were working, were quite happy to remain in Tepelik, at least until marriage. Since they were able to form weak ties at work and during leisure activities, they were free to maintain whichever strong ties they chose to in Tepelik, without having any expectations beyond friendship and neighbourliness from them.

As noted earlier, Vanlı migrants make use of networks of relatives, friends, co-villagers, and more generally *hemşehris* in order to get by in urban centres. This chapter has given the example of a localised network of Vanlı in Istanbul that offers migrants strong ties, or bonding social capital. The neighbourhood of Tepelik is only one example in the study of migration of people settling in clusters that are ethnically and/or socio-economically homogeneous. While the strong ties of such a cluster can be of great help in everyday life, ties forged outside of such clusters, that is, weak ties, represent bridging social capital with a wider variety of people, be it ethnic or socio-economic.

Although the Vanlı in Tepelik represent a localised cluster of migrants, they are also part of the wider translocational migratory social field that includes relatives, friends, and co-villagers in Van province and in other cities around Turkey. They have maintained strong ties with Vanlı relatives and co-villagers living in different locations. Some Vanlı in Tepelik have also created weak ties in Istanbul through school, work, neighbourliness, mosque visits, or local activism related to the *mahalle*. The next chapter discusses the use of such strong and weak ties in the forging of marriage ties, both before and after migration.

7

TRANSACTIONS OF A
SPECIAL KIND: MARRIAGES

Crossing Ethnic and Religious Borders

Transactions and relations between Kurdish Vanlı migrants, as well as between migrants and sending communities, have been discussed in previous chapters. I would now like to turn to a discussion of how migration has affected the institution of marriage. Lévi-Strauss once termed marriages the exchange of 'that most precious category of goods, women' (1969: 60–1). Indeed, even if one balks at describing women as 'goods', it is undeniable that Kurdish (and Turkish) expressions reflect the fact that marriage is an exchange between families. When Gundî and other Vanlı speak of marriage, they speak of '*qiz xastin*'/'*kız vermek*' (giving a girl) and '*qiz dayin*'/'*kız almak*' (taking a girl) in Kurdish and Turkish respectively.[1]

Marriages involve material and emotional transactions between groups. In the cases where Kurdish families still pay a bride price to the family and 'milk money' to the mother of the bride, this is most obvious. However, even marriages without such payments involve a transfer of money to the couple at weddings in the form of gold and cash prestations and purchases of household goods, perhaps even a home. Marriages also represent a reordering of the social universe of families as women leave a household to enter a new one and in-laws are added to the family. Acknowledging the active role women have in arranging these marriages and contesting the reduction of women to 'goods', one can nevertheless consider many Vanlı betrothals as the forging or strengthening of links between groups, lineages, or families rather than just individuals.

Just as the exchange of goods and services is based on a network of trust and generalised reciprocity, the contracting of marriages also requires such a network of relations. In Van city, as pointed out earlier, ethnicity is often also an indicator of social class, meaning that networks form more easily within ethnic groups than across them. Thus, the following two examples of interethnic marriages from Van province are still exceptional for Kurdish Vanlı in Van province, particularly if they are recent rural-urban migrants.

When Haci Fahrettin Çetin's second-oldest son Ahmet saw Ayşe, he fell in love with her and decided that he wanted to marry her. His feelings were requited. However, Ayşe's family were not Kurdish, but Turkish. Her family considered themselves '*öz Vanlı*' (original Vanlı) or '*yerli Vanlı*' (local Vanlı). Although Haci Fahrettin had by then lived in Van for around ten years, his family were still '*sonradan gelme*', 'latecomers', and thus still considered villagers. It was thus with a certain amount of trepidation that Ahmet's family went to ask for Ayşe's hand in marriage. They felt inferior (*ezik* in Turkish), aware of the cultural gap between the families. How would her family react to such a request? In fact, how did Turks phrase such a request?

Ahmet and Ayşe have now been married for over 15 years, and have had time to get used to each other's family's differences. These differences have mostly translated into a greater proximity of their nuclear family to Ayşe's side of the family than a Kurdish bride might have been granted at that time, as well as less control exerted by Haci Fahrettin over the comings and goings of his son and daughter-in-law.

In a second case, Haci Kasım Çetin's grandson Tahir was living in the district town of Muradiye (where he had been born) when he fell in love with a Turkish nurse, Şenay, who had been sent to work there. He once described the same feeling of being '*ezik*' when he went to his own wedding among the bride's family in Thrace, the very west of Turkey. A worry about the disregard in which her relatives might hold Kurds made him and his few relatives who could travel there[2] extremely uncomfortable.

In both these marriages, the wife and her natal family have had considerable influence on postmarital residence. Ahmet and Ayşe moved into a flat a bit further away from Haci Fahrettin's compound after marriage; after several years of marriage, Tahir and Şenay moved to the west of Turkey in order to be able to live closer to members of her family.

Both of these marriages still represent exceptions among my Kurdish interlocutors in Van province. The first is a direct result of migration as Ahmet would not have met Ayşe otherwise, or, even if he had, she and her family would never have consented to a marriage into a Kurdish village—both the Kurdishness and village life being incompatible with Ayşe's upbringing. The fact that the Turks in Van have long been settled in the city and that villagers are almost exclusively Kurdish means that there have been few marriages between them. The urban and rural lifestyles have been thought to be irreconcilable. Thus, even rural migrants to the city move in different circles from the more established urbanites; this prevents the establishment of ties that lead to intermarriage. Thus, most marriages of villagers and former villagers in Van province have been and are between Kurds, Turks representing the ultimate strangers because they are not only not acquaintances, but also culturally different. As some Kurdish families are upwardly mobile, however, there are likely to be more interethnic unions in the future. A total marriage taboo still seems to be in place between Kurds and Roma, called *mirtip* in Kurdish. The prejudices many Kurds (as well as Turks) hold about the *mirtip* make such marriages inconceivable to most.

In the big cities in the west of Turkey that have attracted labour migration from all over Anatolia, interethnic marriage is much more common. It is important to note that the socio-economic status of the families concerned is often more likely to determine the likelihood of intermarriage than their ethnicity. Researchers in the 1970s found that 'inter-ethnic marriages between people of the same religious affiliation have become more frequent with time' (Magnarella and Türkdoğan 1973: 1628). A more recent study estimates that there are 2,708,000 marriages between Turks and Kurds/Zaza, representing 3.7 per cent of the population ('Biz Kimiz?').

However, as Magnarella and Türkdoğan imply, Alevi and Sunni divides make it likely that these interethnic marriages are mostly between couples with the same religious orientation. There is still some reluctance among my Kurdish Vanlı interlocutors to accept marriages between people of different religious affiliation, that is, between Alevis and Sunnis (cf. Magnarella and Türkdoğan 1973: 1628). This is a relatively new issue that Vanlı have to face, since the Vanlı villages and Van city are populated by Sunni Muslims.[3] It is only through migration to other cities, such as Istanbul, that the Vanlı Sunni Muslims have shared quarters, schools, jobs, and universities with Alevis. Through these interactions, some marriages between Kurdish Vanlı and Alevis have taken place.

Below, I discuss marriages of Kurdish Vanlı in more detail, arguing that the principles according to which marriages are contracted have not really changed, but that migration has 'widened the circles', as one woman in Tepelik put it. Vanlı today have a greater choice of marriage partners as migration has dispersed the people they have strong links with and has thus provided more access to weak links.

Gundême Marriages

In the following, I first discuss past marriages in the village of Gundême, also considering the concepts of kin group endogamy and father's brother's daughter (FBD) marriage, both posited as common in Muslim and Kurdish societies. Then I move on to a discussion of more recent marriages in relation to migration.

Studies of Arab and Middle Eastern societies have often noted a preference for marriage of patrilateral parallel cousins, that is, children of father's brothers (e.g. Baumann 1996: 83, Harris 2004: 33, Khuri 1970, McCabe 1983, Murphy and Kasdan 1959: 17, Pfluger-Schindlbeck 2005: 29). More general kin group endogamy has been found to be relatively common in different parts of Turkey (e.g. Béller-Hann and Hann 2001: 32, 145). For instance, a study carried out by Tunçbilek and Ulusoy in Turkey in 1983 found that *akrabalık evliliği* (kin group marriage) amounted to 10.18 per cent in western Anatolia, and 32.86 per cent in eastern Anatolia (in which they included southeastern Anatolia). The average for Turkey was 20.92 per cent (Altuntek 1993: 39 and 2001: 22). The data thus show that kin marriage is not rare in Turkey, and that it seems to be even more common in the east of Turkey.

Eastern and southeastern Anatolia are of course Kurdish-majority regions (with also a considerable Arab population along the Syrian border), and studies of Kurdish society have long emphasised tribal and clan endogamy and a preference for FBD marriage. Barth discussed the 'strong emphasis on the father's brother's daughter as preferred spouse, and marked tendency to close family endogamy' (1954: 167), providing data for the Kurdish region around Kirkuk and Suleimani, cities in Iraq. He argued that the reason for tribal Kurds preferring such marriages was that men offered their daughters in marriage to their brothers' sons so that they could rely on their nephews as allies in disputes (1954: 168).

Bruinessen writes of a preference for marriage with (real or classificatory) FBDs. While he was unable to study this preference statistically, he proposes that tribes in northern Kurdistan (i.e. in Turkey) may have an even higher incidence than that quoted by Barth for southern Kurdistan—an estimated 40 per cent among tribal members and 10 per cent among non-tribal Kurds. Bruinessen posits a gradation of endogamy, with a preference for FBD, then other patrilateral cousins, and then relatives rather than non-relatives. He also suggests that village endogamy is common in some areas (1978: 87–9).

In her village study in Hakkâri, Yalçın found that of 65 marriages, 41.5 per cent were with patrilateral relatives, 13.8 per cent with matrilateral relatives and 33 per cent with non-relatives (1986: 299). Çağlayan, too, speaks of the common occurrence of FBD marriages among her Diyarbakır interlocutors (2007: 53), and Ammann mentions the 'traditional manner [of marriage] between son and daughter of two brothers' among her Kurdish interlocutors in Europe (2000: 212, author's translation).

Despite such data pointing to a preference of marriages between patrilateral parallel cousins and, more generally, patrilateral relatives among Kurds, there is also evidence to the contrary. In 1993, Altuntek carried out a study on kin marriage in the Van region, in which she found that of 400 marriages, 5 per cent were with FBDs, while marriages with other cousins made up around 2 per cent each (1993: 68). She states that the 'right of the brother's son' to a daughter in marriage that some researchers discuss does not exist in the Van region; rather, she argues, 'marriage with a FBS [father's brother's son] is only one of the marriage options' (1993: 82, author's translation). She does point out however, that marriages are ideally contracted with families whom one trusts to look after the daughter well after she moves into that household (1993: 83).

Bourdieu's extensive discussion of the portrayed ideal of marriages between patrilateral parallel cousins in Arab and Berber countries is instructive here. Emphasising the theory of *practice*, he warns of classifying all marriages with a FBD as a 'genealogically unequivocal marriage'. The decision of two brothers (or even of their father) to marry their children is arrived at for a multitude of reasons; as Bourdieu points out, it may be 'the best kind of marriage' or the worst (1977: 48–9).

While he is right to point to the different motivations behind marriages between patrilateral parallel cousins (and, by extension, among patrilateral kin), this still does not explain why the prevalence of FBD marriages found by Barth and of patrilineal endogamy found by Yalçın was not found by Altuntek or, indeed, in my data. One argument, pursued below, is that migration has offered a wider choice in marriage partners. However, if patrilineages were mostly inclined to marry endogamously, then pre-migration data should show a high occurrence of such marriages, and even migration would presumably not convince them of the desirability of marrying outside of the lineage. I thus argue below that the particular make-up of the area, where villages may contain members of several patrilineages, has made strict patrilineal endogamy difficult to practice, due to a small number of marriage partners to choose from.

First of all, I consider past marriages in Gundême, where one can see a variety of marriage patterns. There is no single observable—or observed—rule. I counted 319 marriages over the last three generations in Gundême until 2006. Of these marriages, 83 (i.e. 26 per cent) were contracted among fellow villagers.[4] Of these 83, 48 marriages (i.e. 15 per cent of the total number of marriages) were within the patrilineage.

Table 7: Inter- and Intra-Lineage Marriages in Gundême

'Giving a Girl'	'Receiving a Girl'										
	1	2	3	4	5	6	7	8	9	10	11
1											
2											
3										2	1
4					1				1	1	1
5					1						1
6										1	1
7			1				5		1		1
8								2			3
9							1		7		3
10					1			1		1	4
11	1			1			1	3	1	2	32

Table 8: Marriage Preferences of Different Lineages in Gundême

Lineage	Intra-Lineage Marriage	Intra-Village[5] Marriage	Inter-Village Marriage	Marriage to Cities	Total
1	–	1	1	–	2
2	–	–	9	–	9
3	–	3	6	–	9
4	–	2	3	1	6
5	1	2	10	–	13
6	–	3	20	–	23
7	5	3	38	2	48
8	2	7	10	5	24
9	7	4	20	2	33
10	1	10	27	3	41
11	32	20	95	6	153

Table 7 shows both the intra-village and the intra-lineage marriages. In 2006, there were eleven patrilineages in Gundême. The matrix should be read as the vertical axis 'giving a girl' to the horizontal axis; the numbers in bold thus show instances of lineage endogamy.

The patrilineages in Gundême have differed in their marriage preferences, as summarised in Tables 8 and 9.

Table 8 lists the number of marriages that each lineage contracted within the lineage, within the village, between villages, and with

Table 9: Marriage Preferences of Different Lineages in Gundême, Percentages

Lineage	Intra-Lineage Marriage	Intra-Village Marriage	Inter-Village Marriage	Marriage to Cities
1	–	50%	50%	–
2	–	–	100%	–
3	–	33%	66%	–
4	–	33%	50%	17%
5	8%	16%	77%	–
6	–	15%	87%	–
7	10%	6%	79%	4%
8	8%	29%	42%	21%
9	21%	12%	61%	6%
10	2%	24%	66%	7%
11	21%	13%	62%	4%
Average	6.4%	21.0%	67.3%	5.3%

cities other than Van. Note that for each lineage I have counted the 'girls given' and the 'girls taken', so that a total count would exceed the 319 marriages.

Because the lineages are of such different size, it is more meaningful to look at which percentage of its marriages was of which kind (Table 9).[6] Intra-lineage marriages were popular to varying degrees. Five lineages in Gundême had contracted none in the last three generations, a fact that can maybe be explained with their relatively small size, which would have limited the choice of potential marriage partners severely. On the other hand, two lineages (9 and 11) contracted 21 per cent of their marriages within the lineage. I believe that there are two conflicting values at work, which Gundî themselves have expressed to me numerous times. On the one hand, it is generally desirable to marry one's daughters to relatives (patrilateral or matrilateral), since, the argument goes, one can be sure that they will be treated well. Her natal family will have the power to protect her and even to threaten with sanctions if there should be problems. Even better, if the relatives are of the same patrilineage, then the daughter will be living in the same village as her parents. On the other hand, there is also an awareness of the genetic dangers of frequent relative-marriage, and some disabled children are pointed to as evidence of the dangers of *akraba evliliği*. In her study of Vanlı women, Tunç noted that 34 per cent of the marriages in the survey were relative marriages, but that 53 per cent of the women opposed relative marriage because of the risk of disabilities in children (2004: 7). Similarly, Birkalan describes four Turkish sisters in Istanbul debating the merits of marriage with an *akraba* (relative) versus a *yabancı* (stranger); they discuss worries about genetic defects, but note that marrying a relative often means settling in the proximity of one's natal family, a distinct advantage (1999: 205–6). In addition to these two considerations, some young women and men have expressed doubt about whether they could marry a relative they have known from childhood and consider 'a brother' or 'a sister' (cf. McCabe 1983).

In the case of lineage 9, the relatively high degree of lineage endogamy may be explained with the attitude towards women in this lineage; they are said to be freer in their behaviour than those of other lineages. They dance with men in the *halay* (folk dance where all dancers hold hands in a great circle), get dressed up more at weddings, and are said to joke more freely with men. What is emphasised is that this free behaviour happens in public. Depending on the view of the commentator, these women are either considered lucky and their menfolk enlightened, or their reputation as modest, chaste women is questioned. In such an environment, there is reluctance by some other lineages to ask for the girls, and in turn, the families of lineage 9 are probably just as unwilling to marry their daughters to 'spoilsports'. In addition, because members of this lineage have done well for themselves, there is no urgent need to strengthen ties with others through marriage.

The issue of whom to marry (or in the case of the Vanlı often rather whom to marry one's children to) can also be considered in terms of social capital. Frequent intra-lineage marriage results in close-knit networks whose members are likely to support each other. However, this kind of network is high in bonding rather than bridging social capital, so if the socio-economic status of the lineage is low, it is likely to be isolated. It is more advantageous for wealthier and more influential lineages to practice intra-lineage marriage as the contacts within that close-knit network will be sufficient for a good and secure lifestyle. In Gundême, lineages 9 and 11, which have practiced most endogamy, are relatively well-off. For weaker lineages it may be more advantageous to seek new connections through exogamy.

Apart from the small lineage 2, which contracted all its marriages in the relevant time span outside of the village, all patrilineages have contracted marriages with patrilineage 11. This is not surprising as 11 is the largest patrilineage in the village. However, the data also show that there is not exact reciprocity in marriages as girls are 'given' in one direction only at times.

A larger sample of marriages would be necessary in order to gauge numerically what I have been told frequently: that certain lineages prefer not to marry members from other ones. Anecdotal evidence suggests, however, that these prescriptive rules (e.g. 'My mother and father would not let me choose a girl from lineage X' or 'We don't give our girls to lineage Y') are not necessarily enforced.

To return to the earlier discussion of patrilineal endogamy, which has been posited as typical for Kurdish society, and village endogamy, described by Bruinessen, my data on Gundî marriages contradict this. As stated above, 26 per cent of marriages were within the village, either between or within lineages, while all but one lineage (8) contracted more than half of its marriages with other villages—the village average being 67.3 per cent. Because the wider area has seen great population changes in the last 80 years, it is of course possible that people are marrying dispersed members of their tribe from other villages. However, I was never offered this explanation by interlocutors, and in the cases where I did know the tribes that *bûks* had come from, they did not correspond to that of their husbands. It is more likely that marriages to other cities, not villages, have been with patrilineal relatives who migrated for work.

It thus seems unlikely that marriages between villages are marriages between distant patrilineal relatives. However, often they are also not marriages with 'strangers'. While it is quite appropriate for the families of young males to make enquiries about unrelated young girls in other villages, many marriages are contracted on the basis of previous acquaintance or relatedness. Let me give the case of the Çetin lineage, lineage 7, as an example. Of the 38 marriages that they contracted between villages, ten marriages are with villagers from the neighbouring village, Pembegelin, eight of them with women from one patrilineage.

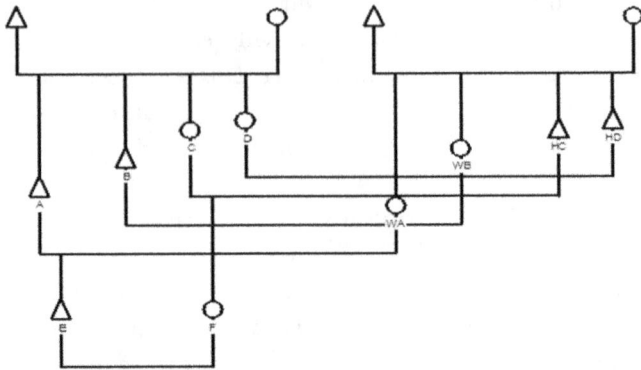

Figure 3: Four Siblings from Gundême Marry Four Siblings
from Pembegelin

Indeed, in one family of the Çetin lineage (Figure 3), two brothers A and B were married to two sisters, WA and WB, from Pembegelin. In turn, their two sisters, C and D, were married to two brothers of the Pembegelin brides, HC and HD.[7] The connection has not been severed; a son of A and WA (E) has married the daughter of C and HC (F). So, although E has married a girl from another village, she is in fact his bilateral cross-cousin (his father's sister's daughter and his mother's brother's daughter at the same time).

It is quite common in Gundême to marry a young woman or a young man from one's mother's village, even if such multiple sibling marriages are not the norm. Over the generations there is often a to-and-fro of women who follow their matrilateral kin of a previous generation. If, for example, a young man marries his mother's brother's daughter, she comes to him in marriage from his mother's natal village. Their daughter in turn may marry her mother's brother's son and so move back to her mother's natal village.

Marriages are not necessarily with first cousins, but also with more distant matrilateral relatives. Over the generations, as young women have come to Gundême or gone from Gundême to those villages, they have often married into their matrilateral family or have created new bonds of relatedness that will lead to further marriages in the future. It has not been possible for me to give a breakdown of inter-village marriages into those contracted with relatives and those with non-relatives, but anecdotal evidence suggests that many are with matrilateral relatives. Thus, patri- and matrilateral relatives, as well as other inter-village acquaintances, form networks within which potential marriage partners may be found.

Again, to return to the discussion of preferential patrilineal endogamy, my data do not fit the commonly-held view of Kurdish marriage preferences. It might be that the dispersal of tribes in the area, which has led to a relative irrelevance of tribal membership and instead more emphasis on lineage membership, has decreased the choice of marriage partners among patrilineages to such an extent that matrilateral connections are also exploited. It is impossible to find a clear reason, and I am guided by comments made by Vanlı interlocutors when I suggest that marriages are preferably with families whom one knows and trusts (cf. Bruinessen 1978: 89, Altuntek 1993: 83). If we recall the possible consequences of patrilocal patrilineal family structures for young women, as discussed in Chapter 8, it is not surprising that families want to use existing relations with others to ensure that their daughters are treated well after marriage.

Figure 4 shows the village Gundême (G) and its neighbouring villages. As far as I could ascertain, I have noted which villages there have

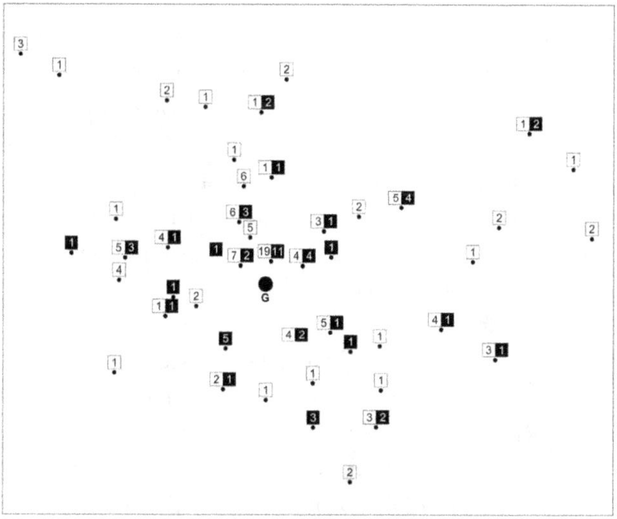

Figure 4: Marriages Contracted with Villages around Gundême

been marriage relations with. In order to keep the villages anonymous, I have not used either the Kurdish or the Turkish village names, but have depicted them as dots on a map in scale to depict distances. The villages are all within a radius of about 50 kilometres from Gundême. Black numbers in white squares denote the number of women who came from a certain village to Gundême, whereas the white numbers in black squares represent the number of Gundî women who moved to other villages in marriage.

The village of Pembegelin just north of Gundême is notable because eleven Gundî women married there, and 19 came from there to Gundême in marriage. In general, it can be seen that there is no exact correspondence between the number of women 'given' and 'taken'. There are thus villages from where young women have come to Gundême without any young women from Gundême going there, and vice versa. The 50 kilometre radius of the many inter-village marriages of the past represents the distance that people have travelled for visits, trade, weddings, funerals, and other occasions, creating social networks that could also lead to (further) marriages.

'A Widening of Circles'

Since more and more families have left villages to move to Van or even further away, the pool of potential marriage partners is ever-widening. In the city, young people see each other in the street or meet relatives of their same-sex friends, though they will still go through the 'correct channels' to make marriage offers. Neighbouring women come for glasses of tea and eye up the single daughters of a household, making a mental note of ages and accomplishments, potentially suitable men in their own surroundings, and people they should mention this to.

More recent marriages of interlocutors and their relatives in Van city and Istanbul have shown that there is now a wide range of possibilities. There thus seems to be no particular preference for endogamy or exogamy; rather, young people marry patri- or matrilateral relatives *or* people whose families have been vetted and approved of. This increase in marriage partner choice can be illustrated with a Vanlı patrilineage from Çaldıran, a district neighbouring Muradiye.

Table 10: Marriages Contracted by the Derman Lineage in Tepelik

Type of Marriage	Frequency	Percentage
Patrilineal Endogamy	7	23%
Marriages with Matrilateral Relatives	3	10%
Marriages with Non-Relatives from Van Province	11	37%
Marriages with Non-Relatives in Istanbul	7	23%
Details Unknown	2	7%
Total	30	100%

Gülşen Derman from Tepelik had come from Gundême in marriage around 20 years before. The patrilineage she married into was from Çaldıran, and it showed a distinct favouring of lineage endogamy. She herself was married to her mother's brother's son (i.e. her husband married his father's sister's daughter). Of the 30 marriages I could ascertain in her husband's patrilineage over the last two generations, seven were within the patrilineage. This may not sound much, but one should remember that it concerns 14 members of the lineage, and thus more than any other of the marriages. Table 10 summarises marriage choices.

Of the eight siblings (seven men and one woman) in the generation before Gülşen, everyone married someone from Van. This is not surprising as all the marriages preceded migration to Istanbul. One man married his FBD, another his maternal uncle's daughter, while at least three of the siblings married non-relatives from the province.

Table 11 shows most of the marriages of the children (generation 1) and grandchildren (generation 2) of Abdurrahman and Melike Derman, who were Gülşen's husband's paternal grandparents (and at the same time Gülşen's maternal grandparents). There was no information on the children of Kutbettin, three of whom are married.

This patrilineage has contracted more lineage-endogamous marriages than any other I have met, even lineages 9 and 11 in Gundême. Nevertheless, it has still contracted the majority of its marriages outside of the family, whether with people from Van or, in Istanbul, with people from a variety of regional backgrounds. Matrilateral relations were sometimes also exploited to find a marriage partner. This variety of choices, I believe, is a fair representation of the manner in which Vanlı families, migrant or not, now use strong and weak ties to contract marriages.

Table 11: Details on Marriages of Derman Lineage

Generation	Name	Marriage
1	Şemsettin/FBD	patrilateral parallel cousin marriage
2	Mehmet	wife from Muradiye
2	Tahir/Gülşen	patrilateral cross-cousin marriage[8]
2	Ibrahim	wife from Muradiye
2	Ömer	wife from Istanbul
2	Abdullah	wife from Istanbul
2	Ahmet	wife from Istanbul
2	Fatma	husband from Istanbul
1	Necmettin	matrilateral cross-cousin marriage
2	Perihan/Yusuf	patrilateral parallel cousin marriage
1	Muhittin	wife from Van
2	Figen/Ramazan	patrilateral parallel cousin marriage
1	Izettin	relative from Van
2	Mevlüde/Bayram	patrilateral parallel cousin marriage
1	Nurettin	unknown
2	Ayşe/Muhammed	patrilateral parallel cousin marriage
2	Güler	husband from Istanbul
2	Emin	wife from Istanbul
1	Alaattin	non-relative from Van
2	Ismail/Serap	patrilateral cross-cousin marriage
2	Mahmud	wife from Istanbul
2	Ercan	matrilateral cross-cousin marriage
1	Kutbettin	non-relative from Van
1	Sanem	non-relative from Van
2	Musa	non-relative from Van
2	Elma	non-relative from Van
2	Adile	non-relative from Van
2	Vekile	matrilateral relative (MMZDS)
2	Hatice	non-relative from Van
2	Elif	non-relative from Van

It is of course not surprising that all the marriages with non-relatives in Istanbul have taken place between younger members of the second generation. They were either born in Istanbul or came there for work. Indeed, in the case of Mehmet's younger brothers, his wife said that she had helped them find suitable spouses in Istanbul after they had come to work there as single men.

From what interlocutors have told me, I have gained the impression that marriages in Van city now cross tribal lines more easily than before and that there are also marriages contracted between families who did not know each other previously. Just as interactions between villages paved the way for marriages within a certain radius for Gundî, new interactions in Van city with migrant neighbours from different provinces, tribes, and villages also make new marriage choices possible. However, as rural-urban migration has affected virtually every family, matrilateral and patrilineal relatives are also close at hand and may offer a marriage opportunity as well.

When I asked Mevlüde Derman, a young woman with two children in Tepelik, if she wanted her daughter to marry a relative, she said, 'Not necessarily.' Her nine-year-old daughter intervened, saying that relative marriage could lead to damaged children. Mevlüde said that she was not concerned about that, but that marrying non-relatives 'widened circles'. She was thus pointing out the importance of bridging social capital that can be gained through marriages. I would argue that past and present marriage behaviour shows a balance of basing marriages on existing relations of trust and of forging new relations. This is perhaps the reason why 66 per cent of my questionnaire respondents, all of them Vanlı living in Istanbul, would like their child to marry someone from Van. The shared province origin seems to offer some guarantee that the future spouse, although perhaps a 'stranger', can be vetted through existing translocational networks.

Recent Gundî Betrothals

In Van city, there is evidence that people are 'widening their circles' beyond those of patrilineage, matrilateral relatives and fellow villagers to include unrelated neighbours from all districts of Van and even from villages in neighbouring provinces, such as Hakkâri. Recent engagements and marriages of young people from the Çetin and other lineages who have migrated from Gundême to Van have included both relatives and 'strangers'.

Alaaddin Çetin's son Mehmet married a patrilateral relative, his paternal grandfather's sister's daughter (FFZD), in 2008. Süleyman Çetin's daughter Mevlüde got married to a matrilateral relative and moved to her mother's village. Her brother, Yusuf, married a non-relative whose family had also moved to Van from a village. When I asked his sister how the match had come about, she said, 'She was recommended to us.'

Similar matches through recommendations by intermediaries were made for Gamze, daughter of Tacettin Çetin, Erhan, son of Haci Fahrettin Çetin, and İhsan, son of Tacit Çetin. In these matches tribal membership has been much less important than the perceived 'quality' of the families. Sevgi, daughter of Musa Çetin, married an unrelated fellow Gundî in 2007. The marriage was arranged after both families had moved to Van, where they are next-door neighbours.

Elif, an unmarried daughter of Tacit Çetin, has recounted that, since moving to Van, her family has received many enquiries about marriage by people in Van, either neighbours or other families who have heard about her. Similarly, her cousin Gülay, the teacher, has even received indications of interest from her pupils, who ask about her marital status on behalf of relatives. Migration to Van has thus widened the circle of potential marriage partners.

It has to be emphasised that marriages with 'strangers' are subject to a careful vetting of the in-laws-to-be through enquiries made in the neighbourhood and city. What the Vanlı do is similar to what Stirling and İncirlioğlu found in central Anatolian villages. They speak of parents 'working outwards through their network of social relations', starting with relatives and moving towards acquaintances when looking for a suitable spouse for their children. They add, however, that claims by relatives are becoming rarer as the importance of the patrilineage is in decline (1996: 69). I would also warn against assuming that relatives are automatically successful in their requests for marriage. I am aware of cases where patrilateral cousins were refused or where parents themselves resisted the desire of related children who wanted to marry.

Changing Attitudes towards Marriage

As far as marriages are concerned, it seems that most families today are more concerned about their children's, particularly their daughter's, preferences than in the past. While many middle-aged men and women remember getting married to people they did not know and were not consulted about, these days it is common practice to consult with the daughter before the young man's family comes for a visit and to let the two young people have some time alone in order to discuss whether they find each other suitable. Indeed, efforts may be made to head off visits from suitors who are bound to face rejection. Middle-aged men of the Çetin lineage often jokingly recite the list of men from their lineage who have 'married with their heart' (in Kurdish: 'bi dilê xwe zewicîn'), that is, they had insisted on marrying the women they had fallen in love with. Because young people are now allowed time alone to gauge the potential for attraction and to discuss whether their expectations of marriage are similar, almost all recent marriages are considered to be in this category, even if the arrangements are confirmed through formal channels.

In the urban context, arranged marriages are making way for marriages among young adults who have met and decided on marriage themselves. As mentioned above, in Van (and also in Istanbul) young people may have seen each other before and have taken a liking to each other. As young women have more access to education now and may even go to university or work, marriages can also result from the mixed-gender circle within which young people socialise. Even in the village, where the comings and goings of young women may be more constrained, mobile phones have made private communication between young people easier.

At the same time however, one should not consider arranged marriages merely a form of subjugation and marriages decided on by young people as a liberation. Bora and Üstün describe a widespread attitude towards arranged marriage in Turkey:

> [...] Whatever their background, the marriages of both women and men are not contracted based on personal choices and

decisions, but based on agreements between families and the initiative of family elders. Marriage is not seen as a union between two people and is not experienced in that way. The preferences and orientations of the people to be married are not the determining factor; rather, importance is attached to whether the families suit each other or whether the brides have the capacity to meet the needs of the family.

(2005: 59, author's translation)

The key issue here is that many young people still accept their parents' right to suggest or veto marriage partners. Abu-Lughod writes of young Awlad'Ali Bedouins in Egypt, 'They do not object to the fact that marriages are arranged for them, but they do resist particular matches, mostly those which do not promise to fulfill certain fantasies' (1990: 50). Similarly, I have heard young people from Van comment favourably on arranged marriages, as long as the young are allowed a measure of choice. Indeed, I have also heard young men ask their parents or siblings to find them a marriage partner because they do not trust their own intuitions.

Admittedly, however, there is some imbalance in the manner in which men and women experience the process of getting married. Because it is often the families who decide on the suitability of a match or the time of marriage, young women of marriageable age may feel the burden when families of young men in their social circles become increasingly interested in their marital status and intentions. There is considerable pressure on women of a certain age to marry; only pursuing an education, which not all families have enabled their daughters to do, allows them a socially sanctioned delay in matrimony. As can be seen in the case of Elif Çetin above, migration to the city also 'widens the circle' of those who feel entitled to ask for the hand of a young woman in marriage. On the one hand, this may offer a young woman a wider choice of marriage partners. On the other hand, in some cases she only gets to know of their intentions at the first meeting; she thus has no way of preventing such an offer being made even if she has no interest in accepting it. Such awkward situations must be handled with great tact in order to avoid the family asking for marriage losing face or having a young woman branded as arrogant.

Young men are generally considered to be interested in marriage at an early age, and their personal happiness seems to depend less on who is chosen for them or whom they choose in marriage. This is partly because of the postmarital patrilocal residence of young couples. Young brides often still experience rupture from their family and a potentially difficult period of adaptation in their new homes. Even if, as many families insist on now, the young couple will live 'separately', this may often be, as in the case of Haci Fahrettin's brides in Van city, one of several flats or houses in a family compound. Stone points out that wives in patrilineal patrilocal societies are treated ambivalently by their in-laws. They are necessary for the continuation of the patri-lineage, but may also be blamed for strife within the household (Stone 1998: 103). A young woman entering her husband's home or moving near his family is thus still dependent on their goodwill to make her feel welcome. For her, marriage is much more of a risk than for a young man. These sources of tension may decrease as young men and women aim for neolocal residence at least after a certain period of marriage. Such neolocal residence has become easier to achieve earlier by young men since migration as they have often become the main wage earners of the family and are thus not financially dependent on their parents.

To summarise, despite research that posits the FBD marriage or patrilineal marriages as most common among Kurds, I have found that this type of marriage is only one option, and not even the most fre-quent one, for Vanlı. There was some village endogamy in Gundême, but the majority of marriages were contracted between villages, either with matrilateral relatives or with 'strangers'. After migration, Vanlı migrants continue to consider a variety of marriages as suitable. What has changed is that contact with different families has 'widened the circle' to include more young men and women, whose suitability can then be researched.

Although the migration context has offered more opportunities for young women and men to meet on their own terms, this does not mean that young couples did not fall in love or find ways of marrying before or that arranged marriages are today a thing of the past. What seems to be changing, however, is the power constellation in extended families, so that young couples face a marriage in which the constraints of the traditional Kurdish age-gender hierarchy are less salient than before. The changes that migration has brought in this area are discussed in the next chapter.

8

CHANGING GENDER
RELATIONS

How to Deal with Gender

This chapter considers the effects rural-urban migration has had on gender relations among my Kurdish Vanlı interlocutors. 'Gender relations', however, is not a concept without complications, and thus a preliminary discussion is in order. It is first suggested that 'gender' be approached through the concept of paradigm or 'discourse'; then a dominant, 'traditional' Kurdish gender paradigm is presented. This is followed by a discussion of how migration has led to the coexistence of different gender paradigms/'discourses' among my Vanlı interlocutors.

When I told two young women in Tepelik about my research into the lives of Vanlı, their response was, 'If we told you our mother's story, you would not stop crying.' They were not the only ones to offer narratives of female suffering. Many conversations with women from Van either implicitly or explicitly referred to a lack of choice or control that they felt in their lives and the lives of other Kurdish women, even more so in the past.

Middle-aged and older women, for instance, talked about being married at a very young age. The following sentences epitomise the experiences of quite a few of them: 'My chest was as flat as a board when my family married me to my husband,' or 'I was playing football outside with the other children when they pointed out my husband to me.' They emphasised that marriage used to be a matter arranged solely by parents and elders of the family; if the husband-to-be was not

Illustration 6: An Elderly Widow from Gundême

a (close) relative, they might not have seen him before the wedding, let alone spent time alone with him.

Middle-aged and older women invariably had many children, commonly more than ten, and little or no access to birth control. The desirability of sons and of many children in general took precedence over health considerations. Men (and also older women), who had a vested interest in the continuation of a populous patrilineage, often idealised the alleged fortitude of Kurdish village women in childbirth and the ease with which they bore children and soon got on with their daily routines. They glossed over deaths in childbed, dramatic transports of women in labour to the nearest town with a hospital, miscarriages, stillbirths,[1] and the deaths of babies and toddlers from illnesses or accidents; the women involved in these tragic incidents knew better than to expect a sympathetic audience for their experiences once some time had passed. Women also acquiesced in the system because a lack of children, especially male heirs, could mean the arrival of a second wife. Older children were used to looking after younger siblings and sometimes left school for that reason, thus also perpetuating marriage at a young age.

Because of patrilocal postmarital residence, many village women lived and live at a distance from their natal families, a distance that used to be more difficult to overcome due to weather and road conditions and lack of transport. They have thus been dependent on the goodwill of their husbands' extended families to make their lives agreeable. Some stories that women shared about their lives and those of other women thus involved psychological or physical abuse by parents-in-law, brothers-in-law, older fellow brides, or unmarried sisters-in-law. Divorce was never an option as families subscribed to the proverb that 'women enter their marital home in their bridal dress and leave it in their shroud.'

A recent study on levirate and sororate marriages in the Kurdish-majority southeast of the country found that both the women and men questioned agreed that women had more difficult lives than men; indeed, many of the female respondents wished they had been born as men (Sev'er and Bağlı 2006: 43). Although the people questioned in their study were arguably in particularly difficult situations as many were pushed into these marriages, I am convinced that I would have received similar replies from many of my Vanlı interlocutors. 'Men have it easier, no doubt about it,' many would say. This was also the opinion of King's Kurdish Iraqi interlocutors; they showed her the 'doubly bound world' of Kurdish women, who were oppressed both politically as Kurds, and by a 'male-dominated society', in which 'their movements and achievements are restricted' (2003: 1).

And yet, the situation is not always as clear-cut as that. Kurdish men from rural areas often lead hard lives as seasonal labour migrants. Starting as young as 14, they work at gruelling jobs on construction sites, far away from parents, siblings, wives, and children for most of the year. Both women and men agreed on how difficult it was for the many male seasonal migrants to be separated from family and be responsible for earning enough money for both the nuclear and the extended family.

In addition, women shared many happy memories and moments with me, showing me that they did not think of themselves as continuously oppressed. I saw mischief glittering in their eyes, the love between couples, affection between parents-in-law and brides, and the

easy socialising between women. Harris, writing about control and
subversion in the gendered hierarchy of Tajikistan, was struck by the
resilience and humour of the women when talking about their problems (2004), an impression I have shared when speaking with Vanlı
women. Abu-Lughod points to the gender-segregation among the
Awlad'Ali Bedouins in Egypt as an arena of both social power and resistance (1990: 43–8), and the same can be argued for Kurdish women,
who often revel in the intimacy and solidarity that the same-sex environment offers. How then to approach the lives of (Kurdish) women
and how to do justice to this complexity?

Behar reminds us that when gender has been at issue in anthropology, there has been a focus on different issues at different periods. An initial 'anthropology of women' made visible the other half
of humanity in order to redress the imbalance of the (mostly) male
anthropologists' gaze. Then, 'feminist anthropology' posited a universal second-class status of women. However, this generalisation was
later challenged by 'feminist ethnography', a movement that questions
whether women everywhere have the same issues to contend with and
that focuses on the construction of both femininities and masculini-
ties in different cultural fields. Behar herself acknowledges that 'these
approaches, which developed in dialogue with one another over time,
exist somewhat messily within anthropology' (1994: 81).

A possible danger with a purely relativist approach to gender is that
it may leave anthropologists unsure about how to deal with conten-
tious issues such as honour killings or female genital operations. They
may fear that criticism of certain cultural practices will fuel universal condemnation of a culture as 'barbaric' or 'backwards'. Indeed, in
Turkey, this is sometimes the way in which Kurdish culture is dis-
credited by the mainstream media. On the other hand, it is also not
acceptable to distinguish between 'insiders' and 'outsiders' and forbid
any critical analysis by the latter. As in all ethnographic description,
there is thus a tightrope to be walked between generalisations and
contextualisation.

One problem with generalisations becomes obvious with more
long-term involvement. When I heard stories of the lives of Vanlı
women, I became aware of the fact that individuals, including myself,

constantly reframe their personal narratives. Through my long-term acquaintance with some interlocutors, I have seen the same persons at times dispirited or hopeful, frustrated or happy. Thus, a woman who described to me her despair when she first left her natal home at the age of 16 is obviously happily married these days. A woman may at times dwell on restrictions and other times obey them willingly, even demanding that other women do so, too. Friedl, when writing about her long-term fieldwork in the village Deh Koh in southern Iran, says that generalisations become virtually meaningless as interlocutors themselves reframe their past and present their experiences in narratives that change situationally (1994: 88).

In addition to situational variation, I am also aware of variation between people. Thus, 'Kurdish women' have very different lives depending on whether they live in the village or the city, with their husband's extended family or only with their husband and children, whether they have had schooling or not, whether they work or not, and whether their natal family is wealthy and respected or less so. As one gets to know more interlocutors and grows to respect and like them as individuals, it becomes increasingly difficult to generalise about them as a group of people.

However, a mere focus on the individual and the situational would mislead readers into thinking that there are no structural constraints on people's behaviour. If that had been the case, then I would not have read literature on gender among Kurds, in Turkey, and even in other, often Muslim, countries, with a sense of recognition. And, in the context of this study, it would not have been possible to see certain changes in gender paradigms due to migration.

A way forward is to ensure that the relativist approach is combined with the critical awareness that gender inequality exists in some form everywhere. As Visweswaran points out:

> If second wave feminists saw women as fundamentally equal in their subordination, third wave feminists insist on the inequality of women's subordination based upon the particular location of different communities in racial/class formations or heterosexual economies.
>
> (1997: 596)

This approach acknowledges the existence of universal patriarchy yet also argues that patriarchy has a different 'flavour' in different societies. Kurdish scholars Mojab and Hassanpour thus argue:

> Each regime of patriarchy is particular. Kurdish patriarchy is different from Italian patriarchy. Nonetheless, patriarchies form a universal regime insofar as they perpetrate, without exception, physical and symbolic violence against women.
>
> (2002: 89)

In her seminal article on 'patriarchal bargains', Kandiyoti criticises the overuse of 'patriarchy' without such contextualisation and, in order to illustrate her point, describes two ideal-type societies where women face different 'gender paradigms' and thus different 'bargains' with male dominance (1988). This acknowledgement of patriarchal structures with a concomitant cultural contextualisation has guided my approach to Kurdish gender.

Throughout this chapter I will thus refer to a dominant Kurdish gender paradigm in terms of Kandiyoti's 'classic patriarchy'; I have, at different times, found this paradigm to be adhered to, challenged, described, and complained about by female and male interlocutors. Other academics have spoken about 'gender ideology' (Harris 2004) or 'gender regimes' (Bora and Üstün 2005), and together with Kandiyoti's 'gender paradigms' I would like to equate these terms with the term 'discourse' that I introduced in Chapter 2. All these terms, to me, imply four things:

1) At any one time, there is a multiplicity of discourses on gender. Indeed, Friedl speaks of 'gender attributes [...] in assemblages, in clusters, selected by each person from a variety of potential choices' (1994: 88). One may argue, as I do, that networks of strong links, as described in Chapters 5 and 6, make certain clusters, that is, discourses, more likely.
2) The terms 'ideology', 'regime', 'paradigms', and 'discourse' all imply situatedness, meaning that an individual, male or female, old or young, may concur with different discourses at different times.

3) Discourses on gender can be ranked in terms of their pervasiveness or dominance, thus allowing a critical evaluation of gender ideology in a certain cultural field. This is necessary as there is a dominant gender paradigm among Kurds that everyone is aware of, even if they do not adhere to it, or only in certain situations.

4) 'Discourse' implies the potential for divergence between what people *say* and what they *do*, so that there is ambiguity as to whether people internalise or merely 'perform' certain gender-specific behaviour. In her study of Tajik gender relations, Harris says, 'What I call variant gender performances are (semi-conscious) enactments of characteristics associated with the appropriate sexed body, varied by the actors according to situation and audience' (2004: 21). I believe that Harris' description of gender performances as *semi*-conscious is useful to remind us that it is virtually impossible to decide in each instance whether an individual is acting 'as if' or not. However, no matter what the motivation for these performances, they contribute to the reinforcement and perpetuation of a certain gender ideology.

The following part thus first discusses a Kurdish gender paradigm, understood as a dominant, yet malleable, discourse. The large-scale rural-urban Vanlı migration has given rise to alternative discourses on gender that compete with the dominant one.

Kurdish Gender Relations as 'Classic Patriarchy'

Popular stereotypes of Kurdish women have moved between the extremes of portraying them as liberated or as victims of patriarchy (cf. Çağlayan 2007: 20).[2] The image of liberated Kurdish women can already be seen in the writings of European travellers to Kurdish areas in the 19th century. The Kurds were generally depicted as wild and their womenfolk as less secluded than Turkish or Persian women. (Male) travellers further depicted gender relations as equal, also noting that women had a highly developed sense of morality (Begikhani 2000). Indeed, at the beginning of the 20th century, one British traveller, Major Soane, described Kurdish women as 'a type of the only race of

the Near East whose women are nearly as free as the women of Europe'
(Begikhani 2000: 59, author's translation).

More realistically, Kurdologist Bruinessen argues that Kurds were
indeed able to accept strong female leaders, citing several historically
proven examples, but also points out that they initially achieved high
positions as tribal leaders only because of the previously high status
of their fathers or husbands. Once they had power, writes Bruinessen,
men were willing to obey them. However, he reiterates:

> This only means [...] that a high birth was able to make up for
> the disadvantage of being female. It would be a false conclu-
> sion to believe, as some Kurdish authors do, that equality (or
> the 'colour blindness' of society towards gender) went beyond
> such exceptional cases. Women of high status were able to avoid
> punishment for actions that would have been considered serious
> offences among normal women.
>
> (2000: 18, author's translation)

He thus explicitly disagrees with the image that a Kurdish nationalist discourse sometimes tries to perpetuate, that of a relatively egali-
tarian people subordinated only by other nations. He cites Kurdish
feminist writer Karahan, who posits that Kurdish women are only
ever respected as mothers or wives, and that they are often exposed to
violence from consanguineous and affinal males, even their own sons
(Bruinessen 2000: 23).

The militant PKK has offered Kurdish women an alternative to
the roles of wife and mother; 'in the mountains', so Kurdish nationalist images would have us believe, women and men are equal, asexual freedom fighters. According to a study Çağlayan cites, around a
third of the fighters were women by 1993 (2007: 170). Recent years
have also seen more political involvement by women in peaceful pro-
test movements in the cities, but often again in the role of a mother.
The 'Saturday Mothers' protested against the disappearance of their
(politically active) sons and husbands for years in the 1990s, and the
'Peace Mothers', mothers of PKK fighters or political prisoners, have
called for an end to fighting (cf. Çağlayan 2007: 168, Günçıkan 1996).

Arguably, many female Kurdish activists have been pushed into their role by extreme circumstances and an increase in politicisation among Kurds in general rather than long-standing cultural norms of gender equality. Indeed, Mojab and Hassanpour criticise that Kurdish nationalists in Turkey, Iran, and Iraq have only paid 'lip service to the idea of gender equality' and do not follow through with any practical legislation or services to improve the status of women (2002: 3–4).

Many accounts of Kurdish society describe gender segregation as the norm. According to Ammann, Kurds, like other ethnic groups in the region, have traditionally practised gender segregation, with only children moving comfortably between the different worlds (2000: 110–1). Begikhani points out that the 'freer' Kurds depicted by early travellers were rural farmers and nomads, whereas urban women of higher social standing were much more secluded (2000: 64). Çağlayan describes clearly-defined male and female spheres inhabited by her Kurdish interlocutors in Diyarbakır, but argues that gender segregation has declined with migration to the city (2007: 49–50). In all my research locations I found that formal occasions in particular often entailed gender segregation, so that women and men would then eat and socialise separately. More generally, gender segregation has been posited as typical for Muslim societies, even if such cultural delineations are now considered more flexible than in the past (Pfluger-Schindlbeck 2005: 1, 6).

Gender segregation, in particular the confinement of women to the domestic sphere, was one of the criteria considered in early feminist anthropological literature. Rosaldo posited a 'global generalization' of women being associated more with the domestic and men more with the public sphere (1974: 35). Arguing that societies could be arrayed on a spectrum, she said, 'Women's status will be lowest in those societies where there is a firm differentiation between domestic and public spheres of activity and where women are isolated from one another and placed under a single man's authority, in the home' (1974: 36).

Indeed, in Kurdish society, which has often been depicted as very hierarchical, young women are placed under the authority of more than one person. For the southeastern Kurdish province of Hakkâri, Yalçın describes parallel male and female hierarchies with a male and

a female household head, often the oldest couple in the household. The
latter controls the female labour, yet ultimately answers to the male
household head (1986: 94–5, cf. Çağlayan 2007: 42). My own observations and explicit statements by interlocutors on (un)acceptable behaviour of young unmarried and married women have confirmed that
such a hierarchy is maintained and reproduced by both women and
men. Very like my impression of Kurdish society is Harris' description
of Tajik society; she posits that social control in Tajikistan is based on
gender and age (2004: 18). It is thus young women, either as daughters
or as *bûks*, who are controlled the most.

Control often focuses on the interactions of the young women with
the opposite sex. Findings among Kurdish migrants in Europe concur
with this: sexual honour, or *namus*, plays a central role. *Namus* depends
on the behaviour of women, but it is defended by men. Unmarried
girls are to be sexually untouched; even rumours about the loss of vir-
ginity can still be fatal (Ammann 2000: 110). In fact, Delaney declares
that such a preoccupation with controlling the sexuality of women is
the real meaning of 'patriarchy', that is, not the dominance of men in
general, but the dominance of those men who are fathers:

> The protection of women in Muslim societies is [...] intimately
> and essentially related to the protection of the seed [...] A man's
> power and authority, in short his value as a man, derives from his
> power to generate life. His honor, however, depends on his abil-
> ity to guarantee that a child is from his own seed. This in turn
> depends on his ability to control 'his' woman.
>
> (1991: 39)

In the city, this control may be continued through limiting the con-
tact that women have with the outside world (cf. Wedel 1997: 162).
Erman, in her study of both Turkish and Kurdish migrant women to
Ankara argues that control over families is maintained more strictly by
Sunni Muslims (which the Vanlı are) than by Alevis (1998a: 153–4).
The experiences of Çağlayan's interlocutors, women in Diyarbakır, a
Kurdish-majority city in the southeast of Turkey, have led her to con-
clude that gender hierarchies continue in the city. She says that the

modernisation process which has affected the Kurdish countryside through the building of dams and irrigation projects, urban migration and capitalisation, has been a very male-dominated process, not changing the prevalent gender ideology much (2007: 43–7).

The gender ideology of male control over female sexuality and, I would add, labour (cf. Yalçın 1986: 94–5, Çağlayan 2007: 39), is well-described by Kandiyoti, who, while acknowledging that all sexual paradigms undergo change, describes Turkey as a 'classic patriarchy'. She ascribes this system to 'North Africa, the Muslim Middle East (including Turkey, Pakistan, and Iran), and South and East Asia (specifically, India and China)' (1988: 278); her description of the characteristics of this type of patriarchy can be applied to Kurdish society, too.

Classic patriarchy, according to Kandiyoti, is found in societies with patrilineal descent and postmarital patrilocal residence. She argues that 'implications of the patrilineal-patrilocal complex for women not only are remarkably uniform but also entail forms of control and subordination that cut across cultural and religious boundaries, such as those of Hinduism, Confucianism, and Islam' (ibid.). Kandiyoti is thus saying that the move of young women into their husband's patrilineal household after marriage favours a patriarchal gender ideology.

This kinship arrangement, argues Kandiyoti, creates two areas of tension where women 'bargain' with patriarchy. The first bargain is a woman's acceptance of subjugation as a young bride in return for a more elevated position as a mother-in-law later in life, provided that she gives birth to a son. The second bargain is the acceptance of male control of her movements in return for economic security provided by the husband and his family. I argue that 'classic patriarchy' and the bargains it entails are visible in many of the Kurdish Vanlı families I have met in all three research locations. As is described below, the position of the bride, the bûk, is stereotypically considered the lowest in the household, particularly when she has just married. It is the birth of children, and particularly sons, that brings her more respect at a later age, especially when she becomes a mother-in-law herself. The second bargain between spouses is also evident in many households, where women offer domesticity and modesty in return for their husbands offering financial security.

Because of migration, it is possible to see this dominant Kurdish gender paradigm being perpetuated throughout the translocational migratory social field. However, at the same time, arguably because of the creation of more weak links at school, work, associations, and religious meetings, as well as exposure to other public discourses in the media, alternative gender paradigms have been strengthened and now coexist with the dominant one. Women may internalise or at least often 'perform' according to the dominant patriarchal paradigm, but they are also increasingly exposed to different ideas on gender roles. There is thus a marked difference between generations as well as between young women who pursue an education and those who do not, as will become apparent in the following discussion.

The First Bargain: 'Being a Bride'

One implication of postmarital patrilocal residence is that women leave their natal homes, often at a young age, and live with their husbands' families (Kandiyoti 1988: 278). They are the strangers, perceived as a potential threat to the relations between sons and parents, particularly mothers (Stone 1998: 103). The same phenomenon is described in John Campbell's work in rural Greece in the 1960s, summarised by Rosaldo; '[u]pon marriage [the young woman] enters a hostile and distant household, where men and women alike resent any signs that she and her husband are close' (Rosaldo 1974: 36).

Allison quotes the Kurdish proverb *'Bumê bûk, bumê pepûk'* ('I became a bride, I became unhappy') (2000: 36). Although she emphatically points out that this proverb evokes a stereotype and that everyone is aware of its stereotypical nature, it nevertheless refers to a source of potential tension and conflict inherent in Kurdish family structures. Marriage is more of a rupture for women than for men. As discussed in the previous chapter, among my Vanlı interlocutors, there have been marriages within the same village (among relatives and non-relatives), between villages, between village and city, and between cities. In almost all cases, even if the young couple today may live separately from the husband's parents (or at least in a separate flat in the same apartment block), the couple is considered to be aligned closer to the husband's than the wife's side of the family. As Kandiyoti argues, even if a three-generation household is not always achieved, the patrilocal extended household is a 'cultural ideal' (1988: 278).

One of Ammann's Kurdish interlocutors in Europe summarised this integration of women into their affinal families:

> The bride belongs to us now, and we, my brothers and I, decide what she is allowed to do or not, her family has no say in the matter any longer.
>
> **(2000: 211, author's translation)**

Among my interlocutors, this integration could be seen, for instance, in the common disregard of the official shares of inheritance that are due to daughters and sisters from their natal families according to Turkish law. Village women have no expectations of inheriting any land or animals from their family, and I knew several who signed papers handing over their official shares to brothers. The money spent on a daughter on marriage, when furniture and white goods are bought, is sometimes argued to be a premortem inheritance.

Evidence for the 'handing over' of daughters to her affines can also be seen in the refusal to offer daughters or sisters refuge from violent or difficult husbands. Indeed, many women know better than even to ask about such a possibility. There are three hurdles to leaving the marriage; one is the anticipated public disgrace, another is the fact that Kurdish patrilineages have traditionally claimed children as their own and might force a woman to leave without them. Although Turkish courts would in most cases probably award the mother custody, many cases of separation do not make it to court. For one, there might not even be an official marriage (just a religious one), and secondly, a woman might feel pressured into obeying traditional law. A third hurdle is the fact that families may resent the financial burden of taking back a woman, perhaps also with her children, to look after her. She would face lifelong dependence on first her parents and later her brothers. That said, a study in Van found that the divorce average in the province between 1995 and 2005 increased three times as much than in the rest of Turkey ('Van'da Kuma...'). This shows that divorce is not impossible; however, there are cultural and financial constraints.

The proximity to the husband's family—geographical, psychological, or both—means that this family controls how much access a young woman has to her natal family. This uncertainty can make marriage traumatic for young women, particularly true in the past, when they were often not consulted on the parents' choice of marriage partner and when geographical distances were more difficult to overcome. Once at a wedding in Van, when the bride was picked up by her husband's family, I watched a whole room of women dissolve into hysterical tears as part of the wedding tradition that the bride (and others) should cry when she leaves her natal home. There was a sense that all the women present were re-living their own ruptures from their families and crying over the fate of women in general. The marriage was one that the young girl had wanted herself, and the women's tears were indeed spilt more for themselves or 'womankind' than for her fate.

Entering the affinal family as a bride involves certain behaviour. There are different degrees to which women adhere to such expectations, but they are all able to list explicitly behaviour that is involved. Çağlayan describes the behaviour of her female Kurdish interlocutors in Diyarbakır, who all, at least for some time, had followed such rules, and it is identical to the rules I was told about or observed among Vanlı women:

> 'Being a bride' can be evaluated as a marginal status, which, for the woman entering her husband's home, involves not speaking to her father-in-law or any males in the family and any of the females older than her, not eating in front of them, taking on the hardest work, not leaving the house, not taking her children onto her lap in front of anyone, and other behaviour.
>
> **(2007: 24, fn 6, author's translation)**

As the following examples show, Vanlı brides have negotiated differently within the constraints of the dominant gender paradigm. It has often been migration, combined with an increase in schooling, that has made a difference.

In Tepelik, I met Pelin, a woman in her thirties, who grew up in Van city. She finished high school and even sat the university entrance exam once, but then started to work to help her father with his shop after her natal family moved to Istanbul. He was a retired civil servant who opened a wholesale food store. On marriage, Pelin and her husband started to live in the flat next to her father-in-law and she had to get used to rules of modesty that she was not used to from her own family. For one, she stopped working when she got engaged. On marriage, she started covering her hair; her husband and children would like her not to, but she said that she would not change back now. She was able to list 'bride rules' for me: in front of your male elders, do not cuddle your child, do not eat, drink, or talk, and do not address your husband by name. Modest attire and ways of sitting complemented this behaviour. Pelin decided on a compromise: she did not eat with her father-in-law, but she talked to him. In addition, she had regular 'days' with her relatives and sometimes their spouses, thus encouraging her husband to become part of her kin network, too. Although she lived in a separate flat from her widowed father-in-law, she still spoke wistfully about young couples enjoying private time together in order to get to know each other. This, she said, was not really possible in most families.

Gülşen Derman came to Tepelik from the village of Gundême in marriage around 20 years ago. Her family still lived in Van and in Gundême, but she had not been back. She claimed that her husband, who was at the same time her maternal uncle's son, would let her go but that her father-in-law (her maternal uncle), who lived with them during the winter, did not want her to. Gülşen was resentful towards her only brother, who still lived in Gundême, as, she said, 'He never comes to pick me up.' It did not seem to occur to the brother that she needed someone to accompany her to Van or that he could persuade the father-in-law to let her go. Thus, she had not seen her mother or her sisters unless they visited her in Istanbul, and she had never met many of her nephews and nieces. Although Gülşen's husband was the breadwinner in the household, he seemed to have less of a say in this matter than his father. Like several other married women in Tepelik, Gülşen treated her father-in-law with deference and served him in silence.

In Tepelik, I also met Feride Abla, a woman in her fifties from a village near Gundême. She had had no formal schooling but later learnt how to read and write. Until a few years ago, she said, she followed certain rules of modesty with her older brother-in-law, a father figure for the family when the father died early. She did not eat with him, but, on his insistence, spoke with him. When her mother, who lived with a brother in Ankara, fell ill, she spent several months within the same year with her mother, going to and fro on her own, by plane or bus. There was no insistence that she be at home to cook, clean, and care for her husband and grown children during those times, and there was also no issue about her travelling on her own. In her own words, Feride Abla had 'courage' (in Turkish: 'cesaret').

In Gundême village, I once witnessed the gender hierarchy taken to extremes when elderly women of over 70 years of age refused to drink tea or eat in front of their young male relatives, consanguineous or affinal. Generally, women of all ages would stop drinking tea when male in-laws entered the room, but men would also be careful not to intrude on female gatherings in order not to disturb the comfort of guests. Meals or tea-drinking gatherings that involved more than the close family would be gender-segregated, but mixed-gender gatherings of close relatives could be very affectionate and informal. Young brides were expected to be hard-working, and any public display of affection between married couples was unheard of. I talked to a young woman who lived a five-minute walk away from her father and mother. At one point, she complained of hardly ever seeing them. Though she did not say so directly, it was implied that permission was not given easily, and that without permission she would not go. A few years later, however, she was visiting her family much more freely.

In Van, Haci Fahrettin's eldest bûk, Serap, a woman in her mid-thirties, spent several years living under the same roof as her in-laws, and had been married for nearly 20 years. She was married at the age of 16 to her 'cousin' (her father's half-brother's grandson), whom she had known from their childhood in the village. After all these years of marriage and proximity, she still would not eat in front of or speak directly to her father-in-law, something that is not unusual for her generation. If a reply was needed, it was whispered to a person close-by who acted as a mouthpiece; this could lead to five-year-old children becoming the messengers of their mothers. For situations where a direct reply was unavoidable, brides would avail themselves of non-verbal sounds and body language: 'No' was the universally recognised clicking of the tongue with raised eyebrows and a lifted chin; the 'yes' I only ever heard performed by women: a slurping sound with the tongue pressed against the back of the top front teeth and air drawn into the open mouth. For Serap, such acts of respect were so ingrained that she would not even eat with her elder brothers although they had an affectionate relationship and I had witnessed them inviting her to sit down with them. She said that she would feel ashamed.

Serap's fellow bride Muhterem, married to Haci Fahrettin's third-oldest son, also did not eat with or speak in front of her father-in-law or older in-laws either, as was common among many women of their age group and older who grew up in the village. Haci Fahrettin's second bride, however, is Turkish, and she has always eaten and spoken in the presence of her father-in-law. Finally, the fourth bride, newly arrived two years ago, is a young Kurdish woman brought up in the city by parents who had themselves migrated from a village. From the beginning, she has sat down to eat with her in-laws and also speaks to them.[3] There is thus a sense, even within this one extended family, that women are categorised according to their background and face different expectations about their behaviour. Their own socialisation into women of more or less 'voice' and presence in public makes them slip into their expected roles easily.

Many of the women I spoke to contrasted the past to now, saying, 'It used to be that mothers-in-law could make life hell for a bride, but today, you had better beware of the brides.' Implied is that young women today are sharper, less obeisant, and more demanding of certain rights.

The above examples show that no family situation is identical. Indeed, among all the families I observed, living arrangements and the character and 'chemistry' of the family members affected the expectations that a bride faced. However, my observations have led me to believe that migration has challenged the discourse that approves of the subjugation of the young bride by her affinal family. There are

several contributing factors. First, migration from villages to Van city
can mean that even if village women have married into different villages, they may eventually end up in Van, as will their natal families.
Proximity to their natal family then provides women with moral support. Younger unmarried women who have moved to Van city prefer a
marriage to someone living in the city (rather than to a villager), again
ensuring that their parents and siblings are nearby. Sevgi Çetin, for
instance, married the son of a neighbour in Van, who was at the same
time a fellow migrant Gundî. She said, 'I would be so upset if I could
not see my mother every day,' indicating the frequency of her visits.

As in the case of Gülşen Derman in Tepelik, migration to other cities
can of course mean further isolation for a bride. However, here a second
factor comes into play for the younger generation. Migration to cities
means easier access to schooling for both girls and boys, as well as a
discourse that encourages such schooling. With more schooling, young
women are less likely to marry very young and, before and after marriage, are more assertive about their own wishes. Gülşen represents the
generation of women who left the village for marriage on their own, who
received hardly any or no formal schooling, and who have thus had fewer
opportunities to shape their lives as they may have wished. Migrant
women of the next generation are likely to be socialised differently.

Third, migration implies waged labour for the young men who
have left their village and thus a shift in intergenerational relations.
Families may live in smaller units, or, even if in extended forms, with
curbed power of the father. The elder generation may still be accorded
respect, but the decisions of fathers (-in-law) no longer have as much
influence. As young women realise that they are not necessarily going
to replicate the extended patrilocal household of their elders and thus
may not achieve the status of a dominant mother-in-law later in life,
they are less willing to put their own lives on hold.

In summary, due to migration there is a higher likelihood of young
married women having a support network of natal family members
nearby, education levels and thus the age of marriage are likely to rise,
and financial dependence of the young generation on the older one is
lower. All these factors make it easier to challenge the subordinated
position of *bûks*.

The Second Bargain: Deserving Wives and Fastidious Domesticity

A second potential source of tension in patrilineal patrilocal families is the division of loyalty of a married man. According to Kandiyoti, mothers have to rely on their sons to look after them in old age, and it is in their interest to keep the sons bound to them by bonds of affection that are stronger than those that tie the sons to their wives:

> Older women have a vested interest in the suppression of romantic love between youngsters to keep the conjugal bond secondary and to claim sons' primary allegiance. Young women have an interest in circumventing and possibly evading their mother-in-law's control.
>
> **(1988: 278)**

In the case of Vanlı, it is both older women and men who are vying for their sons' primary loyalty. This becomes even more vital when migration has occurred. Before migration, fathers (and through them the mothers) were able to keep sons in line by controlling the land that represented the family's economic survival. With the move to the city, however, the older generation has lost symbolic and economic capital. The elder generation often cannot claim a government pension and is absolutely dependent on the continuing loyalty of their sons. They have even more of a vested interest in continuing a sexual paradigm of female subordination and loyalty to the patrilineage. Young women who marry into the family thus have to 'earn' the economic security that their husbands offer them by conforming to expectations of domesticity, modesty, and seclusion (Kandiyoti 1988: 280); this is the second patriarchal bargain.

Domesticity, says Kandiyoti, is one of the qualities that 'good wives' offer their husbands in exchange for being looked after financially. This is true not only among many of my Kurdish Vanlı interlocutors but has also been found in other studies in Turkey. Bora and Üstün, reporting on gender regimes in Turkey, write that women are judged on their cleanliness and ability to create a home (2005: 43–4). In their work on the Black Sea region of Turkey, the Hanns report a usage of 'dirty' (*pis*) with connotations of dishonour, used as an antonym to '*namuslu*' (honourable) (Hann and Hann 1992: 4). In the same vein, my surprise at the extreme cleanliness and domesticity of Vanlı women was inevitably met with the reply, 'I am sure you are very clean yourself.' Implied was a general approval of my character and that, with such a character, it was unthinkable that my home could be dirty or untidy. This aspect of good womanhood had been internalised by women in all three research locations, but was more notable in Van city and in Tepelik than in the village, partly because other duties took up so much of the women's time there. However, the industry of women would there manifest itself in their performance of agricultural as well as domestic duties. The following examples of such performances are all scenes from 2006:

In Gundême, it is seven o'clock. Elif Çetin, an unmarried young woman in her early twenties, has been awake for quite some time, helping her mother to milk the cows before they are taken up the mountain. She comes back to the house, wakes up her sleeping siblings, tidies away the mattresses, and lays out the *sofra* on the ground of the central living room for breakfast. She goes back and forth between the kitchen area in the house and the *xanî* (where the bread is kept and water has been heating) and then lays out breakfast for the family. After breakfast, it is time to clean the house—only when that is finished will she feel she has earned a sit-down. Most days she hoovers the rooms. Since the nozzle of the hoover is broken, she has to make do with the shortened pipe and vigorously pushes it to and fro along the floor. Vigour is in all of her actions; when she brushes the entrance parlour that gets very dusty, she uses a short straw brush without a stick and sweeps powerfully, bending her tall body to reach the floor and all the corners. Although farm life brings many other duties, too, the basic cleaning of the house is a daily morning ritual. There is no bride in the family to help Elif and her mother, so that she is responsible for more duties than other young unmarried women. What Elif does now as an unmarried woman is what she will do as a married woman, too.

In Van, it is half past seven. Serap Çetin, wife of Mehmet Çetin, wakes her husband so that he can have a shower and get dressed and ready for work. She then goes into the kitchen, heats water on the gas stove for tea, and prepares breakfast. Together with her husband and maybe the children, she has breakfast in the kitchen. Then, she too, starts to clean the house. It has only been two years that Serap and her husband Mehmet have been living in their flat, on the third (and top) floor of an apartment. They first lived with Mehmet's parents, Haci Fahrettin and Melek, and then shared a flat with Mehmet's brother Ali and his family for years. Serap cherishes the fact that the building and a lot of the fittings are new and that the flat is her territory alone. It is a matter of pride and good housewifery for her to keep the place spotless. The place is dusted and hoovered daily and special care is taken not to dirty the cream-coloured carpets in the living room. The bathroom and toilet are cleaned nearly every day, too, as are the two balconies, and Serap often looks critically at her windows to see if they are clean. Serap is also an accomplished cook, but she recounts how she knew nothing about housework when she got married at 16. As she was the youngest daughter, there had been plenty of *bûks*, the wives of her older brothers, who had proven their own domesticity and industry through hard work.

In Tepelik, Hediye prepares breakfast for her husband and two children and herself. They sit around a cloth on the floor in the living room and eat. After the husband leaves for work, it is time for the morning jobs here, too. The place is dusted and hoovered every day. The mirrors, TV screen, and glass fronts of the living room cupboards are also polished daily. The bathroom and toilet are also cleaned most days, as is the balcony, which looks out to the front. For Hediye, cleaning the flat every day is both a pleasure and duty.

The intensity with which the women's bodies are engaged in these cleaning activities is high in all three locations. Skirts may be tied up, old clothes worn, bodies bent and stretched in pursuit of cleanliness. Detergent is used generously to ensure absolute hygiene. In Van and in Tepelik, especially where the women often have no animal or bread-baking duties, the 'morning duties', the *sabah işleri*, are taken very seriously. Walking up the staircases in the apartment blocks in Tepelik in the mornings, I was able to hear the sound of hoovers coming from behind different doors.

The *sabah işleri* were activities that women chose to perform every day, in which they compared themselves to others, and in which they also took pride. To this everyday cleaning was added spring cleaning (after the coal stove had been put away) and also a special clean before the two *bayrams* (religious festivals), which involved washing the inside walls and curtains, too. In the summer, carpets and woollen duvets were washed outside or on balconies, a strenuous activity visible to all the neighbours; of course, these neighbours would notice a lack of activity.

The discursive construction of a 'good' wife is embodied in the housework she does. The knowledge that other women may judge her character by the cleanliness of the house fuels this enthusiasm for cleaning. When a woman is described as *'temiz'* (clean), this refers both to her sense of hygiene and her moral worth. One woman in the Tepelik blocks was praised as being *'titiz'* (fastidious), both a compliment to the cleanliness of her house and her general character.

As has been indicated above, village women have less time to spend on housework as they may also tend gardens, milk animals, bake bread, prepare *sergîn* (the fuel made from cow dung), and make dairy products. Furthermore, cleaning the house in the village routinely seems more of a necessity in an environment where more dirt is carried into the house from work on fields, with animals, in the *xanî*, and often from a more crowded household. The—to my eyes—excessive cleaning in the city thus seems a new way of validating oneself, of showing one's ability for hard work. Just as women in the village may be praised for being quick-footed and hard-working (cf. Yalçın 1986: 96), women in the city are praised for being fastidious. Implied in both manners of praise is the idea that a woman kept busy with worthwhile activities has no time to stray.

Returning to Kandiyoti's concept of classic patriarchy, these women are keeping up their side of the bargain by embodying the ideal of a 'clean', hard-working woman concerned with and keeping herself to the domestic sphere.[4] In Turkey in general, women as home makers are still preferred (Bora and Üstün 2005: 48), as can also be seen in official statistics: 72.9 per cent of the paid workforce in Turkey is male (TÜİK 2008).

Men are thus pushed towards keeping their side of the bargain. The discourse on a 'good wife' is matched by one on the 'good husband'. Several women in Tepelik described their satisfaction with their husbands purely in terms of the absence of negative attributes: '*Çok şükür,*[5] he doesn't hit me,[6] he doesn't drink, and he doesn't gamble.' The ultimate bonus was if a husband also prayed five times a day, but this was not considered as important as female piety. One middle-aged woman was able to tell me about different Vanlı men in the blocks whether they drank alcohol (which she disapproved of) or not, showing that the behaviour of men is also monitored, if not controlled as much as that of women. A good husband did not stay out late, did not gallivant around with other women, did not waste the income needed to look after home and children, and did not beat his wife.

Some of these concerns may be a corollary of urban life. In Gundême at least, alcohol is not sold in the village shops and drinking in public is inconceivable. In addition, although a patrilineal extended family can potentially make a *bûk's* life misery, her parents-in-law may also play an important role in moderating a husband's negative behaviour towards his wife or discouraging him from being unfaithful. Domestic violence of husbands is thus just as likely in the nuclear households that are becoming more common in the city.[7] Opportunities for gambling are more frequent in the city, too. If a man becomes unemployed in the city, either through misfortune or laziness, this affects his wife and children much more than in the village; there, women produce a lot of foodstuff themselves, but without money the city quickly becomes a nightmare. Finally, away from the confines of a small village it is easier for men to have affairs if they so choose.

Çağlayan points out that women who have migrated to the city from villages consider being a 'housewife' a gain in status, since the work they have to carry out is much less strenuous than village work (2007: 47). She clearly says, however, that this sense of status gain is only observable among those who migrated voluntarily. The catastrophic proportions of the forced migration in the 1990s, particularly to Diyarbakır, have created immense urban poverty (*ibid.*). Çelik cites Erman's interlocutors, who were happy that they had more leisure time compared to the village, but also points out that Kurdish-speaking women tied to the home with no acquaintances were very lonely (Çelik 2005: 146).

If, as was also the case for my Vanlı interlocutors, the work of women has been reduced, an undesired consequence of this may be that women face the threat of becoming 'dispensable'. This, to me, explains the vigour of urban domesticity for the middle generation: away from the village, women have recourse to fewer acts of labour and domesticity to prove their worth, yet there are perhaps more temptations for men to give up on the bargain.

As will be discussed below, migration has meant that the new generation of women is likely to complete high school and many may even go to university and work later. It is foreseeable that acquiescence in both patriarchal bargains is then reduced, which may result in less influence of the discourse idealising female domesticity.

Portable Seclusion

As Vanlı women keep their side of the bargain in the home, they also extend their performance of acceptable gender behaviour to the public sphere. In the following discussion, I make use of Abu-Lughod's adoption of anthropologist Hanna Papanek's term 'portable seclusion' for the veiling of women (Abu-Lughod 2002). While Papanek used the term to talk about the *burqa* in Pakistan in the 1980s, Abu-Lughod extends the term to describe 'markers, whether *burqas* or other forms of cover, that were supposed to assure [women's] protection in the public sphere from the harassment of strange men by symbolically signalling that they were still in the inviolable space of their homes, even though moving in the public realm' (2006). Inspired by Harris' ethnographic description of Tajik women, I would like to extend the term even further to include not only the attire of women but also other aspects of their behaviour in public, such as the avoidance of certain spaces and situations and body language that women adopt in order to keep up the appearance of modesty.

Harris discusses the fact that traditional gender norms were impossible to maintain in Sovietised Tajik society as seclusion and veiling became impossible. However, she notes that new gender performances took the place of old ones, speaking of 'material veiling giv[ing] way to the virtual veiling of gender masks' (2004: 58). Among my Kurdish interlocutors there was awareness and performance of both material and virtual veiling. Female modesty outside of the home was maintained through clothing, a subdued manner of speaking and walking, the tendency to keep to the neighbourhood, and an avoidance of eye contact and conversation with unknown males.

In the village, Vanlı women were often outside of the home to perform agricultural tasks. The relatively small population of a village meant that their behaviour outside of the home was controlled by the gaze of members of the gender-age hierarchy. When women walked through the village to other houses, they would do so in the manner considered appropriate. They would walk in pairs or groups, keeping their voices low and their eyes on the path ahead, choosing the most direct route. Should they meet someone they knew, they would greet them quietly and modestly. There was a gradation of acceptable ventures outside for different age groups of women. Young unmarried women and new brides in particular were kept closer to the home, and their behaviour in public was observed more closely. As a *bûk* myself, I realised that I felt uncomfortable breaching these conventions and thus restricted myself to visits to neighbouring and relative households (cf. Abu-Lughod 1985: 638).

Because of this emphasis on the control of public female behaviour, men (and older women) may feel that a move to the city brings with it manifold threats and temptations 'out there' waiting to target their wives, daughters, sisters, and daughters-in-law. Considering the fact that they feel entitled as well as obliged to guard the honour of 'their' women, this can lead to a great deal of tension as women in the city almost inevitably enter the public sphere. In the city, women go outside to do the shopping (cf. Çağlayan 2007: 50–1), whereas in the village, much less shopping is done as much of the food is produced by the women themselves—there is no need to buy milk, yoghurt, cheese, butter, eggs, meat, or bread, and many households have become increasingly successful at planting a variety of fruit and vegetables. In Gundême, men used to bring certain goods, such as tea and sugar, from the city in bulk. I often witnessed children rather than (younger) women going to the grocery store when something was needed. The children sometimes had to go twice, once to ask a price and once again to buy the goods, but this seemed preferable to the women going themselves and looking at the wares. However, in the city, shopping becomes an almost daily chore and is mostly left to the women as the men are ideally working. Women in Tepelik would also take their children to school and interact with the teachers there. They would also venture further afield to visit other women in their homes, to go to the doctor's, or to meet for a religious gathering.

Women who adhere to the dominant Kurdish gender discourse have internalised the fact that there should be no 'stain' on their honour (Çağlayan 2007: 61), so they act accordingly, adopting a kind of 'portable seclusion' (Abu-Lughod 2002: 785) with their attire and demeanour. All of the middle-aged and elderly women I met in Tepelik wore headscarves, thus making their ventures outside acceptable. Some wore the village covering at home, but outside (and even inside), many women wore more 'urban' headscarves. In the city, if only in the presence of women in a home, they might take their head covering off. In Gundême, the light cotton *laçık* or *yazma* was so much part of women's basic clothing that they would only use the absence of men to adjust their head coverings if they were slipping, but never felt the need to take them off. Clothes in these age groups were of a baggy nature in the village, often with many layers worn on top of each other. In the city, women might choose a more tailored look, but most still wore a *pardesü*, a long coat, over their clothes. Trousers were rarer, but the more urban style of *tesettür* (being covered) may include a tailored *pardesü* over trousers. One young woman in Tepelik who was being encouraged by her mother to cover said she was willing to do so if her mother would buy her three sets of matching headscarf, skirt, shoes, and bag; this shows that urban manners of covering are not devoid of fashion trends and not cheap.

Apart from attire, another aspect of portable seclusion, as put forward by and also controlled by both men and women, may involve the avoidance of certain spaces or situations. It is, for instance, considered unacceptable for members of the opposite sex who are not close family members to spend time together alone in an enclosed space, lest they be accused of inappropriate behaviour. Women may also withdraw from large gatherings of men even in their own home, the women sitting in one room while the men gather in another. Thus, even in urban areas, women create pockets of female space or avoid particular male spaces, such as a *kahve*, a men's hairdresser's, or the area for males in the mosque. When in contact with males, such as with salespersons in shops or at the market, familiarity is discouraged.

Portable seclusion is also practised by closing off part of the body with modest body language. This may involve averting one's gaze from passers-by or not looking directly in the eyes of someone from the opposite sex. Delaney describes the same behaviour in a Turkish village, 'In order to preserve her reputation, a girl participates in her own enclosure: she averts her eyes when unrelated men are around' (1991: 42). The same was found by Campbell in rural Greece, where '[a]n adolescent girl is taught early to limit her movements, to walk modestly, and never to run [. . .] if she so much as looks eye to eye with a man she is thought to invite assault' (Rosaldo 1974: 36).

I was able to witness the difference in male and female body language very clearly in Tepelik in two particular incidents. One day Doğan Bey, the head of the Vanlı hometown association at Tepelik, offered to introduce me to his unmarried niece Ceylan, a woman in her early twenties. She lived with her brother and his family in close neighbourhood to the blocks. To get there, Doğan Bey and I walked slowly up the hill, passing the Vanlı housing blocks to the left and right, turned right and passed the Vanlı association building, then walking straight on, past the local primary school and the local mosque, then turned right again and went down the hill to where Ceylan lived. Doğan Bey was greeted by many people on the way, and it was clear that this was the route he was used to taking, and that he enjoyed being seen and making eye and verbal contact with people. The housing blocks, the association building, the mosque, and the school all represented places where he was known and respected.

I experienced a very different way of walking when, after a second visit to Ceylan's house on my own, she accompanied me back to Doğan Bey's house. I was prepared to use the route I had walked with him and had also used on my own to find her home, and I was surprised when she pulled me in the opposite direction. We walked to the bottom of the hill, and took a route along a narrow road between houses. It turned out to be a shorter route, and Ceylan walked with a determined stride, a serious expression on her face and her eyes fastened to the ground or on me. The contrast between her and her uncle struck me as enormous. Doğan Bey had savoured the attention he received by walking slowly and on a more 'public' route. Ceylan, on the other hand, was trying not to attract attention by walking fast, choosing the shortest and most 'hidden' route, and by controlling both clothing (wearing *tesettür*) and her body language in order to portray herself as a modest woman. Indeed, in her case, control over her movements went beyond Tepelik; she mentioned that her parents living in Van would get to hear of inappropriate attire or behaviour.

How much other men and women feel they have the right to interfere with or talk about a woman's public behaviour depends on three criteria. The first is age; elderly people are accorded the right to criticise younger people, and in turn become more immune to criticism themselves. However, both in Van city and Tepelik young women and men could also keep up appearances by listening politely to their elders and then acting as they saw fit. A second criterion is how close-knit a network of relations is. If, for instance, a family owns a business that serves the community of their relatives and neighbours, they will be much more sensitive to insinuations that a daughter, daughter-in-law, or wife has behaved inappropriately in public. Lastly, the dependence of a woman on approval by her environment lessens dramatically when she herself has access to weak social ties, through work for instance.

To summarise, women both in the village and in the city use physical and symbolic veiling as a means of 'portable seclusion' when leaving the house. Migration has made a difference in the translocational migratory social field in that it has led to more schooling for children, both in migrant families and 'back home', as well as exposure to different kinds of lives in the city. This in turn has led to exposure to a competing gender paradigm, so that every woman and every family now negotiates their own adherence to or disregard for rules. A guiding principle here, both to her and her environment, is whether she is going to school or working professionally or whether she spends most of her day at home. This distinction, which has emerged through migration and social remittances, is discussed further below.

In the following, I discuss how rural-urban migration of Vanlı has meant that alternative gender discourses have been created. The domesticity and portable seclusion of the married middle-aged and elderly women today represent only one role model that young women have. Through schooling and work, and thus more independent networks of friends and colleagues, that is, weak links, they participate in the creation of different norms for women.

Renegotiating Domesticity after Migration: 'Housegirls' or Education and Work

Migration has played an important role in the current coexistence of competing sexual paradigms. There are, broadly speaking, two types of woman recognised in Kurdish (and also Turkish) society, both in villages and cities. One type is the 'ev kızı', the 'housegirl'. Following more traditional gender expectations, she may go to school for some time until she becomes 'too old' (i.e. until she matures into a young woman) or until her parents decide that she should take over certain domestic duties (such as helping with the care of animals, the production of dairy produce, looking after younger siblings, or relieving the mother of cooking and cleaning).

The second type is that of the young woman who has completed high school and may also strive for a university education. As pointed out earlier, seasonal migration, combined with concerted efforts by the state, has led to a dramatic increase in schooling among Vanlı, and many girls are sent to school for a longer time, both in rural areas and in cities. According to a recent study with 200 women in Van city, 62.5 per cent of the women, most of whom had had very little formal education themselves, would like their daughters to have as much education as they want. Only 9 per cent of these women believed that a primary school education was enough for their daughters (Tunç 2004: 8). Parents of teenagers will today consider paying money for private cram schools that prepare their daughters (and also sons) for the central university exam; in Van and Istanbul, many Vanlı children attend such cram schools.

The girls who are sent to high school (and university) are taught a very different gender paradigm at school. They have female teachers as role models, socialise in mixed-gender classes, and they are exposed to a strongly Kemalist discourse on gender equality.[8] Their parents are well-aware of these differences, and allowing a daughter to continue school is thus an implicit acceptance of the fact that 'times are changing.' Indeed, if one looks at statistics nationwide, one sees both the effect of the traditional sexual paradigm, which kept girls at home (and out of education), and a change in attitudes over more recent years (Table 12).

Thus, in the age group of 44 and upwards, 29.37 per cent of women, but only 7.28 per cent of men are illiterate, a rather large gap. The difference in literacy rates does not necessarily mean that all the men in the oldest age category attended school. Rather, for male Kurdish villagers, the obligatory military service was often the time when they learned how to speak, read, and write Turkish before the advent of television and more widespread migration made Turkish more commonplace. Although the percentage of illiteracy is still higher for women of younger ages than for men, the difference is today much less dramatic.

In an increasing number of quite conservative families in Turkey there is now a sense that if young women adhere to a code of relatively modest public behaviour (i.e. if they 'keep up appearances'), they will be granted the support to continue their education and shape their future lives. This attitude is also becoming apparent in Van as more girls are attending high school. These young women hope for professional employment as a result of their efforts and they are then also judged by a different sexual paradigm from that of the 'housegirls' (cf. Çağlayan 2007: 53).

Table 12: Illiteracy Rates according to Age and Gender in Turkey

Age	Women	Men
18–28	3.54%	1.05%
29–43	8.33%	1.52%
44 and older	29.37%	7.28%
Turkey Average: 3.39%		

Source: 'Biz Kimiz?' Research by Milliyet/KONDA

As rural families have moved to Van, new standards have been set as to what kind of freedom is given young women to move around outside of the house. Those continuing their education go to school and may also attend cram schools in the city centre at the weekends. *Ev kızları* may visit neighbours and relatives, go to the corner shops in the neighbourhood, while others, voluntarily or involuntarily, confine themselves to the house and garden for most of the time.

In Van city, I have only met three young unmarried women who worked outside of the home for some time. Two cousins spent a summer working in a small factory, preparing little mosaic tiles to be stuck onto housing fronts. For one of the girls, it was an opportunity to earn much-needed money for the family while the father was unable to work, and this allowed her to continue her high school education. Her cousin had left school at an earlier age; it might be that the two girls going to work together was more acceptable to the families than one going on her own. The work was almost exclusively done by girls, and the workshop was near their homes. Another young woman with incomplete schooling, a daughter of a widow living in Van, spent some time working at a health centre, but later gave up the job and has not worked since.

In the city of Van, the arrival of national and international clothing and supermarket chains has meant that there has been an increase in demand for female labour at check-out desks and as sales assistants. Although this kind of work does not carry any stigma in itself, there is a sense among many of my Vanlı interlocutors that the young women of their own family should either stay at home if they have left or finished school, helping their mothers with the housekeeping tasks, or continue their education in order to achieve a more professional status as, for instance, teachers or nurses (both considered ideal employment for women). Since it is the young generation of women who are achieving or have achieved professional status, it remains to be seen what will happen when they marry. There may be, as is the case among many Turkish families as well, pressure put on the women to stop working when they marry, or at the latest when children arrive. On the other hand, these young women may insist on continuing to work.

Among families in Van, there is usually a striking threshold visible within one generation, a threshold before which many young women (and men) married early and after which their younger siblings have received much more schooling. This threshold is related to migration from the village to Van. This can be exemplified with cases from the Çetin lineage.

In Süleyman Amca's family, all his daughters were well grown up before this change in attitude. One of his daughters never even had her own ID card before marriage and was given that of an older sister who had died, an indication that there was never much concern with getting her registered for school or for any other purposes. The two youngest daughters were in their twenties before they married (the last one in 2008), which is still considered quite a late age for young women without much schooling. Süleyman's oldest son Abdullah has continued with 'the old mindset'. He and his wife have had nine children, which, even now that they have their own flat in Van, makes it difficult to make ends meet. However, their oldest child, a girl, has just been admitted to university, after her parents and some relatives supported her studies, both financially and morally. The second child, also a girl, has also set her sights on a university education, and it is widely thought that she will succeed. These two daughters were spurred on to do well at school by seeing the difficulties their own mother faced with too little education and too many children. In turn, it was only the girls' success at school that prompted other relatives to offer support—they would probably not have been allowed to stay at school as only average students. Finally, it was only migration that made it possible for them to attend secondary school and then private cram courses in the first place.

In Haci Fahrettin's family, there was also a distinct change after the family moved to Van from Gundême. The older children all left school early or had no formal education, and the oldest son and daughter were married with little say in the matter. The next daughter, Dilan, was a bright pupil who gained a scholarship for middle school (sixth to eighth grade in the old system). However, as she still recounts with bitterness more than 15 years later, she was unable to take up her place as her birth had been registered incorrectly and not enough was done to rectify the mistake. Dilan has had to watch as her two younger sisters have gone all the way to university, the youngest one even leaving

Van to study in Ankara. However, Dilan has registered in adult education classes and is working on completing a high school diploma and then aims for a distance learning university degree. She is in her mid-twenties, but her parents have made no particular efforts to find a husband for her. I sense in their reluctance and in Dilan's quiet waiting a certain dilemma. Dilan has grown up in the city. Besides her remarkable housekeeping skills she has also made efforts to educate herself further. A suitable husband would have to match her intellectually, which might mean a university education, but such a young man may prefer a wife with a university education. In any case, it is still difficult for women who are at home to meet suitable husbands themselves; rather, they have to wait until a suitor and his family come for a visit.

There is no question that Haci Fahrettin's grandchildren, be they boys or girls, will all be offered the opportunity to finish high school, if not more. One granddaughter, in her second-last year of school, is dreaming of studying medicine at a renowned university in Ankara. Her brother, a year older, on the other hand, was not interested in school and even had to resit some classes of the last year in order to obtain his high school diploma. There has never been much disappointment expressed in his lacklustre performance, but the whole extended family has high hopes for his sister. Again, growing up in Van, in close proximity to schools and in an environment where schooling for girls and boys is now taken for granted, means that the young women of the family are offered the same educational opportunities as the young men. Indeed, they may be even keener to take up these opportunities.

In Tacit Amca's family, the oldest girl, Fatma, was also married young, at the age of 16, and again, there was not much concern for her wishes. The next daughter, Elif, now in her mid-twenties, had some primary school education, but was taken out of school to help her mother look after the younger children. Later, when still in the village, she started adult education classes with her younger brother Ihsan. Although there have been offers of marriage, neither she nor her parents are in a hurry to accept any. In all the families mentioned so far there seems to be more reluctance to let go of the younger daughters.

They represent help and companionship for mothers, who are slowly ageing after a life of hard work and many children. In addition, I believe, the increase in education among girls has raised the age after which parents worry that their girls will 'stay at home' (i.e. not find a husband). The study in Van mentioned above also found a correlation between the years of schooling and marriage age (Tunç 2004: 12).

Elif's younger sister Hatice has had a circuitous route to education. She grew up in the village and attended the village school for five years. Her parents were then encouraged to send her to the boarding school in the district town, from which she would come home at the weekend. Hatice was very unhappy there. There seems to have been a distinct lack of psychological care for the young girls (11 or 12 years old), who were scared at night, and having to travel home every week-end was also a financial burden. Most importantly, probably, Hatice's parents were at that time also exposed to the pressure of village opinion, which held that Hatice 'had grown too much'; presumably, they did not offer much moral support for Hatice to continue her education. In short, she left school after sixth grade and enrolled in the same adult education classes as her two older siblings. When her older brother Abdullah moved to Van after finishing university, he took her and her younger brother Tahsin to live with him and enrolled them in school in Van. Hatice then completed school there two years later than normal and, supported by her brothers, also attended university exam preparation classes. She then came to Istanbul, where she lives with four of her brothers and a cousin and works in her eldest brother's company as a bookkeeper. Parallel to her work, she has started a distance learning degree course in business, which will later give her the choice to work in different companies or to qualify further as a chartered accountant. Finally, her youngest sister Güler, aged 14, is being handed her education on a plate. Tacit Amca's family has now moved to Van completely, and she can walk to school in ten minutes.

Tacettin Çetin (middle son of Mahir) is a small wiry man, who has been tired out by working on building sites for many years. In his late forties, he has got seven children, and the first five are daughters. The first daughter married in her late teens, and has now got two children herself. The second daughter, Gamze, is now also going to marry young. I do not mean to imply here that they have been forced to do so; rather, when a girl is not preoccupied with schooling, there is a universal sense that 'she might as well' marry. The two older sisters were both excited and happy before their weddings. The three younger daughters, however, one of whom had to give up school when the family still lived in the village, have continued school and are successful pupils; they have even gained scholarships to support their schooling. They all have visions of studying for the university entrance exam and of going to university, and their parents are supporting them. Although this vision will probably mean financial sacrifices, the parents believe that education will offer their daughters a better life.

Musa Amca (son of Haci Kasım Çetin) has eight children; the first five and the last one are girls. At one point, he was urged to remarry in order to have sons (since the blame for the many girls was laid at his wife's door). His first five daughters are all vivacious self-confident young women, who have had little formal schooling but are very accomplished in handicrafts and other home-making skills. They all married in their late teens, and the last three daughters all married within two years. Again, in this family there is no sense that the girls were forced into marriage early; indeed, the second daughter insisted on her choice of partner in the face of initial family resistance. The youngest daughter is six years old, and it is likely, especially now that the family has moved to Van, that she will go to school for as long as she wants.

This striking difference in education levels within one generation is not limited to the Çetin lineage, but can be seen repeated all over Van. The wife of Haci Fahrettin's son Erhan, Gülnur, for instance, is the second of five daughters. She and her sister have married, though not at a very early age. Gülnur married in her mid-twenties. Her three younger sisters all managed to pass the university exam and enter university in 2008, and all of them are studying outside of Van. Like Haci Fahrettin's own daughter in Ankara, they live in student dormitories. Allowing an unmarried daughter to live away from the family home, let alone in a different city, is a very recent concession to the competing gender paradigm that migration has encouraged.

I would like to reiterate that not every young woman who has married at a young age or has not had much schooling leads an unhappy life. Rather, there is a sense that new values have been offered, which allows families and young women to choose between different lives. There is thus no stigma attached to women choosing to stay at home and marrying early, just as there is often no longer a stigma attached to sending an adolescent girl to school. In Gundême, this can be seen in the high percentage of girls sent to school in Beyazlı, and in Van anecdotal evidence abounds, although there are still many cases of girls being taken out of school early. Critical is the question of whether the wishes of daughters and parents always coincide.

In Tepelik, where I taught English to Vanlı children, the majority of my pupils were female, and nearly all the girls in the blocks were aiming for at least a high school diploma. One girl dropped out of school by herself since she wanted to wear a headscarf,[9] but she continued her secondary school studies through an adult education programme. Another girl left school because her family said they could not afford her education. The girl worked in a textile workshop for a while and then gave it up to do piece work at home. Finally, however, there was one girl whose parents had withdrawn her from school after eight years, despite her protests. The mother said that her own parents had not let her learn how to read and write, to which the daughter replied, 'Well, why did you not let me go to school then?' The mother shrugged her shoulders helplessly and answered, 'The people around us, you know, they said that girls who go to school are prostitutes.' Since different value systems currently coexist, there may thus be conflicts between young women and their parents and extended families as to their future, as well as different expectations harboured by young women themselves.

Returning to the description of 'being a bride' above, my observations in different families in all three research locations have convinced me that higher education levels among women (and the men they marry) lead to an abandonment of many of the avoidance rules that *bûks* are expected to follow; the women themselves are perhaps older when they marry, and thus less cowed by the experience of entering a new family; in addition, their education level leads their affines to expect, in Friedl's words, different 'assemblages' of gender attributes.

The widespread migration from village to city among Vanlı has led to a questioning of the dominant gender paradigm for the younger generation. While young women are still held to standards of modest public behaviour, they are also increasingly offered educational opportunities. The current situation is one of different gender discourses coexisting. Thus, within the same age group, one can see young women already married with a child or two, others helping their mothers at home and 'waiting for a husband', others (in the city) working in semi-skilled jobs out of financial necessity, and others again continuing their education. Migration has definitely enabled more young women to go to school longer if they wish to do so and if their families let them, and this in turn has encouraged different ideas on appropriate female behaviour.

Work inside and outside of the Home

As was pointed out above, migration has led to the coexistence of different discourses on gender, which are then used to expect different behaviour from Vanlı women considered to be in different categories. Similarly, Çağlayan reports on the differentiation into two types of working Kurdish women in Diyarbakır. Those with professional jobs, she reports, have gained status, also among the families of their husbands, and they have been freed from many restrictions and burdens. Those, on the other hand, who work as unskilled labourers out of financial necessity do not achieve any status gain, and housework awaits them as a second shift when they return home (2007: 53). This distinction of types of working women is common in Turkey (Bora and Üstün 2005: 77–9), discouraging the work of many women in unskilled or semi-skilled labour.

Of the married women in Tepelik I talked to none worked outside of the home at the time. Many of the 'housewives' did however take part in the piece work market. In Tepelik, as well as in the city of Van, some women gave other women the opportunity to earn money by preparing items for the trousseau of young girls. The trousseau is still considered an essential part of a young woman's possessions, even if she herself does not know how to make all the things in it any longer.[10] If the mother cannot cope with the workload, or if a neighbour or friend is known to be particularly skilful, then work is handed out. During my fieldwork in Tepelik, Hediye, for instance, completed seventeen *lif*, a kind of face cloth crocheted out of synthetic wool. She was given the wool and was paid 3 Turkish Liras (around 1.5 Euros) a piece. Although the price was standard, the degree of workmanship may differ depending on the relationship the two women have. In this case, Hediye was making the *lif* for a close neighbour from the same district, and she spent a lot of time and energy on making each *lif* special.

In Istanbul (and other cities), women also have the opportunity to earn money by taking piece work from women who act as 'middlemen' for larger textile companies whose products may then be exported to other countries. The pay is worse, but the flexible arrangement suits many of the women with small children. If a woman has taken on too much work, she can call on other women to help her finish the sewing. I often came across several women sitting busily, trying to meet a deadline. The understanding was that such favours were returned or that the woman asking for the favour would pay the other woman her share at the end of the month.

White analyses this kind of piece work very perceptively as an exploitation of culture-specific gender roles of the urban poor by globablisation forces. Women are underpaid as they are considered to be doing something considered 'natural'. Since they are working at home, their work is not seen as 'real' work. This illusion allows men, who want to remain the main wage earners, to permit this work and simultaneously allows middlemen to underpay the home workers (1994: 1–8). Kandiyoti also points out that women forego economically more advantageous work outside of the house in order to remain respectable; they are thus exploited by the labour market (1988: 280). As Wedel says about Kurdish migrant women doing piece work at home in Istanbul, 'with this ideology, their production is devalued and a relationship of exploitation is concealed' (1997: 161, author's translation). In Tepelik, husbands did not seem to appreciate the money earned by women through piece work. Several of my interlocutors packed away beads and threads as soon as their husbands came home, saying that they complained about it. Nevertheless, the women felt that their earnings allowed them to spend some money on clothes for their children or kitchen items they could not otherwise afford.

As for the younger generation of Vanlı in Istanbul, some young women in Tepelik worked in professional jobs. One woman in her twenties, divorced and living with her parents, worked as a lawyer. Another young woman worked in an insurance company, and yet another had an office job, too. There was a real sense that these women were judged by different standards from their non-working peers. The first, for instance, was able to divorce her husband and return to her parents' home, an act not all parents would countenance, partly because of what others might say. The second woman, Aynur, also in her twenties, lived with her mother's father, her mother's brother, and his wife and children. Aynur's sister-in-law reported that the older man had previously tried to have more control over his granddaughter's movements, but that Aynur had always resisted. She socialised with friends outside of work and did not see why she should have to be accountable to her grandfather. The third woman was also free in her movements, and married a young man of her choice. Her husband was an Alevi, a choice that raised some people's eyebrows, but was accepted by her family, another indication of how much trust was placed in educated girls being able to make informed decisions.

There is thus a marked contrast in the way women with different education levels are treated. Indeed, the concept of *ev kızı* shows that the expectation of a girl with little education is that she help her mother at home until she marries and becomes an *ev hanımı*, a housewife. It is often only financial necessity that pushes families into letting their daughters work. In Tepelik, I met one young woman who worked in one of the several grocery stores her family ran; her case was not one of financial necessity, but she was working under the supervision of her father and uncle. Two other young women, less well-off, worked in textile workshops. These workshops are often in cramped, badly lit locations where women and men work long hours for meagre wages, often without being insured.

As touched upon earlier, according to the dominant Kurdish gender discourse it is acceptable for unmarried girls to work, but they should cease to do so after marriage, as was the case for Pelin in Tepelik. Pelin worked for three years, but stopped when she married and has not worked since.

Had Pelin gone to university, she might have continued to work after marriage. However, depending on character and family circumstances, a woman with less education can also persuade her husband and in-laws that she can be a wife and mother *and* work. Ayla, another woman in her thirties in Tepelik, was a case in point. She was still bitter about the fact that her parents did not let her complete high school (she only went to school for five years, despite the school being very close) and that she had to start working at a young age. When she got married at the age of 19, her father told her that now she was married she should not work any longer. This made her very angry. She told me that she asked her father, 'When I was working under your roof, was I prostituting myself that now you consider it dishonourable to work?' She *did* work, first in textile workshops and later at a government office. Her mother looked after her children when she went to work. However, Ayla was later forced to stop working when her mother gave up the child care. Ayla was bitter as she felt that her mother's health problems were an excuse that masked the general disapproval of her working. She repeatedly told me that she wanted to provide her children with a happier and wealthier childhood than she had had herself, and she saw herself engaged in a struggle with financial difficulties and ignorance around her in order to achieve this. She was willing to work at any job to provide a good living standard for her children (she repeatedly and dramatically said 'I wouldn't do anything dishonourable, I would not steal, I would not prostitute myself, but I would clean sewers'). It is foreseeable that Ayla will work again, but both her desire to work outside the home and her determination to overcome obstacles on the way are exceptional among the housewives and mothers of her age and above.

Through migration, women who grew up in the village and had little or no education were freed of a lot of hard work, yet at the same time, the value of their labour decreased. As described above, many of the migrant women engaged in fastidious daily housework to prove their domesticity. Because they came to the city too late, they did not continue their education or find professional work. Only if family finances were strained, did they work outside of the house, with no status gain involved. Otherwise, most women did some kind of piece work, be it through middlemen or on their own.

For the younger generation, however, the changing gender ideology has meant that it is more likely that a young woman will complete high school and even aim for university. If she works in a white-collar job, it is less likely that she will give up her job after marriage or children as different expectations of domesticity are applied to her category of woman. If a young migrant woman is an *ev kızı*, however, she, like most women of her mother's generation, is still unlikely to work unless the family needs the money.

Male Experiences of the Patriarchal Bargain

The dominant Kurdish gender paradigm that idealises female domesticity and male control over female sexuality of course means that the burden of making a living falls on the men, at least in the city. In the village, women's labour makes a considerable contribution to the household finances, even if not officially acknowledged, but in the city, men often have to shoulder great economic responsibility. In many cases, they are financially responsible for their wife and children as well as their parents, a duty that has up to now not been expected from daughters. It will be interesting to see whether the increase in the number of professional women will cause parents to expect support from their daughters as well. Currently, most young men are still trained to think of themselves as the only future breadwinner in their marriage and as the supporters of their parents in old age.

Among rural migrants to Van, there are still many families where several generations live together or in close proximity and share a budget. The oldest male gradually retires from seasonal migration to let his son(s) work, or, in the case of some families that moved away from the village later, the father may have never worked outside of the village but sends his sons away to earn money. A son might then be charged with looking after his parents, wife and children, and unmarried siblings. The following examples from the families of three brothers show that young men are not offered many choices within the dominant Kurdish gender discourse either. Ironically, the emergence of alternative gender paradigms may mean that sisters may receive more education than brothers.

Tacettin Çetin, mentioned above, has two young sons and thus still has to go to work on construction sites himself. It remains to be seen whether he will let his sons finish school or whether he will be so worn out from work that he will eventually expect them to take over and start working to support their parents and sisters. The fact that he is encouraging the education of three of his daughters may mean that he will do the same for his sons; on the other hand, he is ageing and has not been able to pay social security contributions, which in turn means that he will not receive a pension. Thus, his sons might have to take over, sacrificing their own chance for upward mobility in order to support the family. This may lead to very different pathways in marriage of the sisters and brothers. If the sisters went to university and worked professionally, they could marry someone in a similar situation. The brothers, on the other hand, would most likely replicate the more traditional gender paradigm by marrying an *ev kızı*. Their own lack of education would mean that their own nuclear family would be destined for a life of seasonal labour migration or a move somewhere else where they could find work. Like many other young men who work on building sites, they might also not be insured, thus in turn condemning their own sons to having to start work early.

In the family of Tacettin's older brother Alaaddin, the oldest daughter married at a young age. The following three sons (one married, one engaged and one single) are all working on building sites outside of Van, sending remittances home, allowing Alaaddin to 'retire'. So far, the married son has left his wife and three children with his parents, but this year, as the next son is marrying, they are planning to complete a second storey for the oldest married son. It remains to be seen how long the family of the second son will remain with the parents, and whether the wives of the migrant workers will want to move with their husbands to their cities of work. Alaaddin has taken his younger daughter out of school, despite the wishes of herself and her older brothers, who now support the education of the younger brothers financially. This case shows that although the father's economic capital has been reduced by the move to the city and by the wage labour of the sons, he still has a lot of symbolic capital that allows him to override his children's wishes. In other families, the sons would perhaps have been able to prevail. Alaaddin's sons will all endeavour to school their own children, boys and girls, for as long as possible in order to break the cycle; for themselves, however, this means having to keep working in physically taxing and potentially dangerous jobs and being financially responsible for parents, siblings, spouses, and children.

Tacettin and Alaaddin's youngest brother Feyzettin has the fewest children (four), and they are still young. Feyzettin spends a lot of time working away from home and his wife has remained in the village with the children. Feyzettin is currently saving money to build a house in Van. It is foreseeable that he will eventually move to Van. If he is then still young enough to work and if his children have attended school until then, the sons (and the daughter, who is the youngest), may complete high school. However, it is also possible that his sons may be called upon to fulfil their part of the patriarchal bargain by leaving school and starting to work, while the influence of a newer gender discourse may mean that the daughter will be allowed to stay on at school.

My general impression of families in Van is that if a father is sufficiently well-off to delay sending his sons to work, the family will avoid the gruelling migrant labour life for the sons. However, the very high unemployment rate in Van means that families can only achieve this by setting up their own family businesses, as Musa Çetin did (setting up a store for one of his sons to sell car parts), or by scouring around for apprenticeships or jobs, as Haci Şako Çetin did for his sons, who now work as qualified car mechanics. Prior to the earthquakes of 2011, the building sector in Van was booming, but also fluctuating seasonally and according to the global economy. If Gundî young men want to avoid further migration outside of Van, they need more schooling. However, the current coexistence of different gender discourses means that while young women may be sent to school, it is less acceptable to let them work in unskilled or semi-skilled jobs. They are thus not required to contribute financially to the family budget and are in some cases granted more schooling than their brothers, who may have to give up education in order to support the family.

Even in cases where no such pressure to leave school is exerted on young men, I have witnessed some in Van city and Tepelik leaving school voluntarily, having become bored or disillusioned with education. In both locations, I talked to several mothers who were at their wits' end as regards how to keep their teenage sons at school. They were financially able to do without their sons' labour, but the sons were not motivated to continue at school, in marked contrast to their female peers.

One reason for this lack of enthusiasm among some young men, I would argue, is due to the traditional Kurdish age-gender hierarchy. Compared to young women of the same age, young men experience fewer controls on their behaviour by their family. This may make it more likely for them to reject the control exerted and the expectations expressed by the school system. The Turkish education system requires competition for high schools and further competition in a central university entrance exam, so that young people are forced to study hard from the age of 14 onwards if they want to succeed. As girls are used to more control from family and the environment and know that perseverance will result in less control later, they are arguably more motivated to do well than some of their male schoolmates. Young men in the city still have to observe certain forms of respect and obeisance towards their fathers, and some may thus decide to forego future upward mobility (through education) in favour of earning money immediately, thus offering them more independence from their fathers.

Particularly young men in families that could manage to do without their labour seem to want to drop out. The reason may be that these young men have seen the relative success of their fathers, who themselves most likely did not have much education. Thus, there are fathers who have managed to go beyond unskilled labour by, for instance, opening a shop or a business. They may be successful at forming networks and even moving into brokering positions, showing their sons that it is possible to be successful without even a completed high school education. For some young men, all of these factors weigh heavier than the admonitions of parents that 'times have changed.' Unemployment is rife even among high school and university graduates, and high school drop-outs of this generation will have a harder time finding work than their parents.

Traditional gender ideology can thus have different effects on young men's lives. In some instances the financial situation of the family forces them into a life of early unskilled labour, which in turn may condemn their future family to a similar life, even though their sisters (and some younger brothers) might be granted more educational opportunities. Indeed, I have often heard the following utterance by male Vanlı interlocutors:

> 'It is more important that the girls get an education, so that they can save themselves. Men can always find work, but women are given to strangers (in marriage).'

Thus, while education is becoming increasingly highly valued and many young women and men strive for university education, there are also families where the young men sacrifice potential upward mobility for the good of the family. On the other hand, in families that are better off, some young men do not seem to feel the need to face the difficulties of study and competition. They opt for an early start into work life since their own fathers have shown them that this can also lead to success.

This chapter has discussed the concurrence of different gender discourses, the more 'traditional' Kurdish gender ideology that stresses an age-gender hierarchy and seclusion and the more 'modern' paradigm of gender equality that has gained influence through migration. I have discussed potential tensions due to the 'patriarchal bargain' that the more traditional sexual paradigm entails and its effects on female and male lives. I have also argued that because of social remittances from migration, Kurdish Vanlı throughout the translocational migratory social field, that is, in villages and in cities, now recognise and accept different categories of women, the *ev kızı/ev hanımı* and school girls/professional women and apply different standards of expected behaviour to them, both within and outside of the home.

Discourses on gender roles among my Kurdish interlocutors were often entwined with discourses on piety and religion. Based on my observations in Van city and Tepelik, I argue that migration has caused an increase in communal religious activities among women; however, there is also intergenerational difference in the degree of participation. The next chapter will discuss the gendered piety I found among Vanlı.

9

RELIGION IN THE CITY

Contextualisation: Islam in Turkey

In this chapter, I discuss the role that religious beliefs and practices play for Vanlı villagers and migrants and the changes migration has brought in religious practices of women. Although I would describe my Vanlı interlocutors as generally pious, the reader should be aware that such religiosity is not necessarily a 'tradition' carried on unchanged from the past. The current portrayal of Islam in Turkey, particularly in cities, is as constructed as is, say, Turkishness or Kurdishness. Navaro-Yashin argues that both laicist and Islamic camps have reconstructed themselves as 'Turkey's locals', that is, the ones with a claim to authenticity (2000: 90).

Both laicist and Islamic people in Turkey engage in reconstructions of the past, portraying the present as a continuation of a long tradition. The laicist discourse sees the foundation of the Turkish Republic as a liberation, particularly for women. Kemal Atatürk's top-down reforms (abolition of the caliphate, clothes reforms, alphabet reform, introduction of a new legal system, voting rights for women, etc.) are seen as a mobilisation against ignorance and backwardness. An increase in the visibility of headscarves (*türban*) and even the *çarşaf* in the cities is cited as a dangerous slide back in time (cf. Özyürek 2006).

Islamists, on the other hand, have resorted to other discursive themes in order to portray a continuation of—and a justification for—'true' Muslim lifestyles. The Republican era is portrayed as a short historical blip in the long history of Muslim life on the land that today is Turkey.

The Ottoman Empire is seen as the epitome of just ruling, caring for the poor, and religious observance. This discourse camouflages the fact that even in some more provincial areas, where head coverings were always more common than in the city, there has been a move towards more conservative dress, and perhaps also religiosity, in the last decades.

Among women whom I know in Van city, pictures from before the 1980s reveal mid-shin-length tight skirts, make-up, and in some cases uncovered hair; most of these women today have eschewed that dress style for long wide skirts, headscarves, and no make-up. While village dress rules seem to have changed less, I would argue that the whole of Turkey has experienced more explicit teaching and discussion of what it means to be a Muslim since the 1980s. Saktanber speaks of the 'increased popularity acquired by Islamic circles' in the 1980s and 1990s (2002: 20). One reason for this was the military junta that took over in Turkey in 1980; it encouraged the spread of Muslim piety as a useful antidote to political clashes between leftists and rightists, as well as to Kurdish identity politics.

The initial contrast between a politicised younger generation and the more religious elder generation was observed by Yalçın-Heckmann in Kurdish-majority Hakkâri, where '[t]he politically active youngsters before 1980 used to draw hostile reactions from the local people by their refusal to fast during Ramazan and by smoking in public when others were fasting' (1991: 117). The young generation was soon also targeted, one policy of the military junta being the introduction of compulsory religious education classes at school. This compulsion is still enshrined in Article 24 of the Turkish constitution; the classes have been criticised (particularly by Alevis) for instructing pupils *in* Sunni Islam rather than teaching them *about* Islam and other religions. The 1980s and 1990s saw an increase in mosques being built, also in Alevi areas, where people do not worship in mosques (cf. Ammann 2000: 257, Bellér-Hann and Hann 2001: 160). Although there was no dramatic rise in the number of religious *imam hatip* high schools after the coup (Çakır et al. 2004), there is a general perception that religiosity was highly encouraged by the establishment at that time before it later became perceived as a threat.

My general impression is that in the whole of Turkey, there is today more explicit conversation about religious rules and meanings than in the past. There are a variety of private religious TV channels, founded in the last 15–20 years, which show discussion programmes on religion or series with a religious message. In several households in Van and Tepelik these channels were on when I visited.

Religious groups have also targeted the educated elite. An offspring of the 'Nurcu'[1] movement, headed by Fethullah Gülen (who lives in the USA), has become ubiquitous in Turkey and has grown in strength by encouraging the development of social and economic capital necessary for getting on in the modern world and by recruiting young people into the religious movement through volunteers. Thus, for instance, FEM, a successful nation-wide chain of cram course schools preparing young people for the central university exam, is also a place where young people are encouraged to join study and prayer groups and spend time with 'abis' (older brothers) and 'ablas' (older sisters) outside of class time. A branch of this cram school also exists in Van city, and there are many branches in Istanbul. Young people who participate are offered help with accommodation and even living costs if they move to another city for study. Indeed, several of my young male interlocutors recounted being approached by Nurcu members on their first day at university in different cities. The cram schools are gender-segregated, so that one branch will offer only courses for female students, who will be taught exclusively by female teachers. Hatice Çetin, who attended the cram school for a year in Istanbul, reported how the teachers, who like to do a home visit to discuss an ideal learning environment for the students, refused to visit her home as she lived with her brothers and a cousin, all of them single men. According to the traditional/religious gender paradigm, it would have been inappropriate for a female teacher to visit the home.

Kemalists around Turkey express their fear that there has been an invasion of religiosity into the public sphere; it is said, for instance, that 'the volume of the ezan is becoming louder' and that 'there are more women in headscarves now than 15 years ago.' Interestingly however, according to Çarkoğlu and Toprak, who carried out two studies for the TESEV foundation in 1999 and in 2006, there was a decline in the number of women who covered their heads in those seven years. At the same time, however, their study found that both women and men seem to *believe* that there has been an increase in women covering their heads (2006: 58–9). Perhaps this impression is due to the increasing visibility of women who cover. For one, with rural-urban migration, there are more women with rural background (who, according to the statistics in the TESEV studies, are more likely to cover) in the city, entering the public sphere more for daily errands, school runs, and other tasks. In addition, there has also been a rise in a religious bourgeoisie that partakes in education,[2] employment, and consumption. The women of this class are less confined to their homes, and one can see women in headscarves going to work, driving cars, going shopping for pleasure, to cinemas, restaurants, and other leisure facilities. There are arguably also more private businesses willing to employ women in headscarves, from the exploitative textile workshops to offices, some hospitals, shops, and certain supermarket chains. It is, however, still not permissible for civil servants to wear headscarves, nor can women wear headscarves at university, although since 2010 this ban has been relaxed at quite a few places of learning.[3]

As so often in life, although there are polarised discursive positions on religion and laicism, 'ordinary' people tend to muddle through without too much confusion. Many researchers agree that in Turkey there is no absolute divide between Kemalists and Islamists beyond the polarised discourses of politicians and some institutions (e.g. White 2002, Bellér-Hann and Hann 2001, Çarkoğlu and Toprak 2000 and 2006). Although the polarised positions do exist and simplify the matter when one wants to describe tensions existing in Turkish society, people's personal feelings on religion and women's attire are arranged on a broad spectrum. Thus, for instance, if one takes women's attire as one indication of religiosity, it is possible to see women of the same neighbourhood or even family with different attitudes towards covering, as well as friendships between women with different attire and thus presumably also different religious attitudes.

Islam among Kurdish Vanlı

Keeping in mind that the salience of a Muslim identity may have fluctuated for Kurds over time, it is nevertheless true to say that self-identification as a Muslim was universal among my Vanlı interlocutors, and quite strong among some of them. This self-identification has not been eradicated by migration, and it often implies a contrast to others. The first implication of such self-identification is a differentiation from Alevis. As Kreyenbroek points out, 'The majority of modern Kurds are Sunni Muslims; no attempt to examine the religious side of Kurdish cultural identity could be valid unless this central fact is accepted' (1996: 85). The Vanlı I met in Van city, Tepelik, and wider Istanbul were all migrants from homogeneously Sunni villages and thus unused to the Alevi Islam practiced by other Kurds and Turks in Turkey. While a majority of my questionnaire respondents in Istanbul said they would let their children marry an Alevi (56 per cent),[4] my impression was that many of my Vanlı interlocutors would not ever have to face such a decision in the first place. In the village of Gundême there were only Sunni Muslims, and there are, to my knowledge, no settlements of Alevis in Van province that would have resulted in an Alevi presence in the province capital through rural-urban migration. When a young Gundî man from lineage 9, who had gone to university outside of Van and whose family lived in Van, wanted to marry his Alevi girlfriend, this is said to have been resisted by his family for a long time.

In Istanbul, Sunni Muslims and Alevis are more likely to meet on an everyday basis, yet they may still form smaller clusters in neighbourhoods. The migrant Vanlı Kurds in the blocks in Tepelik, for instance, form a small enclave in the ethnically and religiously diverse quarter. While the Vanlı in Tepelik have friends and neighbours among non-Vanlı, the majority of socialising is done within a network of multiplex relations: the most frequent contacts, at least among many women, are with people who are *hemşehri* and neighbours, neighbours and relatives, and relatives who live further away. Many of the Vanlı men who are retired or unemployed socialise in the Vanlı *dernek kahvesi*. Admittedly, men form social relationships with non-Vanlı at the mosque in Tepelik and with non-Vanlı and non-Sunnis at their workplaces, as do children at school. Most women, however, do not go to work and keep close to the home, and thus within the confines of the blocks, in their daily routines.

In Tepelik, rather than explicit antagonism,[5] I became aware of a kind of 'non-consideration' of Alevis. When asking a long-term resident of the blocks about other residents, she was able to recall most of the Vanlı, the names of husband and wife and the district of origin. However, when I asked her about certain flats, she would say apologetically, 'I am not sure, they are from Sivas [a province with a high percentage of Alevis],' or 'that's the Alevi family, but I don't know their names.' Intermarriage was still rare enough for it to set tongues wagging. Two young Vanlı women in Tepelik were engaged to Alevi men (not from the blocks); although the families were reconciled to the matches, they still provoked occasional remarks from outsiders. One should add that in one case, the Alevi family was also wary of the connection and that both sets of parents had had a serious talk with their children about the possibly problematic nature of this union prior to the marriage. Among the teenage girls in my English class, I witnessed the following discussion. One girl said, 'What is wrong with Alevis? My aunt is married to one and he is great.' Another girl clicked her tongue disapprovingly, and a third girl started teasing her: 'Maybe you will end up marrying one!' to which the second girl replied '*tövbe, tövbe*' (literally meaning: 'repent, repent', a phrase often used by the elderly or the more religious to express moral disapproval). I asked Zeynep Abla, a middle-aged woman in Tepelik, whether she could imagine her daughters marrying an Alevi. She said she wanted her daughters to marry a Sunni Muslim, adding that 'if it is written that they marry an Alevi or a non-Muslim, there is nothing I can do,' but, she repeated, it should really be a Sunni Muslim.

A second distinction implied in Kurdish religious identity is that of being from the Shafi'i rather than the Hanefi school (*mezhep*), which the majority of Turks belong to. Indeed, the question about what *mezhep* one belongs to is often an indirect way of finding out whether a person is Kurdish or Turkish (Kreyenbroek 1996: 93, McDowall 1997: 11). In Turkey, the Shafi'i school is considered more conservative. If religious conservatism can be partly measured by 'women's dress and attendance at Koran courses' (Béller-Hann and Hann 2001: 160), then the majority of my interlocutors could indeed be considered religiously conservative. One difference between Hanefis and Shafi'is is that the latter proscribe a renewed ritual cleaning (*abdest*) if two adults of the opposite sex touch each other,[6] thus encouraging men and women to keep a certain distance from each other. Hanefis, on the other hand, may touch without having to repeat *abdest*. This touch could be that between a shopkeeper and a customer when money and goods are exchanged or unintended hand contact in a bus.

A differentiation between Kurdish Shafi'i Muslims and Turkish Hanefi Muslims and Turkish or Kurdish Alevis becomes salient when Kurdish Vanlı migrate outside of Van, potentially encouraging the creation of tight, homogeneous networks with bonding capital, that is, strong links with others of the same religious persuasion.

Irrespective of location, a Muslim cosmology underlay the everyday lives of my Vanlı interlocutors, something they had in common with other Kurds. The above-mentioned TESEV study of 2006 found that 57.4 per cent of those who spoke Kurdish to their parents defined themselves as 'Muslims first', a percentage well above the national average (2006: 44). Indeed, researchers on Kurdish society have noted that it is difficult to separate religiosity from ethnic identity. Thus, Bruinessen argues, 'To many pious Sunni Muslim Kurds, Islam is an essential element of Kurdish identity' (1999b: 21); Yalçın-Heckmann, writing of Kurdish villagers in Hakkâri, posits, 'Islamic practices and beliefs, and the teachings of Islam, form a fundamental, if not the most important, part of the local cultural discourse' (1991: 110).

The salience of religious identity among Kurdish Vanlı was particularly visible among those of relatively recent village origin. In Tepelik, Zeynep Abla summed up the feelings of many migrant Vanlı Kurds, particularly women, when she said: 'First of all, I am a Muslim, *çok şükür.*' This is similar to observations on the importance of religion in rural Turkey in general. Delaney, for instance, says:

> For villagers of my acquaintance, Islam is the taken-for-granted context in which life is lived. This does not mean that all villagers are necessarily devout in their religious practices; rather, Islam sets the widest stage for their action by specifying the kind of world they live in and the kinds of action appropriate in the world. [...] I am trying to indicate that for villagers without much formal schooling, the world is built upon a foundation of Muslim cosmology.
>
> (1991: 514)

Decades before Delaney, anthropologists Magnarella and Pierce also discussed religion as an important frame of reference for people living in rural areas. Magnarella, who observed life in the small town of Susurluk in northwestern Turkey in the 1970s, wrote of the 'all-encompassing, traditional value system of Islam' (1974: 163), adding that 'even today many Turks do not differentiate between things Turkish and things Islamic' (1974: 164). Pierce, who spent time in the Demirciler village in central Anatolia in the 1960s, wrote that 'Islam is a way of life and is the dominant factor in the making of any decision, no matter how slight, in the mind of a villager' (1964: 87).[7]

This 'taken-for-granted' religiosity as a frame of reference has not been lost through migration. In conversations in Gundême, Van and Istanbul, I became familiar with semi-formal Kurdish phrases of greeting, blessing, expressing wishes and thanks that included references to Allah (*Xwedê* in Kurdish) (cf. Yalçın-Heckmann 1991: 110). Religiosity also manifested itself in a mindset that could hardly imagine someone not being or not wanting to be a Muslim.

The fact that religion and Kurdish identity are often inextricably linked can also be seen in the voting behaviour of Vanlı. Election results show that the religious AKP is as successful in the province as it is nationwide, if not more so. In the 2007 general election, the AKP gained 53.2 per cent of the votes in Van province, an above-average success for the party when compared to its national average of 46.57 per cent. While the pro-Kurdish Democratic Society Party (DTP) and then the Peace and Democracy Party (BDP) have gained increasing support, there are still many Kurds who do not support identity politics based on a Kurdish identity that excludes religiosity.

Houston distinguishes three discursive Islamic attitudes towards the 'Kurdish issue' in Turkey. Kurdish Islamism (i.e. the discursive fragment that insists on the possibility of a Kurdish identity as well as a Muslim one) clashes with statist Islamism (which shares the state's silencing of the issue and often represents the Turkish-Islamic synthesis) and Islamism (which subordinates Kurdish *and* Turkish identities to an Islamic one, emphasising the *ümmet,* the Muslim community) (2001a: 147–89). An example of the latter discursive fragment is given by Erder, who points out that aid to Kurdish migrant families in cities is often couched in a religious idiom (1997: 155). The sense of a religious community in Turkey has often been strong enough to bridge ethnic divides, as anthropologist Nur Yalman found:

> It is a matter of considerable good fortune for Turkey that religious affiliations remain more important than linguistic affiliations. If the religious affiliations were weakened, they would have given way possibly to Turkish-Kurdish opposition of a more divisive kind. As it is, this latent structural cleavage is bridged by numerous institutions, among which religious ties play a cardinal role.
>
> (McDowall 1997: 408)

The ruling AKP has been quite successful in appealing to Kurdish voters by combining the last approach with the first, that is, an emphasis on a religious brotherhood with some acknowledgement of Kurdish identity; the party thus competes with the more laicist identity politics of pro-Kurdish parties.

Generally then, for most of the Vanlı men and women I spoke to, migrant or not, Muslim identification offered 'frames of meaning' (Bora and Üstün 2005: 11). It was only from two men that I heard anything coming close to a disparaging comment about religiosity. These comments were made by men who were most involved in the pro-Kurdish movement. Like many Turkish Kemalists, they believed that there was an increase in religious practices, particularly among women; for them, this represented a hurdle for 'modernisation' (cf. Göle 1996: 7–8) and Kurdish ethnic mobilisation. One of them expressed this by saying, 'Kurds are trapped by religion and custom.'

Of course, had I chosen to study Vanlı migrants and non-migrants with more political involvement (more likely to be found among those forcibly displaced from their villages), a discourse critical of religiosity would probably have emerged as more dominant, and religiosity would have featured less in daily life. The same would have been true for Vanlı of higher socio-economic standing. A TESEV report from 2000 showed that primary identification as Muslims (rather than as Turks or citizens of Turkey) decreased with increasing education, and that religiosity was higher among people who had less formal education (Çarkoğlu and Toprak 2000: 30, 43). A 2007 study similarly found that while most people in Turkey identified themselves as citizens of Turkey before expressing a religious identity, those without high school education identified themselves most frequently as Muslims first ('Biz Kimiz?'). In the same vein, Yalçın-Heckmann reported on a decline in the frequency of Islamic expressions used in the Kurdish spoken by more educated and urban Kurds in Hakkâri (1991: 110).

The differing degree of religiosity according to socio-economic class means that shared religious beliefs and practices may overcome ethnic divisions among migrant Sunni Kurds and Turks, but that they only form bonding capital between people of similar classes. In large cities like Istanbul, men going to Friday prayer at their local mosque encounter others with similar incomes and educational backgrounds as neighbourhoods are relatively homogeneous in socio-economic terms. Women attending prayer meetings (see below) also meet other women of similar income and education. If one compares religious activity to membership in hometown associations, activism in Kurdish groups, or relations formed at work places, the latter three are social fields with much more potential for offering social capital that bridges socio-economic levels. However, it is likely that the rise of the religious bourgeoisie under the AKP will increase the potential of religiosity (real or displayed) as a means of creating weak links to more influential networks for rural-urban Vanlı migrants.

Female Piety as Part of the Patriarchal Bargain

Among my female interlocutors, religiosity was held up as being something to aspire to, both in practice and in mind, and the traditional gender paradigm still current among many Kurdish Vanlı approved of religious activity as an appropriate 'leisure pastime' for women and of piety as an appropriate mindset. It is thus acceptable for Kurdish housewives and housegirls to devote time left over from domestic duties to religious activities; the combination of domestic and religious activities reinforced the image of women as 'clean' in both the literal and metaphorical sense and set a standard for Kurdish womanhood.

I have argued that a basic Muslim 'frame of meaning' was apparent among both villagers and migrants. Migration to the city has allowed women to take part in more religious activities than before. This does not represent a major rupture, however, as migrant women have either increased the frequency of previously existing practices or have elaborated on them. In some cases, the urban lifestyle has offered middle-aged housewives the opportunity to carry out activities that only the elderly had time for in the village. In other cases, an increase in leisure time and contact with more learned women teachers has led to more women learning how to read the Qur'an and spending time pondering and discussing its implications.

Readings of the Qur'an as the most holy Muslim text have always been valued highly. However, elder women in Gundême would have been illiterate in Kurdish and Turkish and very few would have been able to read any Arabic, necessary for the Qur'an readings. Younger women, who may also have had some schooling—and thus literacy—in Turkish, may have learnt how to read Arabic letters and go through the Qur'an from the wife of the village *mele,* whereas the boys learnt from the *mele* himself. In Van and Tepelik, parents encouraged their sons and daughters to learn how to read the Qur'an at more organised courses during the summer holidays. Sometimes adult women learnt how to read the Qur'an from their children or from other religiously trained women in the neighbourhood. Apart from the schoolbooks of children, the Qur'an was often the only book in the homes I went to in all three research locations. Treated with reverence, it was kept in hand-made and embroidered cloth bags, hung from a nail in the wall, or on a high shelf, so as not to be below the waist level of people in the room. It was not kept in the bedroom, and when married visitors staid overnight, it was taken out of the room they slept in. Older children were taught not to touch it if they had not carried out *abdest,* the ritual cleaning, and menstruating women did not open it or read aloud from it, although they could attend prayer meetings and listen.

Such prayer meetings were much more common among women living in the city than in the village, and the women in Tepelik were more active than those I knew in Van. They took part in prayer meetings for special occasions (where parts of the Qur'an were read), *mevlüds,* where a poem in celebration of the prophet's birth was recited, or so-called *sohbets* (literally meaning 'chats') on religious themes. These meetings could take place in private homes or at a room under the mosque and would be led by a female *hoca*, or religious teacher.

Regular prayer, *namaz*, was ideally to be performed by all Muslim men and women. In Tepelik, all the married housewives of different ages I met performed *namaz* five times a day. Hediye described it as a *'rahatlatıcı'* (comforting or relaxing) routine that made her feel better. In Van, too, most married housewives did *namaz* regularly. All the Vanlı women I talked to agreed that performing *namaz* was a commitment it was not good to go back on. Once one started, one should continue. Several girls and young women in the Çetin lineage in Van have voiced disappointment in themselves when they have not been able to keep up their praying routines. Several interlocutors described the difficulties of regular *namaz* in the village, particularly in the past, when numerous children, care for animals, baking bread, cooking, and carrying and heating water made it virtually impossible for young and middle-aged women to carry out *abdest* and do *namaz* regularly. There, it was the elder generation, both men and women, who prayed regularly as they had 'retired' from much of the daily work. In Van city and Tepelik, more schooling today means that young people, who have been freed of farm and domestic duties, are nevertheless busy with studies and thus less likely to pray regularly. It is thus generally the generation of housewives with relatively little education as well as the elders who commit to *namaz*.

For Vanlı in all three research locations, Ramazan was a month of particular religious importance, a time 'when more than at any other time, the goal is to gain spiritual excellence and control over the body', as Torab describes it for Iran (2007: 27). Fasting from sunrise to sunset was seen as similarly comforting as the *namaz*. People often fasted even if they could have exempted themselves, for instance when they travelled or took medication on a regular basis. Even if doctors warned against fasting, some people adjusted the times of their medication so that they could fast anyhow. Women with high blood pressure or diabetes insisted that they were well enough to fast. Similarly, pregnant and breastfeeding women, who are exempt from fasting, often did so in Van. Whenever I questioned this practice, I was told by the woman that she would rather fast as fasting is considered meritorious. In one case in Van city, a young new mother was fasting, but her baby was crying of hunger. Her fellow bride then advised her to breastfeed, and the mother decided to fast only every second day. A comparable observation was made by Béller-Hann and Hann, who said, 'Heavily pregnant women with urgent work to carry out in their tea gardens in the 1983 Ramadan would not consume even a glass of water in the course of a long hot day' (2001: 162). Only when menstruating did Vanlı women refrain from fasting, but they were conscientious about 'making up' the days before the next Ramazan.

Several elderly women in Gundême and Van fasted at other times, too, in order to gain extra merit. Thus, a six-day fast immediately after the Ramazan fasting period, the şeşik, and a nine-day fast called nehik just before the Feast of Slaughter were thought to bring extra merit. Muhterem in Van city told me that these two fasting periods have become more popular among younger women in the city as they have fewer chores to do and can bear such a fast. This again would mean housegirls or housewives as parents and daughters who are committed to education do not want to endanger their studies.

Women who were post-menopausal could also fast every day during the three holy months of Recep, Şaban, and Ramazan for seven years in a row in order to obtain further religious merit. It is predictable that this practice may remain popular among Vanlı migrant women who are housewives and mothers, but will not be continued among those young women aiming for higher education and employment.

Covering their heads was also behaviour of Vanlı women related to Islam. Although one can argue in Turkey that there is a distinction between a more 'traditional' way of covering one's head and more self-conscious 'veiling' since the 1980s (cf. Göle 1996: 2–5), even women who do not cover their heads do so during religious activities, such as going to pray at a graveside, taking part in a funeral, attending a prayer meeting, reading from the Qur'an, or entering a mosque, indicating that it is considered integral to religious activity. While covering their head in Gundême village was the norm for all women, migration has changed the way they cover, as discussed earlier. For the younger generation of women in Van and in Istanbul, their ongoing education has challenged the norm of veiling, and many girls who have completed high school have chosen not to wear headscarves. One young woman in Tepelik continued her high school education but, with the encouragement of her mother, began to veil outside of school.

For the married housewives in Tepelik covering their hair was a commitment similar to deciding to perform *namaz*, that is, one should not reverse one's decision. There were three married women in Tepelik who covered their hair later in life (one after marriage, one after a large earthquake, and one because she felt ready for it in middle age); they all said that they would not go back to uncovering their hair although one of them, Ayla, would do so if she went back to work, but still cover outside of work. In Tepelik, there were two Vanlı women wearing the black *çarşaf*, a very prominent expression of religious devotion.

The TESEV study of 2006 asked women in Turkey why they wore headscarves and men why they wanted their fiancées or wives to wear headscarves. The majority of women and men (71.5 per cent and 59.3 per cent) said that it was a condition of Islam to cover. Many fewer said that they covered or wanted their partners to cover because everyone else did (7.6 per cent and 7.8 per cent), while even fewer said that covering was a condition for *namus*, that is, sexual honour (3.4 per cent and 1.5 per cent). The researchers took these statements at face value, saying, 'As can be seen from these percentages, it is clear that whether women cover or not is generally not related to *namus*' (Çarkoğlu and Toprak 2006: 26, author's translation). However, in the same text, they later concede the possibility that the high number of respondents who said that Islam ordered women to cover were likely to have been influenced by their families. The researchers argued that young women may question the need for covering before later accepting such an 'order' from Islam because family and others believe it to be an order, too. Others may be forced more directly (2006: 27).

I would argue that it is virtually impossible to unravel ideas on *namus*, religious duties, or 'traditions' in the Kurdish gender paradigm. Thus, the 'traditional' ideal of a Kurdish woman entails modest attire and physical modesty (i.e. material and virtual veiling), religious piety, Kurdish language use, and hard work. The following description of a short encounter shows all of these elements being embodied. I was at a Vanlı couple's house in Tepelik, when another Vanlı, who, like the host, was a hometown association activist, came for a visit. After he had sat down, Hediye, the wife of the host came into the living room to greet him. She was wearing her white *laçik* headscarf, the chin and mouth modestly covered, and she greeted him in a low humble voice. The visitor asked after her family, and she answered in a low voice again, bowing slightly and putting her right hand to her chest in a humble gesture of gratitude, and saying 'Xwedê ji te razi be' (May Allah approve of you), the traditional Kurdish phrase and gesture used for thanking people. For her, speaking Kurdish, displaying modest behaviour, and being a Muslim were inextricably intertwined. Allah, *Xwedê*, was never far from her thoughts and utterances. She did not sit down with the visitor, but rather immediately went into the kitchen to make tea for the guest, following the ideal of a Kurdish woman seeing to the needs of others. When she brought the guest a glass of tea, he thanked her by saying 'spas', a newly-coined word for 'thank you' that is used by urban, more politicised, and secular Kurds. The phrase, to my ears, was jarring, a self-conscious way of expressing a Kurdishness devoid of religiosity that, to my mind, Hediye could not relate to.

When I listened to women chatting in Gundême, Van city, and Tepelik, I often noted explicit approval of modest attire, piety, and hard work, particularly when older women were commenting on younger ones.[8] The ideal of female piety is thus one element in the traditional gender discourse that permeates Kurdish society, at least as far as the *ev kızları/ev hanımları* are concerned. Arguably, piety and associated behaviour are important for such women to achieve societal recognition and to hold their husbands to their side of the 'bargain'. This piety is however not just an 'act', but a part of the women's value system (cf. Saktanber 2002: 37). Migrant housegirls and housewives differ from those in the village in that they have intensified their religious involvement by learning to read the Qur'an and taking part in communal readings and in prayer meetings. Migrant and non-migrant women alike continue to fast and encourage their own children to become religiously active through Qur'an courses. In return, a pious woman can expect a religious, or at least a dutiful, husband.

Socio-religious Capital and Agency

While female piety can be seen as part of the means of keeping men to their promise of looking after their wives and children, it arguably also offers women the opportunity to create socio-religious networks and to create a gendered religious identity that is based on interaction with religious texts.

While religion was also important in village life, extensive pre-occupation with religion, I argue, is essentially an urban phenomenon that has emerged with migration. It is in women's religious behaviour that there has been most change after migration. Here I would like to apply a concept called 'location-specific religious capital', used by sociologist Myers. While he uses it to refer to socio-religious networks that people have prior to migration (2000), it also serves as a useful concept for post-migration networks. More extensive religious involvement has offered migrant women who do not work outside of the home a means of accumulating socio-religious capital in a manner not possible in a village. Next to piece work and exchanging visits with neighbours and friends, involvement in religious activities was the most common leisure time activity of many of the housewives I met in Tepelik; indeed, visiting or socialising with others could be combined with prayer meetings and religious chats.[9]

During the Ramazan month of fasting in 2006, many of the middle-aged Vanlı housewives in Tepelik gathered to read the Qur'an under the leadership of two young women in their twenties (also from the blocks). They were *hocas*, that is, they had spent the last years studying the Qur'an and other religious texts intensively, albeit not in official, government-sanctioned courses. Another time, I attended a prayer meeting at Gülşen's house. Her son had decided that he would not go to school anymore, and in her despair she held a prayer meeting. A female Qur'an teacher was invited, as were women from the blocks whom Gülşen was friendly with. Food was cooked by her and her sister-in-law to be eaten after the prayers. The gathering was a *41 Yahsin* meeting, meaning that the *Yahsin* sura of the Qur'an was read 41 times. The Qur'an teacher read aloud, but any woman reading along silently was counted as a reader, thus making the process faster and easier. The prayer was hoped to be effective in changing the son's attitude towards education. Prayer meetings are also held on more joyous occasions, such as the birth of a child. Hediye planned to have one to give thanks after her family survived a fire in their home unscathed.

There was often little distinction between social and religious networks, which meant that one could hardly opt out of one kind of activity and only partake in the other. It has to be emphasised that women not working outside of the house partook in these activities in Tepelik. Just as villagers have to decide for themselves whether they have time for regular individual prayer, there is no pressure on working women in the city to join the religious activities. Women with smaller children or those with too much work were also 'excused' from attending meetings.

There were two women who were the most striking examples of accumulation of location-specific religious capital—the two Qur'an teachers, who worked as volunteers at the local mosque. I find the term 'location-specific' apt here, since they would have been much less likely to accumulate this kind of capital in a village. I met one of these women, Nur, when I was teaching her niece English in Tepelik. Nur was 28 years old, and she knew virtually all of the students in my English classes as she had taught them in Qur'an classes before.

Nur can be compared to the 'professional freelance female religious leaders' that Torab found in working-class Teheran (1996: 235). In her position, she acquires more social capital than other Vanlı women and more of a different kind. Although she is 'freelance', her social standing as a person of knowledge, a 'professional', allows her to create a wider network of acquaintances. The difference between her and some of the women she teaches parallels the difference between 'veiled' and 'headscarved' women that Turkish sociologist Göle describes.

Göle sees a difference in the veiling of young women after 1983 and contrasts it with the 'traditional' wearing of headscarves by older women. The young women who wear a veil (*türban* in Turkish) are more educated than their mothers, 'who are perpetuating traditions and traditional religion within their domestic lives without any claim to knowledge and praxis'. The young women, in contrast, are taking part in an 'active reappropriation [...] of Islamic religiosity and way of life' (1996: 4–5). Nur wears a black *çarşaf*, the chador, which is arguably a kind of veiling that expresses absolute commitment to such a way of life. Saktanber, in her study of Islamic life in Ankara, speaks of women who self-identify as 'conscious' (*'şuurlu'*) Muslims (2002). Nur is certainly one of these, and it is due to women like her that other women in the neighbourhood become more religiously active, even if they do not aspire to the same degree of commitment or to the same kind of self-representation with a *çarşaf.*

Nur was born in a district of Van but came to Istanbul with her parents and siblings when she was six. Two of her brothers had moved into separate flats in the blocks after marriage, as had she. When I first met Nur, she was wearing a headscarf and a *pardesü*, but during the summer of 2006, she began wearing the *çarşaf*, covering her forehead and lower face up to the tip of the nose, and also buttoning the sleeves at the fingers in order to cover her wrists and the backs of her hands. Nur was an eloquent self-assured young woman, tall and good-looking, and to see her in the *çarşaf* was a great shock for me.[10] In order to go beyond my initial reaction, I decided to ask Nur to tell me her story herself. It turned out that her self-representation was a narrative of personal reinvention and liberation rather than subjugation. She described her current situation as the climax of a long search for happiness.

When Nur was 17 years old, she got married to her mother's nephew, a young man who had grown up in Istanbul, too. She had been going to an *imam hatip* boarding school and said she was not interested in boys. She said that her family was much more ignorant then, and that neither her parents nor her siblings knew better than to have her married at an early age. She made it sound as if she slipped into marriage almost by accident. Her husband was an understanding man and had encouraged her to develop herself further and to venture out of the domestic sphere. He himself, though working as a security guard, had just completed a distance learning degree in law.

Nur described her life since marriage as a constant search for meaning. She spent some time writing a book and reading a lot. After a period of voluntary work, she started taking seminars on pedagogy and psychology. As her marriage remained childless, Nur started a discussion group that would meet and discuss religious books in the members' homes. After a while this led to her teaching other women at home. Yet she was still looking. Finally, a friend suggested that she help set up a learning centre at the local mosque. She was ecstatic, and they set to cleaning the basement of the mosque and turning it into a Qur'an course centre. For the last three years she has been working at the mosque as a volunteer Qur'an teacher (*hoca*). Technically, her courses are illegal as only the Ministry for Religious Affairs is allowed to organise lessons. However, in practice, every city quarter has its own courses and they are very popular with local families.

Every day, Nur taught women how to read the Qur'an at the mosque. During the day, she also organised *sohbet*s (religious discussions around a theme), and she attended or led prayer meetings at other people's houses. During the summer holidays many families sent their children to Qur'an courses and Nur taught the girls. When I visited her at her flat just before the holy month of Ramazan, she later went off to a prayer meeting she and her friend had organised in an empty flat in her block. Women from this and neighbouring blocks had cleaned the flat, and they came together every day during Ramazan. Their aim was to read the Qur'an through from start to finish (*hatım etmek*).

Nur felt that she had gradually gained a new identity, and this was due to the fact that she had 'fallen in love'. She declared this with great drama and watched me to see if I understood what she meant. She was in love with Allah and she was also in love with her *örtü*, her covering. It was only quite recently that she had changed her name from the worldlier 'Gülşen', meaning rose garden, to 'Nur', meaning divine light. The new name and her *çarşaf*, she said, were outward expressions of her love.

Although most of the Vanlı women in Tepelik were covered in some way or other, the *çarşaf* was considered a radical way of dressing. Indeed, Nur said that her family told her not to wear 'that ugly thing', and her husband was dismayed, too. A mother of one of Nur's students expressed concern that the girl would take Nur as a role model later. Nur herself acknowledged that the *çarşaf* had brought her many

negative reactions; she said that people who did not know her considered her ignorant, backward, and helpless. At the same time, however,
the *çarşaf* symbolised her 'professional' status. Although many of the
Vanlı women may say that the *çarşaf* is 'not for us' and criticise it as
exaggerated, they did accord respect to those wearing it and acknowledged their religious commitment and insights.

Wearing a *çarşaf* made Nur unemployable in the secular world.
Her husband expressed ambitions for her to work and do well for
herself, and Nur herself agreed that she had the intelligence and
self-confidence to do well in a career. However, she had no interest
in any other work than her current one, and in many ways, she *was*
a 'working woman'. Every morning, she went to the mosque and to
other women's houses. She said she often left the house even in the
evenings, when her husband was at home, and hardly came home on
holy nights (*kandil geceleri*), something that would have been inconceivable for most of her fellow Vanlı women. She had a wide social
network of her own, which went beyond the neighbourhood and
relative relations that other Vanlı women had. Although she worked
voluntarily, she did sometimes receive money or presents of gold
from her students. So, despite the misgivings that some may have
expressed at her wearing the *çarşaf*, her occupation with religious
affairs and her attire both gave her the license to ignore certain discourses on appropriate behaviour for women. If, as Kandiyoti argues,
female modesty and a confinement to the domestic sphere are part
of the patriarchal bargain (1988), and if the headscarves of the Vanlı
women represent an assurance to the men folk that modesty is being
preserved despite the widening of the female sphere, then, arguably,
the more extreme *çarşaf* has allowed Nur to widen her sphere far
beyond that of many of her fellow Vanlı women (cf. Abu-Lughod
2002, 2006).

Nur's choice of attire may seem like the ultimate obeisance of male-
dominated discourses on appropriate (religious) behaviour for women.
Some people may argue that by wearing the *çarşaf*, Nur has internalised the male hegemonic discourse on appropriate female dress and is
deluding herself if she feels that it is her own choice. This is a point
that needs contextualisation and has troubled many social scientists

studying 'Muslim women'. It is a question of cultural relativism versus the insistence on universal human rights. Taken to an extreme, the former perspective accepts anything, in this case the veiling of women, as 'part of their culture', whereas critics say that the 'culture' label is being used to excuse violations of human rights. Abu-Lughod is highly critical of the Western perspective, perpetuated in scholarly and media circles, that 'Muslim women' need to be 'rescued' from the veil: 'First we need to work against the reductive interpretation of veiling as the quintessential sign of women's unfreedom, even if we object to state imposition of this form, as in Iran or with the Taliban' (2002: 787). She points to the variety of veiling practices and asks her readers to respect them. She argues that a constant reduction of 'Muslim societies' to the 'veiling issue' blinds observers to transnational political and economic processes which create inequalities, such as the American support for the Taliban in reaction to the invasion of Afghanistan by the Soviets. Similarly, Mojab synthesises a particularist approach (which sees women first and foremost as individuals) with feminism, arguing that we 'can respect the voluntary choice of any woman to wear the veil, and we can oppose forcible unveiling (e.g., in Iran in 1936–41), yet we can at the same time criticize veiling or any segregation of human beings along sex lines' (1998: 4). The issue of women's veiling is still being hotly debated in academic and political circles in Turkey, as well as in Europe. However, unlike several other women in Tepelik who hinted at how good it would be for me to convert to Islam, Nur, the woman with most religious involvement, conversed with me easily, accepting our differences. Her way of life did not seem a result of 'brainwashing', but rather a result of choices.

One may of course point out that these choices were limited by the dominant Kurdish gender paradigm (cf. Kandiyoti 1988). Bourdieu has argued that individuals are aware of what is possible in their lives and act accordingly:

Outlooks on the future depend closely on the objective potentialities which are defined for each individual by his or her social status and material conditions of existence. The most individual

project is never anything other than an aspect of the subjective
expectations that are attached to that agent's class.

(1977: 53)

In this context, I would make two points about Nur. The first is that
she would probably not be so religiously involved if she had young
children. Her 'vocation' would take second place after her duties as
a mother, and there would probably be pressure on her from husband, family, and neighbourhood to put the children first.[11] The female religious leaders in Teheran that Torab describes are women with
grown-up children or grandchildren, and thus freed from maternal
responsibilities (1996: 235). Secondly, as pointed out earlier, the *çarşaf*
and extensive religious studying and teaching are urban phenomena.
Were Nur living in a village, milking animals, cooking, baking bread,
preparing trousseaus, carrying and heating water, and looking after a
vegetable garden, the *çarşaf* would not be practical, and there would
not be great amounts of time to dedicate to reading and contemplating
the Qur'an and other religious texts. Thus, Nur's life is not a mere
product of circumstances, but her choices have been influenced by the
fact that she is living in the city. The religious capital she has accumu-
lated is thus 'location-specific'.

Nur, partly through inclination and education and partly due to
childlessness, has taken religious involvement very far, and she is quite
exceptional among the Vanlı women in Tepelik. However, when one
looks at migrant women in general, an increase in religious involvement can be seen among the married housewives who conform to the
dominant Kurdish gender discourse, partly due to the training and
encouragement they get from women like Nur. An involvement with
religious texts and ideas in an all-female environment in turn offers
women the sense that they are shaping their lives in a meaningful
manner. Migration has thus offered them a way of integrating their
experiences in a religious narrative. The religious behaviour of many
Vanlı women moves between the less explicit 'ways of being' and the
more self-conscious 'ways of belonging', with Nur definitely taking
part in the latter.

The younger generation of migrant Vanlı women is unlikely to pursue religious activities with so much enthusiasm. Through education and perhaps later work, as well as through exposure to a more secular discourse at school, they are encouraged to form social networks that are mostly unrelated to religious activity. They are more likely to frame their lives with narratives of educational or professional success, while still maintaining some elements of the Muslim cosmology learnt from their family and environment.

10

CONCLUSION

This study has depicted Kurdish Vanlı as positioned in a particular social field. Just as transnational migrants live in a social field unconfined by national borders, Kurdish Vanlı migrants, their relatives, co-villagers, and other Kurds are part of a translocational social field within Turkey; sometimes, as is the case with discourses on Kurdishness, national borders are crossed to include Kurds in Europe or in other Middle Eastern states.

I have portrayed different layers of this field, describing networks of people, transactions of goods, favours, and marriages between people, that is, 'ways of being' in Levitt and Glick Schiller's terms (2004: 1010). In some cases, people acted in this social field in a relatively unreflected, even automatic, manner; they helped relatives to find jobs, rushed to the bedside of co-villagers in hospitals in the big cities, attended hometown organisation meetings in the neighbourhood, cooperated on piece work with neighbours, chatted in Kurdish with a fellow Vanlı they met in Istanbul, or kept an eye out for suitable marriage partners for their own children and those of other family members and acquaintances.

At other times, more explicit identifications, that is, 'ways of belonging', came to the fore. Migrants and non-migrants alike took part in the production, dissemination, and modification of discourses. These could be heard among Vanlı, as well as in conversations with me. Young Vanlı, for example, were admonished to treat their elders with respect, women discussed the merits of fasting and praying, political candidates wooed voters with a rhetoric of tribal unity or with discourses on Kurdish ethnicity, or migrants evaluated village life nostalgically or critically.

When describing the life experiences of Kurdish Vanlı, I have sometimes focused on commonalities. While my interlocutors are not forced migrants, they may nevertheless face economic hardship, discrimination as Kurds, and, as rural-urban migrants, a questioning of the legitimacy of their presence in the city. Women may be doubly restricted through their position in the Kurdish age-gender hierarchy, a hierarchy also quite dominant among Turks, which is thus often reinforced rather than challenged by many in the migratory environment. On a more positive note, migrants and non-migrants in the translocational field may share knowledge of village life and the skills required there, a sense of common identity based on village or province origin, a more or less explicit Muslim cosmology, and a desire for upward socio-economic mobility.

The transnational perspective suggests that the position of migrants and non-migrants in their field of relations, actions, and ideas is flexible, yet that this does not lead to a fragmentation of the self. One and the same person may thus evaluate rural life, tribal membership, family relations, or the importance of education, religion, and Kurdishness in different terms at different times, depending on his or her current life situation. In the words of a researcher on Filipino migration to the USA, there exists 'a network of sometimes competing definitions of identities, connections, and loyalties' (Vergara 2008: 3).

At the beginning of the book I introduced concepts from research on transnational migration as a frame for my study. One reason was that rural-urban migration everywhere mirrors transnational migration in that it is a response to inequality, or, in Portes and DeWind's terms, a reaction to 'economic distance' between the 'global North and South' (2007: 6).

Inequality was the impetus for migration from Gundême and countless other villages in Van province. Through migration, young men escaped the age hierarchy that had made their fathers dependent on the land controlled by their own fathers or older uncles well into adulthood. Seasonal migrants moved in the realisation that they could earn wages unattainable in Van, on construction sites in tourism regions and urban growth areas. Ironically, and sometimes tragically, labour migration has made these migrant workers part of new systems of inequality; they often work without their employers paying social security contributions, which means that they are neither insured against work accidents (not infrequent under the unsafe working conditions of building sites) nor eligible for a pension in later life. Working without contracts, these construction workers are also easily laid off when the economy is hit by a recession, as has recently been the case, or when the building season ends.

There is blatant inequality in many respects between the sending villages and the receiving regions, educational opportunity (or lack of it) being a major one. As indicated in Chapter 3, one factor that has turned seasonal migration into the permanent resettlement of complete families has been the desire to have children do better; migrants want to break both with dependence on land and animal husbandry and with exploitation in the construction labour market. Indeed, in conversations my interlocutors themselves often subscribed to the unilineal migration paradigm that considered their integration into cities and education systems a prerequisite for 'modernity', sometimes contrasting it with their own 'ignorance' ('cahillik').

This desire to 'modernise' is based on the realisation that migration has brought with it: village life earns little money and is not a realistic source of income for large families, and schooling in and around the village is inadequate if one wants one's children to do better. Moreover, city life lures with promises of comforts such as running water, washing machines, indoor toilets, and access to more consumer goods. Just as 'the village' can turn into a symbol of nostalgia, 'the city' can become idealised as a place where there are more choices, opportunities, and less hardship.

The goal of 'modernisation' has led to a willingness to educate children in the Turkish education system for a longer time than in the past, which at the same time implies accelerated linguistic assimilation. This willingness to assimilate has been fuelled by public discourses that denigrate both Kurdishness and rural life, discourses that

Vanlı themselves partake in at times. Just as speakers of languages other than English may be denigrated as 'linguistically isolated' in the USA (Graham and Zentella 2010: 6), a categorisation that invalidates other cultural and linguistic experiences, speakers of Kurdish (or other non-Turkish languages in Turkey) do not receive any recognition for their linguistic competence. For instance, a 'modern' CV in Turkey would not list Kurdish language proficiency. Many parents, also those in Tepelik, were keener that their children speak Turkish without a regional accent and learn 'proper English', the knowledge of which is perceived to open doors. When asked about the lack of Kurdish language proficiency, parents did sometimes express fleeting regret, yet they did not take active steps to increase the use of Kurdish at home.

This non-validation of Kurdish is of course influenced by the wider Turkish discourse on the homogeneity of the nation and is one of the social remittances (Levitt 1998) that migrants have 'sent back' to villages and Van province. While in the village children may still speak Kurdish, they are likely to lose the language if they move to Van city or further away for schooling. Other relatives visiting the village, particularly younger ones, will be increasingly monolingual in Turkish. Migrant marriages with non-Kurds or non-Kurdish speaking Kurds brought up in the city are likely to increase, so that the language of communication in many families ceases to be Kurdish.

The decline in the use of Kurdish is accompanied by changes in the understanding of what it means to be Kurdish. For many Vanlı, 'modernisation' is an inevitable process that implies a move to the city, integration into the wage labour market, possibly higher level education, and increasing individualisation. This understanding means that the Kurdishness of the elder and middle generation may soon be a thing of the past. Their Kurdishness seems a somewhat old-fashioned ethic of religious piety, sense of duty, modesty, and hard work. As the economic and symbolic capital of the elder generation declines, the traditional age-gender hierarchy is no longer as strong a determining factor of people's lives.

The values implied in the Kurdish age-gender hierarchy are seen as increasingly unsuitable for urban and 'modern' life. A young man who is modest and obeisant will remain an ordinary painter or bricklayer

who gets work through a foreman rather than negotiating his own
contracts with better wages and conditions. A silent bride is of no use
when she needs to talk to teachers at school about her children's performance. An illiterate woman may piously perform prayers five times
a day, yet she will have problems when she needs to get around the city
by bus. Nor can she support her children with their school work.

Young Kurdish women in particular have been motivated to pursue
an education in order to avoid some of the submission their mothers
endured; this education in turn 'Turkifies' them. Some young men as
well, although not as many as women, are now keen to pursue secondary or even tertiary education; in some cases, however, they are forced
to leave school in order to take over the support of the extended family
from their fathers. An increase in education, particularly in the case
of women, has transformed both their own and others' expectations
of their behaviour. It is true that there is still an insistence on certain
performances of modesty and respect, but, increasingly, young women
and men are being offered more choices in shaping their lives. In short,
there has been some change in what it means to be Kurdish.

A move away from 'traditional' Kurdishness does not, however,
imply an automatic acceptance of certain alternatives. Among the
Vanlı Kurds I have met, many were wary of explicit political expressions of Kurdishness as this often implied an uneasy proximity to the
militant PKK. While they may have voted for the pro-Kurdish DTP
or BDP, any news of fallen soldiers from the Turkish army was greeted
with great sadness and empathy for the families. After all, their own
sons had also done military service or would join the army, and, being
from the less educated working class, were also more likely to be sent
to areas of conflict.

Children and youngsters in Tepelik often identified themselves as
'Vanlı' first, rather than Kurds. In Istanbul, such a label did not have
to imply much more than the fact that a child or its parents were
not born in the city, a situation that the majority of Istanbul resi-
dents have in common. Thus, a 'Vanlı' was not very different from a
'Trabzonlu' (from the Black Sea) or an 'Izmirli' (from the Aegean).
To express 'Vanlı'ness was very different from explicitly expressing
Kurdishness. As ethnic differentiation decreased due to exposure to

the Turkish education system and the decline of Kurdish language use, people were often categorised more according to socio-economic status than ethnicity.

On the other hand, sometimes ethnic prejudice could come to the fore if, for instance, a family rejected a male suitor on the grounds of his Kurdishness, job applicants were not invited for an interview because of their region of origin, or house owners did not want Kurds to rent their flats.

In this context, Esser differentiates between two types of societal assimilation. One type is a weakening of boundaries between groups, that is, 'the dissolution of institutionally complete ethnic communities and/or the decline of ethnic boundaries and collective feelings of social distances and identifications' (Esser 2007: 313). The second type is the elimination of social inequality, that is, the end of a gap in educational, occupational, and income terms (2007: 312).

My observation is that there has been more assimilation of the first type among Vanlı Kurds. On the part of the elder and the middle generation, self-identification as Kurdish was never divisive as it was inextricably linked with religious piety that emphasises shared values with other Muslims. Younger Kurdish Vanlı have been exposed to more Kurdish identity politics since the 1990s, but my interlocutors have responded less to it than others because they have largely been spared the traumata of forced migration and state terror. For many young Vanlı I spoke to, the pursuit of educational and other goals was more urgent than being or speaking Kurdish. Kurdishness could be situationally salient in nostalgic conversations, song singing, and anecdote telling, yet it was one among several self-identifications rather than the only one.

As for the second type of assimilation, it is fair to say that, over the last 20 years, there has been an increase in social differentiation *within* the Kurdish 'community', as exemplified in the different pathways that families of the Çetin lineage have taken. There are thus more university graduates or self-employed Kurdish Vanlı than before, forming a middle class that is growing in size. However, the majority of Vanlı migrants, like rural-urban migrants from all over Turkey, are constrained in their socio-economic rise. The first generation of migrants is one that was brought up with animal husbandry and farming skills, but little formal schooling. In the city, they have moved into the construction sector, an area of the labour market that offers them no improvements in socio-economic terms unless they also display some business skills.

The initial move to the city frames the future paths of migrants: if they follow other migrants to Van city or other cities, they may rent a flat or buy a plot of land near their kin or former neighbours; indeed, they are unlikely to be able to afford anything in a different area. This in turn leads to clusters of migrants living in one place. In Van city, rural-urban migrants are mostly from the same or neighbouring provinces, but tribal membership or village origin is varied. In other cities, such as Istanbul, there may be clusters of Vanlı living in a neighbourhood of migrants from different areas. In Tepelik, for example, there were migrants from Van and the Black Sea region living together. This may widen networks of interaction, even leading to intermarriage at times; however, these networks are made up of people with a similar socio-economic background. Differences between Alevis and Sunnis may still be seen as a hindrance to free communication, even if there is no difference in class.

Kurdish Vanlı migrants, and here I have to reiterate that I am writing about migrants who were not forced to leave their villages, have similar opportunities to, say, a migrant from the Black Sea, but both are hampered by the lack of equality that exists due to their rural origin and lack of education. For migrants of the first generation, urban life usually means having a more marginal status. Exceptional educational success or a determination to succeed in business may offer opportunities for the next generation, but they have to overcome the limitations of the tenuous urbanity that White described. Living in a quarter like Tepelik means attending a school that produces fewer university candidates. State schools are usually underfunded, which is reflected in poorer foreign language teaching, fewer sports facilities, books, and computers, and less science lab equipment. Living in a quarter like Tepelik also means that there are few leisure time activities on offer apart from Qur'an courses and perhaps some football for the boys. Sports, arts, theatre, or music lessons all cost a lot of money and are usually only available in the more middle and upper class areas of the city. The cram schools for pupils studying for the university exams are also located in other quarters and are too heavy a financial burden for many families. One could thus argue that the Vanlı in Tepelik do not differ much from other rural-urban migrants in the cities; they form part of a large section of the population in Turkey that is struggling to maintain or improve socio-economic standards. This 'struggle for bread' often takes precedence over the maintenance of a Kurdish identity.

However, nothing remains static, and a possible future trend to be considered is that the current conflict between state and pro-Kurdish politicians and protesters in the sending community region of Van and other Kurdish areas may become a social remittance of more influence in the western cities. The public denigration of the pro-Kurdish move-ment may lead to Kurdish self-denigration *or* an increase in politicisa-tion. Indeed, there have been protests and riots by Kurdish youth in Kurdish majority and other Turkish cities, including Van, as a gen-eration of traumatised or disillusioned young people, many affected by village clearances and subsequently living in poverty in the cities, have expressed their anger. It is possible that some Vanlı migrants, too, particularly the young men who have given up on schooling, may be influenced by this movement, both in Van city and in western Turkey.

Another possible trend is that the rise of a Kurdish middle class will lead to more awareness of bilingualism and a desire to explore the more literary side of Kurdish. As yet, there are not many educational resources for Kurdish children in Turkey, but this may change. There has always existed a small urban Kurdish intellectual elite able to read as well as speak Kurdish; members of this elite have produced and read Kurdish poetry and prose. The anecdote about the taxi driver crying when a small girl in Istanbul spoke Kurdish to her father shows that there are different ways in which migrant parents hand on their Kurdishness to their children. In the future, some families may thus aspire to instill a sense of Kurdishness in their offspring that is less linked to religion, social hierarchies, or politics and more connected to linguistic or cultural knowledge. There are indications that Turkish universities will develop Kurdish language and literature departments. It is likely that many of the students will be children of Kurdish migrants with a desire to learn more about their language and literary heritage. Of course, in the past the maintenance of Kurdish at a literary level was in itself a political act. As there has now been some public acknowledgement that Kurdish is a separate language that merits teaching and learning, it is likely that bilingualism will represent less of a consciously political stance and thus become more frequent.

Politically, it remains to be seen whether Vanlı migrants and non-migrants, as well as other Kurds, will continue to respond to the ruling AKP's brand of Islamism, which appeals to the *ümmet*, the 'community' of Muslims, yet also allows some space for the expression of Kurdishness. Some Kurds have expressed their frustration with the promises of the government's 'democratic ouverture', saying that the AKP makes do with token gestures of multiculturalism without solving real political issues. Others see steps such as the creation of the Kurdish-language TRT 6 channel as an indication of major change. The general election of 2011 was a success for both the AKP, which received nearly 50 per cent of the national vote, and the pro-Kurdish BDP, which managed to have 36 independent candidates elected. Currently, it is unclear whether the AKP will form any coherent policies towards democratisation and cultural pluralism or if its actions are merely based on political opportunism. An increase in the number of pro-Kurdish politicians in parliament may strengthen the creation of discourses on Kurdishness and democracy that rival those of the AKP, but may not be able to compete with the religious bias of the AKP or, indeed, with the network of connections that affiliation with or support for the ruling party can increasingly bring. The unselfconscious, taken-for-granted piety of Kurdish Vanlı migrants may become a more conscious, elaborated, religious identity which, not unlike the tribal and hometown identities described in Chapter 5, can be fronted in order to create networks of more bridging than bonding social capital.

When looking at the stream of rural-urban migration from Gundême and other villages in Turkey, the question arises whether villages will eventually be totally depopulated. It has been decades since

Mücahit, one of the first labour migrants, left Gundême for Istanbul, and seasonal labour has long since become a rite of passage for most young Gundî men who have not completed high school. A few have tried to avoid the construction sector and work in restaurants, bars, and shops in tourism areas on the western or southern coast of Turkey, but this requires some foreign language skills. Some, often with the support of other migrant relatives, manage to complete high school, and a few even go to university. They, too, however, have left the village, as acquiring a high school education means going to boarding school or lodging with relatives in the city.

The 'ebb and flow' of migratory lives (Levitt and Glick Schiller 2004: 1012) is partly due to extraneous factors, as for instance the prevailing economy. This was visible on my most recent visit to Van province in July 2011. Feyzettin Çetin was preparing to move his nuclear family to Van city, following his two brothers who had already established themselves there. He was encouraged by a construction boom in Van city that had started after 2008, with many people in the centre of Van selling their houses on garden plots in return for flats in bigger apartment blocks which would be built on these plots. Feyzettin's brother Tacettin had found employment on a construction site in Van city. So had the sons of Süleyman Amca, which meant that they were no longer moving between Alanya and Van but rather living in Van city with their nuclear families.

Yet other young Gundî men have made use of the frequent minibus services between village and city, as well as the improved village roads, to commute from Gundême to Van every day for work and have chosen to remain in the village, at least for as long as the current boom continues. Mehmet, the youngest son of Haci Memo Çetin, has just built a new house in the village, tearing down the old one. He and his family now have an indoor bathroom and toilet, as well as running water in the kitchen. They have invested in furniture and curtains for their home and seem satisfied to remain in the village. Despite looking after the elderly Haci Memo and an adult disabled brother of Mehmet's, they are relatively autonomous. The move of many villagers to the city means that the market for dairy produce and meat has changed in their favour. For now, at least, they are not going anywhere.

The earthquakes of 2011 have shown how misleading it is to assume that people's lives are static. Many Vanlı moved out of the city, some of them to the villages, but these also suffered a lot of aftershocks. Others have made use of extensive networks of kin to spend at least the winter in different cities around Turkey, while others again have been supported by the government and have been provided with lodgings outside of Van. Many have become unhappy with their liminal existence as migrants-yet-non-migrants and will have to decide whether to settle more permanently or move back to Van once it is warmer.

There are thus various possible future scenarios for Gundême and Gundî, none of them perfectly foreseeable, even for Gundî themselves. Macro-processes such as a recession, a construction boom, a natural disaster, the possibility of democratisation, and the continuation of army-PKK conflict will all affect migration decisions. People may leave, some may return later, and some may find that remittances and changing circumstances make living in the village viable. Whatever the future of Gundême, it is likely to remain a potent, if ambiguous, symbol around which discourses of village life, modernity, and Kurdishness revolve.

APPENDIX

Questionnaire Handed out to Kurdish and Turkish Vanlı (English Translation)

The information collected with this questionnaire will be used for an anthropology thesis. The researcher is examining factors that affect identity formation in a village of Van, Van city, and among people from Van living in Istanbul. Your name will not be used in this questionnaire or at any point during this research. Your opinions and thoughts are very important for this research and I thank you for agreeing to take part.

1. General Information

Year of birth?

Place of birth? (City of Van, a village in Van, a district town in Van, other)

Gender?

Are you married? If yes, where was your spouse born?

Your level of education? Your spouse's level of education?

Your occupation? Your spouse's occupation?

Have you got children? If yes, how many?

Since when have you lived in Istanbul?

Why did you come to Istanbul? (For work, for education, because my relatives are here, because of the conflict, other)

Do you belong to a tribe? If yes, which one?

Have you got relatives in Istanbul? If yes, how many?

Which area of Istanbul do you live in? Why did you choose to live there?

What languages do you know? (Turkish, Kurdish, Arabic for reading the Qur'an, Arabic for conversations, English, German, French, other)

When did you join the association for people from Van?

Why do you take part in the association's activities?

When did you last go to Van?

Why do you go to Van? (to visit relatives, for business, other)

How often do you go to Van?

2. Your Views

Please look at the following statements and decide to what extent you agree/disagree with them (I agree very strongly, I agree, I am undecided, I disagree, I disagree very strongly). Please only tick one box after each statement.

Being from Van

I am proud of being from Van.
Sometimes I hide the fact that I am from Van.
When I meet someone from Van, I feel close to them.
It is important for me to know where people are from.
People from Van can be good or bad like any other person.
I would like my child to marry someone from Van.

Social Environment

Most of the people I socialise with are relatives.
Most of the people I socialise with are from Van.
The people I socialise with are all Muslims.
I socialise with both Turks and Kurds.
I spend more time with people of my own sex.

Religion

First of all, I am a Muslim.
My religious school (*mezhep*) is important to me.
My child can marry an Alevi.
My child can marry a non-Muslim.
I pray regularly.
Women should be able to wear a headscarf.
Women should wear a headscarf.
I feel close to a religious sect (*tarikat*).
I find religious sects dangerous.

Tribe

In Van, tribes are still important today.
Tribal organisation harms society.
I am attached to my tribe.
I would take care of a stranger if they were from my tribe.

I don't want my child to marry people from certain tribes.
Tribal organisation is more effective than the government in solving people's problems.

Life in Van

If I had a good job, I would like to return to Van.
Life in Van is better than life in Istanbul.
The people living in villages are happier than we are.
I am glad that I grew up in a village/in Van.
It was very difficult to grow up in a village/in Van.

Language and Identity

It's important for me to know Turkish well.
It's important for me to know Kurdish well.
I want my child to speak both Turkish and Kurdish well.
My child should know English rather than Kurdish.
The loss of Kurdish means the loss of a culture.
I see myself as a Kurd.
I see myself as a Turk.
I see myself as a citizen of Turkey (*Türkiyeli*).

Questionnaire Results (Partial)

Number of respondents: 85
Age range of respondents: 18–60
Average age of respondents: 34.6
Number of female/male respondents: 5/80
The answers to some of the questions in part 2 are summarised and shown after the questions. The numbers stand for, in this order: (agreement, disagreement, indecision, an invalid answer)

Being from Van

I am proud of being from Van. (76, 5, -, 2)
Sometimes I hide the fact that I am from Van. (12, 69, -, 4)

When I meet someone from Van, I feel close to them. (70, 7, 5, 3)
I would like my child to marry someone from Van. (56, 10, 13, 6)

Social Environment

Most of the people I socialise with are relatives. (28, 47, 7, 3)
Most of the people I socialise with are from Van. (16, 62, 3, 5)
The people I socialise with are all Muslims. (41, 37, 1, 6)
I socialise with both Turks and Kurds. (75, 4, -, 6)
I spend more time with people of my own sex. (57, 20, 3, 5)

Religion

First of all, I am a Muslim. (64, 14, 4, 3)
My child can marry an Alevi. (48, 18, 13, 6)
My child can marry a non-Muslim. (33, 30, 13, 9)
I pray regularly. (53, 24, 4, 4)
I feel close to a religious sect (*tarikat*). (16, 60, 6, 3)
I find religious sects dangerous. (47, 27, 6, 5)

Tribe

In Van, tribes are still important today. (53, 20, 8, 4)
Tribal organisation harms society. (48, 24, 9, 4)
I am attached to my tribe. (28, 43, 9, 5)
I would take care of a stranger if they were from my tribe. (46, 28, 7, 4)
I don't want my child to marry people from certain tribes. (32, 44, 5, 4)
Tribal organisation is more effective than the government
in solving people's problems. (16, 50, 13, 6)

Life in Van

If I had a good job, I would like to return to Van. (73, 7, 3, 2)

Language and Identity

It's important for me to know Turkish well. (73, 9, -, 3)
It's important for me to know Kurdish well. (79, 3, -, 3)

I want my child to speak both Turkish and Kurdish well. (77, 3, 1, 4)
My child should know English rather than Kurdish. (15, 63, 4, 3)
The loss of Kurdish means the loss of a culture. (76, 6, -, 3)
I see myself as a Kurd. (72, 3, 1, 9)
I see myself as a Turk. (12, 60, 4, 9)
I see myself as a citizen of Turkey (*Türkiyeli*). (71, 7, 3, 4)

NOTES

Chapter 1

1. Nadire Mater and her publisher were put on trial for 'degrading and accusing the armed forces' in her book *Mehmed'in Kitabı* (1999) (*Mehmet's book* – 'Mehmet' is the generic name for soldiers). Although the prosecution asked for two to twelve years imprisonment, they were later acquitted.

2. The *Cumartesi Anneleri* met every Saturday since 1995. Despite police pressure, the protests continued until 1999. For more details see Günçıkan 1996.

3. Examples of Kurdish MPs are Abdulkadir Aksu, the Minister of the Interior under Özal (ANAP) and in the same position under the AKP until 2007 and Mehdi Eker, minister of agriculture (AKP). Another Kurd, Leyla Zana, famous internationally for her imprisonment in 1994, entered parliament in 1991 with the Social Democrat Populist Party (SHP). Only after she was forced out of the party, did she co-found the Democratic Party with more specific Kurdish interests. In 1994 she and three other MPs (Hatip Dicle, Selim Sadak, and Orhan Dogan) were sentenced to 15 years in prison for separatist activities (Kürkçü 2003). They were released in 2004.

4. It is important to reiterate that Kurdology as a concept is just emerging in Turkey; the following account thus relates to foreign scholars as well as Kurdish and Turkish scholars/writers living abroad.

5. For annotated bibliographies see Kren 2000 (German literature) and Meho and Maglaughlin 2001 (mostly English, some Arabic, French and German literature). For simple bibliographies see Erdem (n.d.), Bozarslan (n.d.), and the Washington Kurdish Institute (n.d.).

6. See for example Chaliand 1980 and McDowall 1997 on Kurds generally and Olson 1996a and Deschner 2003 on Kurds in Turkey. Gunter, a political scientist, has published extensively on Kurds in Turkey (e.g. 1997, 2000, 2001).

7. See for example Barkey and Fuller 1998, Bozkurt and Druwe 1995, and Gürbey 1997.

8. In 1991, the Ministry of the Interior commissioned a report on how Spain and England had dealt with ETA and IRA. The report emphasised the democratic steps taken by the respective governments to resolve the conflicts (Gürbey 1997: 121). In 1993, Prime Minister Tansu Çiller mentioned the possibility of a 'Basque model' (Kirişçi and Winrow 1997: 20). The TOBB report of 1995 also drew comparisons between the PKK and ETA and the IRA.

9. Olson 1996b comments on how Russia uses the 'Kurdish card' to prevent Turkey from intervening in the conflict with Chechnya.

10. Examples are Beşikçi 1977, 1991a, and 1991b.

11. Asked whether they had family members in the PKK, 65 per cent chose not to answer. Over 70 per cent chose not to answer the question of what the effects of the PKK were.

12. Bozarslan says, 'Even in Turkey, the most democratic among those countries [the others being Iran, Iraq, and Syria], some subjects, like the Kurdish issue, are either discouraged or become practically non-existent' (n.d.).

13. Also see interview with Doğu Ergil, the author of the controversial TOBB report. He also discusses the difficulties of doing research on 'sensitive' topics (Ergil 2006).

14. In Turkey, Suryani Christians are/were mostly settled in the Tur Abdin area in the provinces of Şırnak and Mardin (Kreyenbroek 1996: 92, Armbruster 2007). As for Yezidis, who are neither Christians nor Muslims, there was a population of around 100,000 in Turkey before the 1980s, but many have migrated to Germany (Kreyenbroek 1996: 96–7).

15. The armed conflict between the militant Kurdistan Workers' Party (PKK) and the army began in 1984.

16. International intervention has led to a move from absolute denial of the issue to the acknowledgement of some responsibility (Ayata and Yükseker 2005: 32–3).

17. When counting households, I followed local intuitions: when an extended family lived in one building and shared the preparation and consumption of food, they were considered one household (*mal* in Kurdish), with the father or the oldest brother being the household head. If brothers or sons separated, that is, moved into different buildings (adjacent or further apart), they were considered as separate households.

18. See the appendix for the questionnaire in English and for some results.

19. See also Ochs and Capps (1996: 21): '[N]arratives are versions of reality. They are embodiments of one or more points of view rather than objective, omniscient accounts.'

Chapter 2

1. *Haci* is the title given to Muslims who have performed the pilgrimage to Mecca (*hac*) during the Feast of Sacrifice.
2. *Gundî* literally means 'villager', and I use it here to denote people from the village of Gundême.
3. Ammann's study of Kurds in Europe is partly based on interviews with Kurdish interlocutors from Turkey, Iran, Iraq, and Syria. The descriptions of village life by her interlocutors point to transnational, regional similarities in rural Kurdish material culture (2000: 35).
4. Ammann still speaks of woven and knotted floor coverings being made (2000: 105). See Aristova (2002: 180–4) for information on Kurdish carpet designs.
5. As a Sunni Muslim, he had been inculcated with a deep suspicion of Alevis. As many commentators on Turkey have noted, Sunni-Alevi antagonism has often been greater than Turkish-Kurdish antagonism (cf. Ammann 2000: 278).
6. Yalçın-Heckmann writes of the working day being 'divided according to prayer-times' in a Kurdish village in Hakkâri in the 1980s (1991: 110).
7. There may of course also be Kurdish civil servants. However, education levels among Kurds have generally been lower, so they make up a smaller percentage of civil servants.
8. Apparently these Kyrgyz were invited to settle in Turkey after the Russian invasion of Afghanistan in 1979. The inhabitants of one Van village, Ulupamır, came to Turkey from the Pamır high plateau in Afghanistan.
9. Yalçın points out that the concepts of lineage and clan are different in the degree to which common ancestry is traced. She thus argues that *mal* corresponds to both, since a common ancestor is assumed, yet the link is not necessarily clear (1986: 186). I have chosen to use the term 'lineage' only, partly for convenience and partly because it is irrelevant in practice whether my interlocutors assume or can prove common descent as long as they believe they are related.
10. Since it proved difficult to determine the exact number of children in each household without direct access to all of the households, I have decided only to count the married and widowed adults in the table. An official register of village households at the health centre proved to be unreliable as it still listed villagers who were deceased or had long moved away.
11. Here an adult son who will not marry due to a physical and perhaps mental disability has been counted.
12. Here two disabled men who live with their brother have been counted.
13. The term is said to be derived from the Arabic *fallah*, meaning 'peasant' (Wießner 1997: 178).

14. I am using a pseudonym here.
15. Here only about 12,000 of 90,000 soldiers survived (Zürcher 1997: 119). Sarıkamış is around 250 kilometres from Gundême.
16. Although he is referring to transnational migration, the analysis of migration in terms of different social spaces is persuasive.
17. The original German is 'eine institutionell verfestigte Redeweise, insofern eine solche Redeweise schon Handeln bestimmt und verfestigt und also auch schon Macht ausübt.'
18. Since they moved after an earthquake in 1976, they left their villages exceptionally early.

Chapter 3

1. 'Amca' means father's brother in Turkish. He is addressed thus, or as 'Ape' in Kurdish.
2. His mother had been widowed early, and she was left with five children and little extended family. When she refused to leave her children with the patrilineage, she was married to a younger relative of her husband's in a levirate marriage; with him she had two more children. When her sons were old enough to take care of her, she separated from her second husband and let him remarry.
3. One nuclear family from Gundême paid rent in Van after they had to move there in order to get physiotherapy for their severely handicapped son. However, later the husband's father built them a house in Van.
4. Of course Van has very different neighbourhoods. I am here referring to those that have grown with rural-urban migration of low-income, and often large, families.
5. The dilemma of farm succession and farm fragmentation is not limited to Turkey; Canadian researchers speak of the possibility of conflict between 'farm successor' and 'off-farm sibling' (Taylor and Norris 2000). Anthropologist Favret-Saada also points to subliminated intra-familial conflict due to farm succession (Favret-Saada and Cullen 1989).
6. While many Armenian and Syriac names were already changed from 1915 onwards, the vast majority of Rum, Armenian, Laz, Jewish, Arab, and Kurdish names were changed in 1968, when 12,000 new toponyms were introduced, replacing around 30 per cent of village names in Turkey (Öktem 2008: §19, §40).
7. To western Turks, and perhaps to people all over Turkey, Şırnak and Hakkâri are associated very closely with the fighting. If someone is sent to do his military service there, everyone is worried about him. Unlike other provinces which might be associated with agricultural products (e.g. herb

cheese from Van, dried fruit from Malatya, water melons from Diyarbakır), the only thing most people can think at the mention of Şırnak and Hakkâri is the clashes.

8. After the military coup of 1980, villagers had been forced to hand in any guns and shotguns they had. Unfortunately, the *korucu* have been known to exploit their armed status. According to sociologist Yükseker, there were still 58,000 paid and armed *korucu* in 2005, and they have been implicated in 'thousands of crimes, from kidnapping girls to killing people, from roadside robbery to theft' (Düzel 2005).

9. I follow Yalçın (1986) in this usage; fraternal joint means the cohabitation of two or more married brothers and their children, while a paternal joint household refers to a married couple with their children and at least one married son.

10. Like in other societies, milk kinship precludes marriage (cf. Parkes 2004).

11. Ammann posits that the rich land owners were/are mostly to be found in the plains rather than the mountains (2000: 105).

Chapter 4

1. The Turkish '*doğru*' can mean right or true, and he used the opposite of the former.

2. Anderson writes of the power of maps and map-makers in the colonial context (1991: 174).

3. The *millet* were the groups based on religious affiliation into which the population of the Ottoman Empire was divided.

4. In İstanbul, my husband and I experienced this mindset rather concretely; an elderly woman in our neighbourhood we had repeatedly argued with about the rubbish she threw out of her window said to my husband: 'You come here from Van [i.e. you are a Kurd], and marry an infidel [*gâvur*] ... you cannot tell me anything.'

5. In a recent article, Yeğen claims that Turkish nationalism is now going even further. The recent coinage of the term 'Jewish Kurds', first in reference to North Iraqi Kurds and then extended to Kurds in Turkey, indicates, writes Yeğen, that the nationalist project is aiming to end any 'precariousness' in the definition of Turkishness. With this new term, Kurds are not even considered Muslims anymore, and are firmly defined as 'other' (2007).

6. This argument has to be treated with care, however, as it has been used in the past to discredit any claims of the existence of 'Kurds'.

7. Orywal and Hackstein argue that the initial polarisation of primordialist versus situationalist descriptions of ethnicity has moved on to a synthesis stemming from the awareness that an emphasis on primordial characteristics

of an ethnic group is part of the border-drawing process that groups engage in continuously (1993: 596). Sökefeld, too, speaks of 'ein *common sense* des Konstruktivismus' (2001: §6).

8. According to a report on the east and southeast of the country, Van province ranked 67th in 1996 and 75th (out of 81) in 2003 (Kurmuş et al. 2006: 13). Public investment in all the provinces considered was well below the national average (*ibid.*).

Chapter 5

1. Jews had been living in the east of Turkey and other Kurdish-majority regions outside of Turkey for over two thousand years (cf. Kreyenbroek 1996, McDowall 1997: 12). Christian Nestorians lived mostly in the Hakkâri area since at least the 4th century. They were evacuated from the Hakkâri area in 1924 (Yalçın 1986: 139, 170).

2. From 1927 to 1985, Turkish censuses asked questions about mother tongue and second language use. However, from 1965 onwards, these results were not published any longer (Zeyneloğlu et al. 2011: 343).

3. This term (*asimile* in Turkish) is often used by Kurds who lament the effect of assimilationist state policies on their own behaviour. The most important criterion of assimilation is whether or not a person can speak Kurdish. The term is often used regretfully: 'We have become assimilated' (*Biz asimile olduk*).

4. According to Balı, the 250-strong Jewish community of Van city emigrated to Israel in October 1950 (2003: 247).

5. I use this term reluctantly, and thus in quotation marks, as it evokes a boundedness that does not necessarily exist (cf. Baumann 1996: 28–9).

6. Koçak, in an article on parliament in the early Republican period (1925–45), writes of 'leaders of Kurdish clans' entering parliament easily, provided that they had good relations with the party (2005: §37).

7. 'Retribalisation' describes the opposite of what some early studies of African rural-urban migration used to posit: a process of 'de-tribalisation' (cf. Ross and Weisner 1977: 359). However, the term 'retribalisation' was also used by Abner Cohen in his study of Hausa in Nigeria. His emphasis on the instrumentality of ethnic identity for material reasons (Banks 1996: 32–6) is applicable to my findings among Vanlı. A difference is that Vanlı themselves may perceive other ways belonging, too, such as Kurdish ethnicity (see Chapter 4).

8. The three Burukî candidates were Paşa Kurşunluoğlu for the centre-right DYP, Mehmet Kartal for the centre-left CHP, Fethi Eryiğit for the centre-left New Turkey Party (YTP). The Ertuşi candidates were İskender Ertuş for the DYP and Necip Yağizer for the CHP.

9. In the 2002 elections, 258,287 valid votes were placed and seven MPs voted for. Although the pro-Kurdish DEHAP party received most of the votes (over 40 per cent), they could not put a candidate in parliament, since nationally the party scored under 10 per cent. So, the second-placed AKP (with about 25 per cent) entered six, and the third-placed CHP (with about 5 per cent) entered one candidate, the Burukî member Mehmet Kartal (Türkiye Belgenet n.d.).

10. In Narı's study, it was found that in Bursa hometown associations went from representing 2.2 per cent of all associations in the city in 1963–83 to 34 per cent in 1984–90 and 61.1 per cent in 1991–99 (Hersant and Toumarkine 2005: endnote 3).

11. The term 'modern' is often used by non-covered women themselves to describe their dress. There is also the combination of 'modern türbanlı', i.e. a 'modern covered' woman, meaning that she wears tighter-fitting clothes, vibrant colours, and eschews the *pardesü*, an ankle-length loose-fitting coat.

12. Putnam traces the term back to reformer L. J. Hanifan in 1916 (2000: 19), while Palloni et al. point to economist Loury (2001: 1263, cf. Putnam 2000: 19).

13. Not all the wealth in Van comes from remittances. There are also a great number of civil servants, working for the university, the police force, the city, and the army. These civil servants earn a wage which would leave them struggling in Istanbul but offers a comfortable life in Van. Some of the serious wealth in Van also comes from the petrol and heroin smuggling trade.

14. A minibus (or indeed any kind of vehicle) is very prestigious in a village; a saying goes: 'Aldım Ford'un dizeli, sevdim köylü güzeli' ('I have bought a diesel Ford, I have fallen in love with the village beauty').

Chapter 6

1. Primary schools in Turkey used to comprise five years and then pupils went on to middle school for three years. Now primary school means eight years of compulsory education, after which high school (*lise*) is optional.

2. When reading White (2002), I have been struck by the detailed descriptions of women's attire. It is indeed immediately enlightening for anyone familiar with Turkey to know whether a woman is covered or not, what kind of cover she wears, and what she wears indoors and out. Navaro-Yashin writes that 'women's appearance in public is loaded with such deep symbolic meaning' (2000: 90, author's translation).

3. A popular game where four players use playing stones instead of cards and try to get rid of them all by sorting them in groups.

4. The night or a few nights before the wedding, the bride and the women celebrate with songs, food, and henna decorations.

5. Historian Karpat, who wrote a book on *gecekondus* in 1976, says that his book, written in English, was only translated into Turkish 27 years later, an indication of the lack of support for and interest in social sciences, as well as the suspicion that such 'leftist' endeavours were held in (2004: §27–9).
6. But as White rightly points out, with the constant expansion of the city, Ümraniye, too, is now no longer on the outskirts of Istanbul.
7. In my 14 years of contact with Vanlı both in Van province and in Istanbul, I have yet to come across any female Kurdish Vanlı of rural origin who moved to the city on her own. Seasonal migration has mostly been young and male, and permanent labour migration is common among young males, either single or with their families. As women go to university, this will change.

Chapter 7

1. Birkalan notes the same phrases used by a Turkish migrant family in Istanbul (1999: 207).
2. A marriage involves a ceremony at the bride's home first. After she is taken away to the groom's house, there is another ceremony there.
3. Of course there may be Alevis among the civil servants who are posted there and perhaps also some local families. However, the percentage of Alevis in Van province is less than 5 per cent (Washington Institute of Near East Policy 2007). The closest settlement of Alevis seems to be in the district of Varto in the neighbouring Muş province.
4. Magnarella and Türkdoğan say that according to literature from the 1950s and 1960s, over 50 per cent of marriages in the east of Turkey were contracted within villages (1973: 1628).
5. These marriages are between lineages in the same village.
6. Because the figures were rounded up and down, sometimes the total does not amount to 100 per cent.
7. This kind of exchange marriage (*berdel* in Turkish) is illegal in Turkey if a woman or a man is married against her or his wishes. Two fathers from the east of Turkey were sentenced to about 17 years in prison each in 2007 for marrying their underage children to each other against their wishes. In other cases it is debatable whether the marriages are contracted freely or whether families decide for young people. I have seen several examples of happy *berdel* marriages among Gundî, but would be reluctant to generalise.
8. When the marriage is described as a patrilateral or matrilateral cross-cousin marriage, the perspective of the member of the Derman patrilineage is taken.

Chapter 8

1. Nearly every woman aged over 40 that I spoke to in Gundême mentioned 'live' and 'dead' children. The children were either miscarriages, stillbirths, or infant deaths.
2. It has also been argued that different religious affiliations among Kurds have led to confusion about the role of women. The Kurdish Alevis tend to promote more gender equality than the Kurdish Sunnis of the Shafi'i school (cf. Ammann 2000: 277, Çelik 2005: 148, Erman 1998a). The Kurdish Vanlı of my acquaintance are all Sunnis.
3. Landmann reports similar avoidance rules among Circassians in Turkey: new brides were expected to remain silent in front of all males and females older than them and to avoid sharing the same space with the males. These avoidance rules were then gradually lifted by those in authority. Interestingly, young men were held to similar avoidance rules with their in-laws until the latter signalled a relaxation of this behaviour (1981: 121–2).
4. Indeed, the cleanliness of the homes is in sharp contrast with the rubbish-strewn backyards of the blocks in Tepelik or the littered streets in all three research locations.
5. This means 'Thank goodness'.
6. A recent survey on domestic violence in Turkey challenges the commonly-held myth that it is only women in and from the east and southeast of the country who suffer from male violence (Altınay and Arat 2009: xi).
7. A recent survey in Van city, carried out by the municipality's family consultation centre, found that of the 553 women applying to the centre in six months in 2007, 41 per cent had experienced domestic violence ('Erbatur'dan Başbakan'a . . .'). However, it is not clear whether they experience violence in nuclear family or in extended family households.
8. I by no means aim to be uncritical of the Turkish education system, which inculcates a homogenising nationalism, denying the value of pluralism. A recent study of Turkish school books has found many examples of racist, nationalist, sexist, and other discriminatory utterances (Tüzün 2009).
9. Headscarves are not permitted at schools or universities. Some young women choose to unveil during class time and put on headscarves outside of the institution, while others circumvent the ban by wearing hats or wigs. Others, however, choose to leave school completely.
10. There generally is an inverse relationship between level of education and handicraft skills. If a family encourages a girl to go to school, and even to university, she will not be expected to learn all the handicraft skills. Even if she knows how to knit, crochet, and make lace, she will not be expected to spend much time on preparing her trousseau.

Chapter 9

1. The movement began with the Kurdish religious thinker Said Nursi (1876–1960) (Bruinessen 1999b: 15), a native of Bitlis, a province to the west of Van and also bordering Van Lake. 'Nurcu' refers to 'Nur', the divine light.

2. Those women who do not want to take off their headscarves enrol in the Turkish open university, where they only have to take their head coverings off for the central exams. Yet others go to university abroad to avoid the headscarf ban.

3. The government of the Justice and Development Party (AKP), with the support of the Nationalist Movement Party (MHP) voted for constitutional change in February 2008 to allow women in higher education to wear headscarves. However, in June 2008, the Constitutional Court revoked these amendments of Articles 10 and 42, dealing with equality before the law and the right to education respectively.

4. Recent research found that among Sunni Hanefi, Sunni Shafi'i, and Alevi, the latter are the most accepting of intermarriage between religions, ethnic groups and countries. For a majority of Hanefi and Shafi'i, marriage with people of a different religion or from a different country is not a consideration, while over half of the Alevis would accept such a marriage ('Biz Kimiz?').

5. Mainstream prejudice towards Alevis is common. In general, Alevis have been invisibilised in Turkey, so that their exact number is not known. The centre-left CHP (Republican People's Party) has used Alevis as a potential vote-booster and wooed them in order to compete against the Sunni AKP. Up to 2006, religious instruction in schools did not mention Alevis and students had to learn and take part in Sunni namaz.

6. Excluded are close blood relatives.

7. Béller-Hann and Hann do point to regional differences in the degree of religiosity in the eastern Black Sea region, finding religion a 'vital force' in some areas, but of much less importance in others (2001: 160).

8. Among women there is of course also appreciation of intelligence, humour, generosity, hospitality, sensitivity, and good-naturedness.

9. Saktanber spoke of women's reception days being changed into days of religious reading and discussion (2002: 218); however, in the case of Vanlı migrants, reception days seemed to have become common only after moving to the city, and many such days may have been socio-religious from the beginning.

10. My initial discomfort was not unlike Unni Wikan's reaction when she first saw the Northern Omani women wearing burqa face masks. Wikan wondered whether 'an ingenious male mind had [...] invented a device

to distort women's beauty' (1991: 92–3). For me, too, the *çarşaf* had always represented a male invention, one aimed at making women 'safe' (i.e. 'asexual') for anyone but her husband. The Atatürkist discourse in Turkey has interpreted head covering, and in particular the *çarşaf*, as an insidious political symbol in danger of spreading and undermining the secular republic.

11. On the other hand, the other Qur'an teacher living in Tepelik, also wearing a *çarşaf*, takes her six-year-old daughter with her to her lessons.

BIBLIOGRAPHY

2011 Genel Seçim Sonuçları: Van Kesin Sonuçları. *Şehrivan Haber*, 13 June 2011. http://www.sehrivanhaber.com/haber_yorumla.php?haber_no=7836& kat=17.

Abu-Lughod, Lila. 1985. A Community of Secrets: The Separate World of Bedouin Women. *Signs*, 10 (4): 637–57.

——— 1986. *Veiled Sentiments: Honor and Poetry in a Bedouin Society.* Berkeley: University of California Press.

——— 1990. The Romance of Resistance: Tracing Transformations of Power through Bedouin Women. *American Ethnologist*, 17 (1): 41–55.

——— 2002. Do Muslim Women Really Need Saving? Anthropological Reflections on Cultural Relativism and Its Others. *American Anthropologist*, 104 (3): 783–90.

——— 2006. The Muslim Woman: The Power of Images and the Danger of Pity. *Eurozine*, 1 (Sept.). http://www.eurozine.com/articles/2006-09-01-abulughod-en.html.

Adı Değiştirilmiş 12 Bin 211 Köy Var. *Bianet*, 13 May 2009. http://www.bianet. org/bianet/insan-haklari/114489-adi-degistirilmis-12-bin-211-koy-var.

AK Parti'ye 'Brukan' Desteği. *Medya Van*, 2 June 2011. http://www.medyavan. com/index.php?action=haber&haber_no=3198&kat_id=6.

Al-Ali, Nadje and Khalid Koser, eds. 2002. *New Approaches to Migration: Transnationalism and Transformations of Home.* London: Routledge.

Allison, Christine. 1996. Old and New Oral Traditions in Badinan. In *Kurdish Culture and Identity.* Philip Kreyenbroek and Christine Allison, eds. pp. 29–47. London: Zed Books.

——— 2000. Volksdichtung und Phantasie: Die Darstellung von Frauen in der kurdischen mündlichen Überlieferung. In *Kurdische Frauen und das Bild der kurdischen Frau.* Eva Savelsberg, Siamend Hajo, and Carsten Borck, eds. pp. 33–50. Münster: LIT Verlag.

Altınay, Ayşe Gül and Yeşim Arat. 2009. *Violence against Women in Turkey: A Nationwide Survey.* Istanbul: Punto Publishing Solutions.

Altuntek, N. Serpil. 1993. *Van Yöresinde Akraba Evliliği.* Ankara: Kültür Bakanlığı.

—— 2001. Türkiye Üzerine Yapılmış Evlilik ve Akrabalık Araştırmalarının Bir Değerlendirmesi. *Hacettepe Üniversitesi Edebiyat Fakültesi Dergisi*, 18 (2): 17–28.

Ammann, Birgit. 1997. Ethnische Identität am Beispiel kurdischer Migration in Europa. In *Ethnizität, Nationalismus, Religion und Politik in Kurdistan*. Carsten Borck, Eva Savelsberg, and Siamend Hajo, eds. pp. 217–39. Münster: LIT Verlag.

—— 2000. *Kurden in Europa: Ethnizität und Diaspora*. Münster: LIT Verlag.

—— 2004. Die kurdische Diaspora in Europa. In *Die Kurden: Studien zu ihrer Sprache, Geschichte und Kultur*. Stefan Conermann and Geoffrey Haig, eds. pp. 207–46. Hamburg: EB-Verlag.

And, Metin. 1987. *Culture, Performance and Communication in Turkey*. Tokyo: Institute for the Study of Languages and Cultures of Asia and Africa.

Anderson, Benedict. 1991. *Imagined Communities: Reflections on the Origin and Spread of Nationalism*. London: Verso Editions/NLB.

Andrews, Peter, ed. 1989. *Ethnic Groups in the Republic of Turkey*. Wiesbaden: Dr. Ludwig Reichert Verlag.

Aristova, Tatyana Feodorofna. 2002 [1990]. *Kürtlerin Maddi Kültürü: Geleneksel Kültür Birliği Sorunu*. Istanbul: Avesta.

Armbruster, Heidi. 2007. Homes in Crisis: Syrian Orthodox Christians in Turkey and Germany. In *New Approaches to Migration? Transnational Communities and the Transformation of Home*. Nadje Al-Ali and Khalid Koser, eds. pp. 17–33. London: Routledge.

Ayata, Bilgin and Deniz Yükseker. 2005. A Belated Awakening: National and International Responses to the Internal Displacement of Kurds in Turkey. *New Perspectives on Turkey*, 32: 5–42.

Balı, Rıfat N. 2003. *Cumhuriyet Yıllarında Türkiye Yahudileri: Aliya: Bir Toplu Göç Öyküsü (1946–1949)*. Istanbul: İletişim Yayınları.

Banks, Marcus. 1996. *Ethnicity: Anthropological Constructions*. London: Routledge.

Barkan, Joel D., Michael L. McNulty and M.A.O. Ayeni. 1991. 'Hometown' Voluntary Associations, Local Development, and the Emergence of Civil Society in Western Nigeria. *The Journal of Modern African Studies*, 29 (3): 457–80.

Barkey, Henri J. and Graham E. Fuller. 1998. *Turkey's Kurdish Question*. Oxford: Rowman & Littlefield Publishers.

Barth, Fredrik. 1953. *Principles of Social Organization in Southern Kurdistan*. Oslo: Brodrene Jorgensen.

—— 1954. Father's Brother's Daughter Marriage in Kurdistan. *Southwestern Journal of Anthropology*, 10: 164–71.

—— 1969. Introduction. In *Ethnic Groups and Boundaries*. Fredrik Barth, ed. pp. 9–38. Bergen: Universitets Forlaget.

—— 1995. Ethnicity and the Concept of Culture. Paper presented at the conference 'Rethinking Culture', Harvard 1995.

Başlangıç, C. 2003. Sınır'da Kalan Kadın Sosyolog. *Radikal*, 25 August. http://www.radikal. com.tr/veriler/2003/08/25/haber_86413.php.

Baumann, Gerd. 1996. *Contesting Culture: Discourses of Identity in Multi-Ethnic London*. Cambridge: Cambridge University Press.

Bedir Xan, Emir Celadet and Roger Lescot. 2000. *Kürtçe Dilbilgisi (Kurmancî)*. Istanbul: Doz Yayınları.

Bedir Xan, Kamuran. n.d. *Kolay Kürtçe (Kurmancî)*. Istanbul: Doz Yayınları.

Begikhani, Nazand. 2000. Das Bild der kurdischen Frau in der orientalistischen Literatur des neunzehnten Jahrhunderts. In *Kurdische Frauen und das Bild der kurdischen Frau*. Eva Savelsberg, Siamend Hajo, and Carsten Borck, eds. pp. 51–75. Münster: LIT Verlag.

Behar, Ruth. 1994. Gender, Identity, and Anthropology. In *Reconstructing Gender in the Middle East: Tradition, Identity, and Power*. Fatma Müge Göçek and Shiva Balaghi, eds. pp. 81–4. New York: Columbia University Press.

Bellér-Hann, Ildiko and Chris Hann. 2001. *Turkish Region: State, Market and Social Identities on the East Black Sea Coast*. Oxford: James Currey Publishers.

Berkan, İsmet. 2005. Kürtler Var Mıdır, Yok Mudur? *Radikal*, 23 November, p. 3.

Beşikçi, İsmail. 1970. *Doğu Anadolu'nun Düzeni: Sosyo-Ekonomik ve Etnik Temeller*. Ankara: E Yayınları.

——— 1977. *Kürtlerin 'Mecburi İskân'ı*. Ankara: Komal.

——— 1991a Cumhuriyet Halk Fırkası'nın Tüzüğü (1927) ve Kürt Sorunu. Ankara: Yurt Kitap Yayın.

——— 1991b. Tunceli Kanunu (1935) ve Dersim Jenosidi. Istanbul: Belge Yayınları.

Birkalan, Hande. 1999. *Homemaking and Story Telling in a Gecekondu in Istanbul*. PhD dissertation, Indiana University.

Biz Kimiz? *Milliyet*, 19–26 March 2007. http://www.milliyet.com.tr/2007/03/19/guncel/agun.html.

Blau, Joyce. 1996. Kurdish Written Literature. In *Kurdish Culture and Identity*. Philip Kreyenbroek and Christine Allison, eds. pp. 20–8. London: Zed Books.

Boissevain, Jeremy. 1974. *Friends of Friends: Networks, Manipulators and Coalitions*. Oxford: Basil Blackwell.

——— 1979. Network Analysis: A Reappraisal. *Current Anthropology*, 20 (2): 392–4.

Bora, Aksu. 2005. *Kadınların Sınıfı: Ücretli Ev Emeği ve Kadın Öznelliğinin İnşası*. Istanbul: İletişim Yayınları.

Bora, Aksu and İlknur Üstün. 2005. *'Sıcak Aile Ortamı': Demokratikleşme Sürecinde Kadın ve Erkekler*. Istanbul: TESEV Yayınları.

Borgatti, S.P., M.G. Everett, and L.C. Freeman. 2002. *Ucinet for Windows: Software for Social Network Analysis*. Harvard, MA: Analytic Technologies.

Bott, Elizabeth. 1971 [1957]. *Family and Social Network: Roles, Norms, and External Relationships in Ordinary Urban Families (Second Edition)*. New York: The Free Press.

Bourdieu, Pierre. 1977. *Outline of a Theory of Practice*. Cambridge: Cambridge University Press.

—— 1985. The Social Space and the Genesis of Groups. *Theory and Society*, 14 (6): 723–44.

—— 1998. *Practical Reason: On the Theory of Action*. Cambridge: Polity Press.

Bozarslan, Hamit. n.d. Research Guide: Kurdish Studies. *Middle East Review of International Affairs*. http://meria.idc.ac.il/research-g/kurds.html.

Bozkurt, Askım and Ulrich Druwe. 1995. Das Kurdenproblem in der Türkei, in Iran, in Irak und in Syrien. *Orient*, 36: 398–402.

Brettell, Caroline. 2003. *Anthropology and Migration: Essays on Transnationalism, Ethnicity and Identity*. New York: Altamira Press.

Brubaker, Rogers and Frederick Cooper. 2000. Beyond 'Identity'. *Theory and Society*, 29: 1–47.

Bruinessen, Martin van. 1978. *Agha, Shaikh and State*. PhD dissertation, University of Utrecht.

—— 1989a. *Agha, Scheich und Staat: Politik und Gesellschaft Kurdistans*. Berlin: Verlagsabteilung des Berliner Instituts für Vergleichende Sozialforschung e.V.

—— 1989b. The Ethnic Identity of the Kurds in Turkey. In *Ethnic Groups in the Republic of Turkey*. Peter Andrews, ed. pp. 613–21. Wiesbaden: Dr. Ludwig Reichert Verlag.

—— 1994. Kurdish Nationalism and Competing Ethnic Loyalties. Original English version of: Nationalisme Kurde et Ethnicités Intra-Kurdes. *Peuples Méditerranéens*, 68–69: 11–37. http://www.let.uu.nl/~martin.vanbruinessen/personal/publications/Competing_Ethnic_Loyalties.htm.

—— 1997a. Kurden zwischen ethnischer, religiöser und regionaler Identität. In *Ethnizität, Nationalismus, Religion und Politik in Kurdistan*. Carsten Borck, Eva Savelsberg, and Siamend Hajo, eds. pp. 185–216. Münster: LIT Verlag.

—— 1997b. İsmail Beşikçi: Turkish Sociologist, Critic of Kemalism and Kurdologist. Paper presented at the conference 'Kemalismus als Herrschafts- und Staatsideologie', Berlin, Humboldt-Universität, 24–25 October. http://www.let.uu.nl/~martin.vanbruinessen/personal/publications/ismail_besikci.htm.

—— 1999a. Kurds, States and Tribes. Paper presented at the conference 'Tribes and Powers in the Middle East', London, SOAS, Birkbeck College and Iraqi Cultural Forum, 23–24 January.

—— 1999b. The Kurds and Islam. Working Paper No. 13. Islamic Area Studies Project, Tokyo. http://www.let.uu.nl/~martin.vanbruinessen/personal/publications/Kurds_and_Islam.htm.

—— 2000. Von Adela Khanum zu Leyla Zana: Weibliche Führungspersonen in der kurdischen Geschichte. In *Kurdische Frauen und das Bild der kurdischen Frau*. Eva Savelsberg, Siamend Hajo, and Carsten Borck, eds. pp. 9–32. Münster: LIT Verlag.

———— 2003. Innerkurdische Herrschaftsverhältnisse: Stämme und religiöse Brüderschaften. *epd-Dokumentation*, 7: 9–14.

Burt, Ronald. 1992. *Social Holes: The Social Structure of Competition*. Cambridge, MA: Harvard University Press.

Casier, Marlies, Joost Jongerden, and Nic Walker. 2011. Fruitless Attempts? The Kurdish Initiative and Containment of the Kurdish Movement in Turkey. *New Perspectives on Turkey*, 44: 103–27.

Chaliand, Gerard, ed. 1980. *A People without a Country: The Kurds and Kurdistan*. London: Zed Press.

Chyet, Michael L. 2002. *Kurdish-English Dictionary*. New Haven: Yale University Press.

Cliggett, Lisa. 2003. Gift Remitting and Alliance Building in Zambian Modernity: Old Answers to Modern Problems. *American Anthropologist*, 105 (3): 543–52.

Cohen, Jeffrey H. 2001. Transnational Migration in Rural Oaxaca, Mexico: Dependency, Development, and the Household. *American Anthropologist*, 103 (4): 954–67.

Cohen, Robin. 2002. Diaspora. In *International Encyclopedia of the Social and Behavioral Sciences*. Neil J. Smelser and Paul B. Bates, eds. pp. 3642–5. Amsterdam: Elsevier.

Çağaptay, Soner. 2006. *Islam, Secularism, and Nationalism in Modern Turkey: Who is a Turk?* London: Routledge.

Çağlayan, Handan. 2007. *Analar, Yoldaşlar, Tanrıçalar: Kürt Hareketinde Kadınlar*. Istanbul: İletişim Yayınları.

Çakır, Ruşen, İrfan Bozan, and Balkan Talu. 2004. *İmam Hatip Liseleri: Efsaneler ve Gerçekler*. Istanbul: TESEV Yayınları.

Çarkoğlu, Ali and Binnaz Toprak. 2000. *Türkiye'de Din, Toplum ve Siyaset*. Istanbul: TESEV Yayınları.

———— 2006. *Değişen Türkiye'de Din, Toplum ve Siyaset*. Istanbul: TESEV Yayınları.

Çaymaz, Birol. 2005. İstanbul'da Niğdeli Hemşehri Dernekleri. *European Journal of Turkish Studies*, 2. http://www.ejts.org/document410.html.

Çelik, Ayşe Betül. 2005. 'I Miss My Village!': Forced Kurdish Migrants in Istanbul and their Representation in Associations. *New Perspectives on Turkey*, 32: 137–63.

Delaney, Carol. 1991. *The Seed and the Soil: Gender and Cosmology in Turkish Village Society*. Berkeley: University of California Press.

Deschner, Günther. 2003. *Die Kurden: Volk ohne Staat, Geschichte und Hoffnung*. München: F.A. Herbig Verlag.

Devlet Planlama Teşkilatı (DPT). 2008. *Türkiye'de İç Göçler ve Göç Edenlerin Nitelikleri (1965–2000)*. Ankara: DPT.

Düzel, Neşe. 2005. Hakkâri'de Korku ve Gerginlik Var. *Radikal*, 7 November. http://www.radikal.com.tr/haber.php?haberno=169155.

Düzel, Neşe. 2006. CHP'nin Tutumu Dinci Bir Tutum. *Radikal*, 2 October, p. 6.

Edgü, Ferit. 2002 [1977]. *O/Hakkâri'de Bir Mevsim*. Istanbul: Yapı Kredi Yayınları.

Elwert, Georg. 1995. Boundaries, Cohesion and Switching: On We-Groups in Ethnic, National and Religious Forms. *Bulletin de LAPAD*, 10. http://apad. revues.org/1111.

En Pahalı Benzin Türkiye'de. *Milliyet*, 23 July 2008. http://www.milliyet.com. tr/Ekonomi/Son Dakika.aspx?aType=SonDakika&Kategori=ekonomi&Art icleID=970290.

Erbatur'dan Başbakan'a: Kadına Yönelik Şiddet Genelgesi Uygulanıyor mu? *Bianet*, 23 January 2009. http://bianet.org/bianet/siyaset/112117-erbaturdan-basbakana-kadina-yonelik-siddet-genelgesi-uygulaniyor-mu.

Erdem, Engin. I. n.d. Research Guide: A Bibliography of the Kurdish Question in the Middle East. Middle East Review of International Affairs. http:// meria.idc.ac.il/research-g/kurds_biblio.html.

Erder, Sema. 1996. *Ümraniye: İstanbul'a bir Kent Kondu*. Istanbul: İletişim Yayınları.

―――― 1997. *Kentsel Gerilim ve Enformel İlişki Ağları*. Ankara: UM:ag Yayınları.

Ergil, Doğu. 2006. Knowledge is a Potent Instrument for Change: Interview with Doğu Ergil. *European Journal of Turkish Studies*, 5. http://ejts.revues.org/ index762.html#tocto1n1.

Eriksen, Thomas Hylland. 1993. *Ethnicity and Nationalism: Anthropological Perspectives*. London: Pluto Press.

Erman, Tahire. 1998a. The Impact of Migration on Turkish Rural Women: Four Emergent Patterns. *Gender and Society*, 12 (3): 146–67.

―――― 1998b. Göç Olgusunda Kalitatif Yöntem Olarak Etnografik Araştırmasının Düşündükleri. In *Türkiye'de İçgöç: Türkiye'de İçgöç, Sorunsal Alanları ve Araştırma Yöntemleri Konferansı 6–8 June 1997*. Türkiye Ekonomik ve Toplumsal Tarih Vakfı, ed. Istanbul: Tarih Vakfı.

―――― 2004. Gecekondu Çalışmalarında 'Öteki' Olarak Gecekondulu Kurguları. *European Journal of Turkish Studies*, 1. http://www.ejts.org/ document85.html.

Esen, Orhan. 2007. Learning İstanbul: Die Stadt İstanbul: Materielle Produktion und Produktion des Diskurses. In *Self Service City: İstanbul*. Orhan Esen and Stephan Lanz, eds. pp. 33–52. Berlin: b_books.

Esser, Hartmut. 2007. Does the 'New' Immigration Require a 'New' Theory of Integration? In *Rethinking Migration: New Theoretical and Empirical Perspectives*. Alejandro Portes and Josh DeWind, eds. pp. 308–41. Oxford: Berghahn Books.

Favret-Saada, Jeanne and Catherine Cullen. 1989. Unbewitching as Therapy. *American Ethnologist*, 16 (1): 40–56.

Ferguson, James. 1992. The Country and the City on the Copperbelt. *Cultural Anthropology*, 7 (1): 80–92.

Friedl, Erika. 1994. Notes from the Village: On the Ethnographic Construction of Women in Iran. In *Reconstructing Gender in the Middle East: Tradition,*

Identity, and Power. Fatma Müge Göçek and Shiva Balaghi, eds. pp. 85–99. New York: Columbia University Press.

Frisch, Hillel. 1997. Modern Absolutist or Neopatriarchal State Building? Customary Law, Extended Families, and the Palestinian Authority. *International Journal of Middle East Studies*, 29 (3): 341–58.

Gambetti, Zeynep. 2006. The Search for a New Ground: Interview with Zeynep Gambetti. *European Journal of Turkish Studies*, 5. http://ejts.revues.org/index784.html.

Gardner, Katy. 1995. *Global Migrants, Local Lives: Travel and Transformation in Rural Bangladesh.* Oxford: Oxford University Press.

Gmelch, George. 1980. Return Migration. *Annual Review of Anthropology*, 9: 135–59.

Göç Edenler Sosyal Yardımlaşma ve Kültür Derneği (Göç-Der). n.d. *Van: Boşaltılmış Köyler.* http://www.gocder.net/interest.htm.

Göle, Nilüfer. 1996. *The Forbidden Modern: Civilization and Veiling.* Michigan: University of Michigan Press.

Grabolle-Çeliker, Anna. 2009. Construction of the Kurdish Self in Turkey through Humorous Popular Culture. *Journal of Intercultural Studies*, 30 (1): 89–105.

Graham, Laura R. and Ana Celia Zentella. 2010. Language in the US Census: Problems and Progress. *Anthropology News* (May): 6.

Granovetter, Mark. 1983. The Strength of Weak Ties: A Network Theory Revisited. *Sociological Theory*, 1: 201–33.

Gudykunst, William B. and Karen L. Schmidt. 1988. Language and Ethnic Identity: An Overview and Prologue. In *Language and Ethnic Identity.* William B. Gudykunst, ed. pp. 1–14. Clevedon: Multilingual Matters.

Gunter, Michael M. 1997. *The Kurds and the Future of Turkey.* New York: St. Martin's Press.

——— 2000. The Continuing Kurdish Problem in Turkey after Öcalan's Capture. *Third World Quarterly*, 21 (5): 849–70.

——— 2001. The Bane of Kurdish Disunity. *Orient*, 42: 605–16.

Güler, Habib. 2008. 31 Bin Çocuk Sokaklarda Yaşıyor. *Zaman*, 22 November. http://www.zaman.com.tr/haber.do?haberno=762922&keyfield=333120626 96E20C3A76F63756B20736F6B616B.

Günçıkan, Berat. 1996. *Cumartesi Anneleri.* Istanbul: İletişim Yayınları.

Güneş-Ayata, Ayşe. 1996. Solidarity in Urban Turkish Family. In *Turkish Families in Transition.* Gabriele Rasuly-Paleczek, ed. pp. 98–113. Frankfurt am Main: Peter Lang.

Gürbey, Gülistan. 1997. Optionen und Hindernisse für eine Lösung des Kurdenkonfliktes in der Türkei. In *Ethnizität, Nationalismus, Religion und Politik in Kurdistan.* Carsten Borck, Eva Savelsberg, and Siamend Hajo, eds. pp. 113–54. Münster: LIT Verlag.

Hacettepe Üniversitesi Nüfus Etüdleri Enstitüsü. 2006. *Türkiye Göç ve Yerinden Olmuş Nüfus Araştırması.* http://www.hips.hacettepe.edu.tr/tgyona/tgyona.htm.

Haig, Geoffrey. 2004. The Invisibilisation of Kurdish. In *Die Kurden: Studien zu ihrer Sprache, Geschichte und Kultur*. Stefan Conermann and Geoffrey Haig, eds. pp. 121–50. Hamburg: EB-Verlag.

Hajo, Siamend, Carsten Borck, Eva Savelsberg, and Sukriye Dogan, eds. 2004. *Gender in Kurdistan und der Diaspora*. Münster: Unrast Verlag.

Hann, Ildiko and Chris Hann. 1992. Samovars and Sex on Turkey's Russian Markets. *Anthropology Today*, 4: 3–6.

Hannerz, Ulf. 1980. *Exploring the City: Inquiries Toward an Urban Anthropology*. New York: Columbia University Press.

Harris, Colette. 2004. *Control and Subversion: Gender Relations in Tajikistan*. London: Pluto Press.

Hassanpour, Amir. 1996. The Creation of Kurdish Media Culture. In *Kurdish Culture and Identity*. Philip Kreyenbroek and Christine Allison, eds. pp. 48–84. London: Zed Books.

——— 1997. MED-TV, Großbritannien und der türkische Staat: Die Suche einer staatenlosen Nation nach Souveränität im Äther. In *Ethnizität, Nationalismus, Religion und Politik in Kurdistan*. Carsten Borck, Eva Savelsberg, and Siamend Hajo, eds. pp. 239–78. Münster: LIT Verlag.

Hersant, Jeanne and Alexandre Toumarkine. 2005. Hometown Organizations in Turkey: An Overview. *European Journal of Turkish Studies*, 2. http://www.ejtsorg.revues.org/document 397.htm.

Herzfeld, Michael. 1990. Pride and Perjury: Time and the Oath in the Mountain Villages of Crete. *Man*, 25 (2): 305–22.

Houston, Chris. 2001a. *Islam, Kurds and the Turkish Nation-State*. Oxford: Berg.

——— 2001b. Profane Institutions: Kurdish Diaspora in the Turkish City – Istanbul. *The Australian Journal of Anthropology*, 12 (1): 1–16.

Işık, Burhan C. 1992. Depremler ve Türkiye. Harita ve Kadastro Mühendisleri Odası. http://www.hkmo.org.tr/resimler/ekler/54dda4b1ba34c6f_ek.pdf.

Işık, Oğuz and Melih Pınarcıoğlu. 2001. *Nöbetleşe Yoksulluk: Gecekondulaşma ve Kent Yoksulları: Sultanbeyli Örneği*. Istanbul: İletişim Yayınları.

İflazoğlu, Nazif. 2006. Bütün Suçların Anası: Göç. *Radikal*, 9 July, p. 8.

İncesu, L. and S. Meresh. 1995. Aufregung um Kurden-Studie in der Türkei. *Kurdistan Heute*, 16. http://www.navend.de/html/kurdistan_heute/artikel/16_Kurdienstudie_TOBB.htm

İstanbul Büyüksehir Belediyesi (İBB). 2007. *İstanbul'da Görgülü Yaşamak*. Istanbul: Seyyar Kitap.

Jäger, Siegfried. 2001. Diskurs und Wissen: Theoretische und methodische Aspekte einer kritischen Diskurs- und Dispositivanalyse. In *Handbuch sozialwissenschaftliche Diskursanalyse, Band 1: Theorien und Methoden*. Reiner Keller, Andreas Hirseland, Werner Schneider, and Willy Viehöver, eds. pp. 81–112. Opladen: Leske und Budrich.

Jongerden, Joost. 2001. Resettlement and Reconstruction of Identity: The Case of the Kurds in Turkey. *Ethnopolitics*, 1 (1): 80–6.

Just, Roger. 2000. *A Greek Island Cosmos: Kinship and Community in Meganisi*. Oxford: James Currey Publishers.

Kandiyoti, Deniz. 1988. Bargaining with Patriarchy. *Gender and Society*, 2 (3): 274–90.

Karpat, Kemal H. 2004. The Genesis of the Gecekondu: Rural Migration and Urbanization (1976). *European Journal of Turkish Studies*, 1. http://www.ejts.org/document54.html.

Kartal'dan AK Parti Açıklaması. *Medya Van*, 3 June 2011. http://www.medyavan.com/index.php?action=haber&haber_no=3209&kat_id=6.

Khuri, Fuad I. 1970. Parallel Cousin Marriage Reconsidered: A Middle Eastern Practice that Nullifies the Effects of Marriage on the Intensity of Family Relationships. *Man*, 5: 598–618.

Kieser, Hans-Lukas. 2000. *Der verpasste Friede: Mission, Ethnie und Staat in den Ostprovinzen der Türkei 1839–1938*. Zürich: Chronos Verlag.

King, Diane E. 2003. The Doubly Bound World of Kurdish Women. *Voices*, 6 (1): 1, 8–10.

Kirişçi, Kemal and Gareth M. Winrow. 1997. *The Kurdish Question and Turkey: An Example of a Trans-State Ethnic Conflict*. London: Frank Cass Publishers.

Kızılkaya, Muhsin. 2000. *Kayıp Divan*. Istanbul: İletişim Yayınları.

Koçak, Cemil. 2005. Parliament Membership during the Single-Party System in Turkey (1925–1945). *European Journal of Turkish Studies*, 3. http://www.ejts.org/document497.html.

Koven, Michele E.J. 1998. Two Languages in the Self/The Self in Two Languages: French-Portuguese Bilinguals' Verbal Enactments and Experiences of Self in Narrative Discourse. *Ethos*, 26 (4): 410–55.

Kren, Karin. 1996. Kurdish Material Culture in Syria. In *Kurdish Culture and Identity*. Philip Kreyenbroek and Christine Allison, eds. pp. 162–73. London: Zed Books.

——— 2000. *Kurdologie, Kurdistan und die Kurden in der deutschsprachigen Literatur: Kommentierte Bibliographie*. Münster: LIT Verlag.

Kreyenbroek, Philip. 1992. On the Kurdish Language. In *The Kurds: A Contemporary Overview*. Philip Kreyenbroek and Stefan Sperl, eds. pp. 68–83. London: Routledge.

——— 1996. Religion and Religions in Kurdistan. In *Kurdish Culture and Identity*. Philip Kreyenbroek and Christine Allison, eds. pp. 85–110. London: Zed Books.

Kreyenbroek, Philip and Christine Allison, eds. 1996. *Kurdish Culture and Identity*. London: Zed Books.

Kurban, Dilek. 2007. Raporun Söylemedikleri. *Radikal*, 9 March. http://www.radikal.com.tr/ek_haber.php?ek=r2&haberno=6575&tarih=09/03/2007.

Kurban, Dilek, Deniz Yükseker, Ayşe Betül Çelik, Turgay Ünalan, and A. Tamer Aker. 2006. *'Zorunlu Göç' ile Yüzleşmek: Türkiye'de Yerinden Edilme Sonrası Vatandaşlığın İnşası*. Istanbul: TESEV Yayınları.

Kurmuş, Orhan, Ayşe Kudat, Ece Sanal Kılıçözlü, Ertan Karabıyık, İsmet Yalçın, Serkan Ünverdi, A. Halis Akder, Çağlar Keyder, and Nazan Üstündağ. 2006. *Doğu ve Güneydoğu Anadolu'da Sosyal ve Ekonomik Öncelikler.* Istanbul: TESEV Yayınları.

Kürkçü, Ertuğrul. 2003. Defiance under Fire; Leyla Zana: Prisoner of Conscience. *Amnesty Now* (Fall). http://www.amnestyusa.org/action/special/zana.html.

Landmann, Angelika. 1981. *Akifiye – Büyükçamurlu: Ubychen-Dörfer in der Südost-Türkei.* Heidelberg: Esprint Verlag.

Leach, Edmund R. 1940. *Social and Economic Organisation of the Rowanduz Kurds.* London: London School of Economics.

Lévi-Strauss, Claude. 1969 [1949]. *The Elementary Structures of Kinship.* Boston: Beacon Press.

Levitt, Peggy. 1998. Social Remittances: Migration Driven Local-Level Forms of Cultural Diffusion. *International Migration Review,* 32 (4): 926–48.

Levitt, Peggy and Nina Glick Schiller. 2004. Conceptualizing Simultaneity: A Transnational Social Field Perspective on Society. *International Migration Review,* 38 (3): 1002–39.

Lin, Nan. 1999. Building a Network Theory of Social Capital. *Connections,* 22 (1): 28–51.

———— 2000. Inequality in Social Capital. *Contemporary Sociology,* 29 (6): 785–95.

———— 2001. *Social Capital: A Theory of Social Structure and Action.* Cambridge: Cambridge University Press.

MacDonald, Charles G. 1998. Kurdology Conference in Berlin: Between Imagination and Denial: Constructing Kurdology. *Zagros,* 2. http://www.kurd.org/Zagros/Berlin.html.

Magnarella, Paul. 1974. *Tradition and Change in a Turkish Town.* New York: John Wiley.

Magnarella, Paul and Orhan Türkdoğan. 1973. Descent, Affinity, and Ritual Relations in Eastern Turkey. *American Anthropologist,* 75 (5): 1626–33.

Marcus, Aliza. 2007. *Blood and Belief: The PKK and the Kurdish Fight for Independence.* New York: New York University Press.

Marcus, George. 1995. Ethnography in/of the World System: The Emergence of Multisited Ethnography. *Annual Review of Anthropology,* 24: 95–117.

Mater, Nadire. 1999. *Mehmed'in Kitabı.* Istanbul: Metis Yayınları.

Mayer, Philip. 1971. *Townsmen or Tribesmen: Conservatism and the Process of Urbanization in a South African City.* Cape Town: Oxford University Press.

McCabe, Justine. 1983. FBD Marriage: Further Support for the Westermarck Hypothesis of the Incest Taboo? *American Anthropologist,* 85: 50–69.

McDowall, David. 1997. *A Modern History of the Kurds.* London: I.B. Tauris.

Meho, Lokman I. and Kelly L. Maglaughlin. 2001. *Kurdish Culture and Society: An Annotated Bibliography.* London: Greenwood Press.

Mir-Hosseini, Ziba. 1996. Faith, Ritual, and Culture among the Ahl-i Haqq. In *Kurdish Culture and Identity.* Philip Kreyenbroek and Christine Allison, eds. pp. 111–34. London: Zed Press.

Mitchell, James Clyde. 1969. *Social Networks in Urban Situations.* Manchester: Manchester University Press.

Moerman, Michael. 1965. Ethnic Identification in a Complex Civilization: Who are the Lue? *American Anthropologist,* 67 (5): 1215–30.

Mojab, Shahrzad. 1998. 'Muslim' Women and 'Western' Feminists: The Debate on Particulars and Universals. *Monthly Review,* 50. http://www.monthlyreview.org/volume50. htm.

——— 2001. *Women of a Non-State Nation: The Kurds.* Costa Mesa, Cal.: Mazda Publishers.

Mojab, Shahrzad and Amir Hassanpour. 2002. Thoughts on the Struggle against 'Honor Killing'. *International Journal of Kurdish Studies,* 16 (1–2): 83–97.

Moore, Will H. and Stephen M. Shellman. 2004. Fear of Persecution: Forced Migration 1952–1995. The Journal of Conflict Resolution, 48 (5): 723–45.

Muhtarlık Seçimlerinde Akıl Tutulması. *Radikal,* 29 March 2009. http://www.radikal.com.tr/Radikal.aspx?aType=RadikalDetay&ArticleID=928552&Date=06.04.2009&CategoryID=78.

Murphy, Robert F. and Leonard Kasdan. 1959. The Structure of Parallel Cousin Marriage. *American Anthropologist,* 61: 17–29.

Müküs, Burhanettin. 1970. *Ertuş Aşireti.* Graduation dissertation, Istanbul University.

Myers, Scott M. 2000. The Impact of Religious Involvement on Migration. *Social Forces,* 79 (2): 755–83.

Narı, Yaşar. 1999. *Bursa Kent Merkezinde Faaliyet Gösteren Hemşehri Dernekleri ve bu Derneklerin Bursa'nın Sosyo-Politik Yapısına Katkıları.* Master dissertation, Marmara University.

Navaro-Yashin, Yael. 2000. Kültür Kehanetler: Yerelliğin Toplumsal İnşası. In *İstanbul: Küresel ile Yerel Arasında.* Çağlar Keyder, ed. pp. 78–96. Istanbul: Metis Yayınları.

Nestmann, Liesa. 1989. Die ethnische Differenzierung der Bevölkerung der Osttürkei in ihren sozialen Bezügen: Auswertung der 'Köy Envanter Etüdleri' des Ministeriums für Dorfangelegenheiten. In *Ethnic Groups in the Republic of Turkey.* Peter Andrews, ed. pp. 543–81. Wiesbaden: Dr. Ludwig Reichert Verlag.

Neuwirth, Robert. 2007. Security of Tenure in Istanbul: The Triumph of the 'Self Service City': Case Study Prepared for Enhancing Urban Safety and Security: Global Report on Human Settlements 2007. http://www.unhabitat.org/downloads/docs/GRHS.2007.CaseStudy.Tenure.Turkey.pdf.

Neyzi, Leyla. 2004. *'Ben Kimim?' Türkiye'de Sözlü Tarih, Kimlik ve Öznelik.* Istanbul: İletişim Yayınları.

Ochs, Elinor and Lisa Capps. 1996. Narrating the Self. *Annual Review of Anthropology,* 25: 19–43.

Olson, Robert. 1989. *The Emergence of Kurdish Nationalism 1880–1925.* Austin: University of Texas Press.

———— ed. 1996a. *The Kurdish Nationalist Movement in the 1990s: Its Impact on Turkey and the Middle East.* Lexington: The University Press of Kentucky.

———— 1996b. The Kurdish Question and Chechnya: Turkish and Russian Foreign Policies since the Gulf War. *Middle East Policy,* 4 (3): 106–18.

Ortner, Sherry. 1973. On Key Symbols. *American Anthropologist,* 75 (5): 1338–46.

Orywal, Erwin and Katharina Hackstein. 1993. Ethnizität: Die Konstruktion ethnischer Wirklichkeiten. In *Handbuch der Ethnologie.* Thomas Schweizer, Margarete Schweizer, and Waltraud Kokot, eds. pp. 593–609. Berlin: Reimer Verlag.

O'Shea, Maria T. 1996. Kurdish Costume: Regional Diversity and Divergence. In *Kurdish Culture and Identity.* Philip Kreyenbroek and Christine Allison, eds. pp. 135–55. London: Zed Books.

———— 1998. Imagining Kurdistan. Paper presented at the conference 'Between Imagination and Denial: Kurds as Subjects and Objects of Political and Social Processes', Berlin: Kurdistan-AG AStA FU.

Öktem, Kerem. 2008. The Nation's Imprint: Demographic Engineering and the Change of Toponymes in Republican Turkey. *European Journal of Turkish Studies,* 7. http://www.ejts.org/document2243.html.

Öncü, Ayşe. 2002. Global Consumerism, Sexuality as Public Spectacle, and the Cultural Remapping of Istanbul in the 1990s. In *Fragments of Culture.* Deniz Kandiyoti and Ayşe Saktanber, eds. pp. 171–90. New Brunswick: Rutgers University Press.

Örer, Ayça. 2008. Annesi Bir Daha Türkçe Konuşmadı. *Taraf,* 9 November. http://www.taraf.com.tr/haber/21040.htm.

Özdalga, Elisabeth. 1998. *The Veiling Issue, Official Secularism and Popular Islam in Modern Turkey.* Richmond: Curzon Press.

Özer, Ahmet. 2003. *Doğu'da Aşiret Düzeni ve Brukanlar.* Ankara: Elips Kitap.

———— 2008. *Şehrivan.* Istanbul: Doz Yayınları.

Özgen, H. Neşe. 2003. *Toplumsal Hafizanın Hatirlama ve Unutma Biçimleri: Van-Özalp ve 33 Kursun Olayi.* Istanbul: TÜSTAV Yayınları.

Özyürek, Esra. 2006. *Nostalgia for the Modern: State Secularism and Everyday Politics in Turkey.* Durham: Duke University Press.

Palloni, Alberto, Douglas S. Massey, Miguel Ceballos, Kristin Espinosa, and Michael Spittel. 2001. Social Capital and International Migration: A Test Using Information on Family Networks. *The American Journal of Sociology,* 106 (5): 1262–98.

Parkes, Peter. 2004. Milk Kinship in Southeast Europe: Alternative Social Structures and Foster Relations in the Caucasus and the Balkans. *Social Anthropology,* 12 (3): 341–58.

Pierce, Joe E. 1964. *Life in a Turkish Village.* New York: Holt, Rinehart and Winston.

Pfluger-Schindlbeck, Ingrid. 2005. *Verwandtschaft, Religion und Geschlecht in Aserbaidschan.* Wiesbaden: Dr. Ludwig Reichert Verlag.

288 Kurdish Life in Contemporary Turkey

Portes, Alejandro and Josh DeWind. 2007. A Cross-Atlantic Dialogue: The Progress of Research and Theory in the Study of International Migration. In *Rethinking Migration: New Theoretical and Empirical Perspectives.* Alejandro Portes and Josh DeWind, eds. pp. 3–26. Oxford: Berghahn Books.

Putnam, Robert D. 2000. *Bowling Alone: The Collapse and Revival of American Community.* New York: Simon and Schuster.

Rapport, Nigel and Andrew Dawson. 1998. Home and Movement: A Polemic. In *Migrants of Identity: Perceptions of Home in a World of Movement.* Nigel Rapport and Andrew Dawson, eds. pp. 19–38. Oxford: Berg.

Rapport, Nigel and Joanne Overing. 2000. *Social and Cultural Anthropology: The Key Concepts.* London: Routledge.

Riedler, Florian. 2008. Public People: Temporary Labour Migrants in Nineteenth Century Istanbul. In *Public Istanbul: Spaces and Spheres of the Urban.* Frank Eckardt and Kathrin Wildner, eds. pp. 233–53. Bielefeld: transcript Verlag.

Robinson, Richard D. 1958. Turkey's Agrarian Revolution and the Problem of Urbanization. *The Public Opinion Quarterly,* 22 (3): 397–405.

Rosaldo, Michelle Zimbalist. 1974. Women, Culture and Society: A Theoretical Overview. In *Women, Culture and Society.* Michelle Zimbalist Rosaldo and Louise Lamphere, eds. pp. 17–42. Stanford: Stanford University Press.

Rosenthal, Mila. 2000. Rural-Urban Relations and Representations: Comparative Perspectives, 26–28 April 2000. *Anthropology Today,* 16 (5): 23–4.

Ross, Marc Howard and Thomas S. Weisner. 1977. The Rural-Urban Migrant Network in Kenya: Some General Implications. *American Ethnologist,* 4 (2): 359–75.

Saktanber, Ayşe. 2002. *Living Islam: Women, Religion and the Politicization of Culture in Turkey.* London: I.B. Tauris.

Sanjek, Roger. 1996. Network Analysis. In *Encyclopedia of Social and Cultural Anthropology.* Alan Barnard and Jonathan Spencer, eds. pp. 396–7. London: Routledge.

Savelsberg, Eva, Siamend Hajo, and Carsten Borck, eds. 2000. *Kurdische Frauen und das Bild der kurdischen Frau.* Münster: LIT Verlag.

Scalbert-Yücel, Clémence and Marie Le Ray 2006. Knowledge, Ideology and Power: Deconstructing Kurdish Studies. *European Journal of Turkish Studies,* 5. http://ejts.revues.org/index777.html.

Schiffauer, Werner. 1987. *Die Bauern von Subay: Das Leben in einem türkischen Dorf.* Stuttgart: Klett-Cotta.

Scott, John. 2000. *Social Network Analysis: A Handbook (Second Edition).* London: Sage Publications.

Secor, Anna. 2004. 'There Is an Istanbul That Belongs to Me': Citizenship, Space, and Identity in the City. *Annals of the Association of American Geographers,* 94 (2): 352–68.

Seçim Bilançosu: En Az 19 Ölü, 151 Yaralı. *Radikal,* 2 April 2009. http://www.radikal.com.tr/ Radikal.aspx?aType=RadikalDetay&ArticleID=929188&Date=06.04.2009&CategoryID=78.

Seufert, Günter. 1997. Between Religion and Ethnicity: A Kurdish-Alevi Tribe in Globalizing Istanbul. In *Space, Culture and Power: New Identities in Globalizing Cities*. Ayşe Öncü and Petra Weyland, eds. pp. 157–76. London: Zed Books.

Sev'er, Aysan and Mazhar Bağlı. 2006. Levirat and Sororat Marriages in Southeastern Turkey: Intact Family or Sanctified Incest? *Women's Health and Urban Life*, 5 (1): 27–47.

Sevinç, F. 2002. *Van'da AKP'den Aşiret Adayı Yok. NTV*, 2 October. http://ntvmsnbc.com/news/179044.asp.

Sharabi, Hisham. 1988. *Neopatriarchy: A Theory of Distorted Change in Arab Society*. Oxford: Oxford University Press.

Skubsch, Sabine. 2001. Das Bildungswesen der Türkei aus kurdischer Perspektive. *Kurdische Studien*, 1 (1): 65–89.

Skutnabb-Kangas, Tove and Sertaç Bucak. 1994. Killing a Mother Tongue: How the Kurds are Deprived of Linguistic Human Rights. In *Linguistic Human Rights: Overcoming Linguistic Discrimination*. Tove Skutnabb-Kangas and Robert Phillipson, eds. pp. 347–70. Berlin: Mouton de Gruyter.

Somers, Margaret R. 1994. The Narrative Constitution of Identity: A Relational and Network Approach. *Theory and Society*, 23 (5): 605–49.

Sökefeld, Martin. 1999. Debating Self, Identity, and Culture in Anthropology. *Current Anthropology*, 40 (4): 417–31.

———— 2001. Editorial: Identitäten und Ethnizität. *Ethnoscripts*, 3 (1): 1–9. http://www.uni-hamburg.de/Wiss/FB/09/EthnoloI/Artikel/edi3–1.html.

Smith, Michael Peter. 2002. Preface. In *New Approaches to Migration? Transnational Communities and Their Transformation of Home*. Nadje Al-Ali and Khalid Koser, eds. pp. xi–xv. London: Routledge.

Stirling, Paul. 1994 [1965]. *Turkish Village: The Nature of Human Society*. University of Kent. http://lucy.ukc.ac.uk/TVillage/StirlingContents.html.

Stirling, Paul and Emine Onaran İncirlioğlu. 1996. Choosing Spouses: Villagers, Migrants, Kinship and Time. In *Turkish Families in Transition*. Gabriele Rasuly-Paleczek, ed. pp. 61–82. Frankfurt: Peter Lang.

Stone, Linda. 1998. *Kinship and Gender: An Introduction*. Oxford: Westview Press.

Strohmeier, Martin. 2004. Identität und Loyalität in der frühen kurdischen Nationalbewegung. In *Die Kurden: Studien zu ihrer Sprache, Geschichte und Kultur*. Stefan Conermann and Geoffrey Haig, eds. pp. 81–96. Hamburg: EB-Verlag.

Strohmeier, Martin and Lale Yalçın-Heckmann. 2000. *Die Kurden: Geschichte, Politik, Kultur*. München: C.H. Beck.

Szreter, Simon. 2002. The State of Social Capital: Bringing Back in Power, Politics, and History. *Theory and Society*, 31 (5): 573–621.

Şen, Leyla. 2005. Poverty Alleviation, Conflict and Power in Poor Displaced Households: A Study of the Views of Women in Diyarbakır. *New Perspectives on Turkey*, 32: 113–35.

Tarım ve Köyişleri Bakanlığı (TKB). 2005. *Van İli Tarım Master Planı.* http://www.tarim.gov.tr/arayuz/10/icerik.asp?efl=duyurular/bolge_il_master_planlari/bolge_il_master_planlari.htm&curdir=\duyurular\bolge_il_master_planlari&fl=Master_planlari/masterplan/masterplan.htm.

Taylor, Janet E. and Joan E. Norris. 2000. Sibling Relationships, Fairness, and Conflict over Transfer of the Farm. *Family Relations,* 49 (3): 277–83.

Tayman, Enis. 2004. Aşiretler Çeteleşme Yolunda. *Tempo Dergisi,* 11 August. http://www.tempodergisi.com.tr/toplum_politika/06149/.

Ter Minassian, Anahide. 2000. The City of Van at the Turn of the 20th Century. In *Armenian Van/Vaspurakan.* Richard G. Hovannisian, ed. pp. 171–93. Costa Mesa, Cal.: Mazda Publishers.

TOBB. 1995. *Doğu Sorunu: Teşhisler ve Tespitler.* Ankara: TOBB.

Toprak, Veli and H. Ateş. 2004. Van'da Neler Oluyor? *Yeni Şafak,* 12–16 August. http://www.yenisafak.com/diziler/van/index.html.

Torab, Azam. 1996. Piety as Gendered Agency: A Study of Jalaseh Ritual Discourse in an Urban Neighbourhood in Iran. *The Journal of the Royal Anthropological Institute,* 2 (2): 235–52.

——— 2007. *Performing Islam: Gender and Ritual in Iran.* Leiden: Brill Academic Publishers.

Transparency International. 2007. *Annual Report 2007.* http://www.transparency.org/publications/annual_report.

Tsuda, Takeyuki, ed. 2009. *Diasporic Homecomings: Ethnic Return Migration in Comparative Perspective.* Stanford: Stanford University Press.

Tugan, Rojbin. 2009. Kürtçe Ahların ve Ağıtların Dili Olmasın. *Taraf,* 3 March. http://www.taraf.com.tr/haber/29145.htm.

Tunç, Aynur İ. 2004. Van'da Kadın Sorunları ve Eğitim. *Yüzüncü Yıl Üniversitesi Eğitim Fakültesi Dergisi,* 1. http://efdergi.yyu.edu.tr/makaleler/cilt_I/ozetler/aynur_ozet.htm.

Tunçel, Harun. 2000. Türkiye'de İsmi Değiştirilen Köyler. *Fırat University Journal of Social Science,* 10 (2): 23–34.

Turkish Ministry of Culture. 2000. *Van, a Changing City.* http://www.discoverturkey.com/english/yeni/van/changing.

TÜİK. 2007. *İllere Göre İl/İlçe Merkezi ve Belde/Köy Nüfusu.* http://report.tuik.gov.tr/reports/rwservlet?adnksdb2=&ENVID=adnksdb2Env&report=turkiye_il_koy_sehir.RDF&p_kod=1&p_yil=2007&p_dil=1&desformat=html.

TÜİK. 2008. *Hanehalkı İşgücü Araştırması 2008 Eylül Dönemi Sonuçları (Ağustos, Eylül, Ekim 2008).* http://www.tuik.gov.tr/PreHaberBultenleri.do?id=2077.

Türkiye Belgenet. n.d. Türkiye Seçimleri, 2002 Genel Seçim Sonuçları. http://www.belgenet.net/ayrinti.php?yil_id=14&il_id=965.

Türkiye İnsan Hakları Vakfı. n.d. Annual and Monthly Reports. http://www.tihv.org/eindex.html.

Tüzün, Gürel, ed. 2009. *Ders Kitaplarında İnsan Hakları II: Tarama Sonuçları.* Istanbul: Tarih Vakfı.

Uehling, Greta. 2002. Sitting on Suitcases: Ambivalence and Ambiguity in the Migration Intentions of Crimean Tartar Women. *Journal of Refugee Studies*, 15 (4): 388–408.

Unicef. 2005. *Haydi Kızlar Okula! The Girls' Education Campaign 2001–2005.* http://www.unicef.org/turkey/pr/ge6.html.

Van Vakfı Genel Başkanlığı. 2004. *İstanbul'daki Vanlılar.* Istanbul.

Van'da 'Haydi Kızlar Okula' Kampanyası. *Tüm Gazeteler.* http://www.tumgazeteler.com/?a=3016010&cache=1.

Van'da Kuma Artık Boşanma Nedeni. *Milliyet,* 24 December 2007. http://www.milliyet.com.tr/2007/12/24/guncel/gun10.html.

Vergara, Benito. 2008. *Pinoy Capital: The Filipino Nation in Daly City.* Philadelphia: Temple University Press.

Vertovec, Steven. 2004. Migrant Transnationalism and Modes of Transformation. *International Migration Review,* 38 (3): 970–1001.

—— 2007a. Introduction: New Directions in the Anthropology of Migration and Multiculturalism. *Ethnic and Racial Studies,* 30 (6): 961–78.

—— 2007b. Migrant Transnationalism and Modes of Transformation. In *Rethinking Migration: New Theoretical and Empirical Perspectives.* Alejandro Portes and Josh DeWind, eds. pp. 149–80. Oxford: Berghahn Books.

—— 2009. *Transnationalism.* London: Routledge.

Visweswaran, Kamala. 1997. Histories of Feminist Ethnography. *Annual Review of Anthropology,* 26: 591–621.

Wahlbeck, Östen. 1999. *Kurdish Diasporas: A Comparative Study of Kurdish Refugee Communities.* London: Macmillan.

Washington Kurdish Institute. n.d. *WKI Select Bibliography.* http://www.kurd.org.

Washington Institute of Near East Policy. 2007. *Turkey: Alevi Population by Province.* http://www.washingtoninstitute.org/mapImages/4616b6127d683.pdf.

Wedel, Heidi. 1996. Binnenmigration und ethnische Identität – Kurdinnen in türkischen Metropolen. *Orient,* 37 (3): 437–52.

—— 1997. KurdInnen in türkischen Metropolen: Migration, Flucht und politische Partizipation. In *Ethnizität, Nationalismus, Religion und Politik in Kurdistan.* Carsten Borck, Eva Savelsberg, and Siamend Hajo, eds. pp. 155–84. Münster: LIT Verlag.

—— 2000. Frauenbewegung und Nationalbewegung – ein Widerspruch? Gefahren und Chancen am Beispiel der Türkei und Kurdistans. In *Kurdische Frauen und das Bild der kurdischen Frau.* Eva Savelsberg, Siamend Hajo, and Carsten Borck, eds. pp. 105–27. Münster: LIT Verlag.

Werbner, Pnina. 1999. Global Pathways: Working Class Cosmopolitans and the Creation of Transnational Ethnic Worlds. *Social Anthropology,* 7 (1): 17–35.

White, Jenny. 1994. *Money Makes Us Relatives: Women's Labor in Urban Turkey.* Austin: University of Texas Press.

—— 2002. *Islamist Mobilization in Turkey: A Study in Vernacular Politics.* Seattle: University of Washington Press.

Wießner, Gunnar. 1997. *Hayoths Dzor – Xavasor: Ethnische, ökonomische und kulturelle Transformation eines ländlichen Siedlungsgebiets in der östlichen Türkei seit dem 19. Jahrhundert*. Wiesbaden: Dr. Ludwig Reichert Verlag.

Wikan, Unni. 1991. *Behind the Veil in Arabia: Women in Oman*. Chicago: University of Chicago Press.

Yalçın, A. Lale. 1986. *Kinship and Tribal Organization in the Province of Hakkâri, Southeast Turkey*. PhD dissertation, London School of Economics and Political Science.

Yalçın, A. Lale. 1988. Ismail Besikci: State Ideology and the Kurds. *Middle Eastern Report*, 153: 43.

——— 1989. Başka bir Kürt Konferansının Ardından. *Birikim*, 8: 76–7.

——— 1991. Ethnic Islam and Nationalism among the Kurds in Turkey. In *Islam in Modern Turkey: Religion, Politics and Literature in a Secular State*. Richard Tapper, ed. pp. 102–20. London: I.B. Tauris.

Yalçın-Heckmann, Lale and Pauline van Gelder. 2000. Das Bild der Kurdinnen im Wandel des politischen Diskurses in der Türkei der 1990er Jahre – Einige kritische Bemerkungen. In *Kurdische Frauen und das Bild der kurdischen Frau*. Eva Savelsberg, Siamend Hajo, and Carsten Borck, eds. pp. 77–104. Münster: LIT Verlag.

Yeğen, Mesut. 1996. The Turkish State Discourse and the Exclusion of Kurdish Identity. In *Turkey: Identity, Democracy, Politics*. Sylvia Kedourie, ed. pp. 216–29. London: Frank Cass Publishers.

——— 1999. The Kurdish Question in State Discourse. *Journal of Contemporary History*, 34 (4): 555–68.

——— 2005. 'Müstakbel-Türk'ten 'Sözde Yurttaş'a: Devlet ve Kürtler. In *Türkiye'de Azınlık Hakları Sorunu: Vatandaşlık ve Demokrasi Eksenli Bir Yaklaşım. Uluslararası Konferans Tebliğleri, 9 –10 Aralık 2005*. pp. 105–11. Istanbul: TESEV Yayınları.

——— 2007. Jewish-Kurds or the New Frontiers of Turkishness. *Patterns of Prejudice*, 41: 1–20.

Zeyneloğlu, Sinan, H. Yaprak Civelek, and Yadigar Coşkun. 2011. Kürt Sorununda Antropolojik ve Demografik Boyut: Sayım ve Araştırma Verilerinden Elde Edilen Bulgular. *Uluslararası İnsan Bilimleri Dergisi*, 8 (1): 335–84.

Zürcher, Erik J. 1997. *Turkey: A Modern History*. London: I.B. Tauris.

INDEX

A

Abu-Lughod, Lila, 21, 176, 182,
  202–204, 244–245
AKP (Adalet ve Kalkınma Partisi)
  democratic ouverture of, 11–12
  election results in Van 2007, 114,
    232
  election results in Van 2011, 114
  general election results 2011, 256
  and Kurdish identity, 233, 256
  and socio-religious networks, 256
  and tribal support, 115
  see also Elections
Alevis
  and compulsory religious education
    classes, 226
  family control among, 188
  and relations with Sunnis, 11, 34,
    89, 161, 217, 229–230, 254
  in Tepelik, 138, 139, 217
Allison, Christine, 7, 26, 190
Ammann, Birgit, 7, 26, 31, 32,
  33, 70–71, 85, 86, 88, 101,
  102, 129, 134, 162, 187, 188,
  191, 226
Andrews, Peter A., 27, 68, 85, 92
Aristova, Tatyana Feodorofna, 7, 32, 33

Armenians
  and change of village names, 86
  file, 40
  and former presence in Van, 10, 40,
    41–42, 107
  and former villages now occupied
    by Burukî, 42, 110

B

Barth, Fredrik, 7, 21, 90, 103, 162, 163
BDP (Barış ve Demokrasi Partisi)
  general election result in Van 2011,
    114
  increase in support for, 232
  Kurdish Vanlı voting for, 252
  national result in 2011 general
    election, 256
  see also DTP, Elections
Beşikçi, İsmail, 8, 41, 116
Bora, Aksu, 24, 147, 175–176, 184,
  197, 200, 215, 233
Brettell, Caroline, 16–17
Bride, see Bûk
Bruinessen, Martin van, 7, 8, 38, 42,
  70, 76, 89, 101, 110, 111, 115,
  162, 167, 169, 186, 231

www.ingramcontent.com/pod-product-compliance
Lightning Source LLC
Chambersburg PA
CBHW060146280326
41932CB00012B/1656